UNTIL THE FIRES STOPPED BURNING

CHARLES B. STROZIER

UNTIL THE FIRES

*9/11 and New York City in the Words
and Experiences of Survivors and Witnesses*

STOPPED BURNING

Columbia
University
Press
New York

Columbia University Press
Publishers Since 1893
New York   Chichester, West Sussex
Copyright © 2011 Charles B. Strozier
All rights reserved

Library of Congress Cataloging-in-Publication Data

Strozier, Charles B.
Until the fires stopped burning : 9/11 and New York City in the words
and experiences of survivors and witnesses / Charles B. Strozier.
p. cm.
Includes bibliographical references and index.
ISBN 978-0-231-15898-5 (cloth : alk. paper)
1. September 11 Terrorist Attacks, 2001. 2. Terrorism—New York (State)—
New York. 3. Terrorism—United States. 4. Victims of terrorism—New
York (State)—New York—Interviews. 5. Heroes—New York (State)—
New York—Interviews. I. Title

HV6432.7.S774 2011
974.7′10440922—dc22   2011014317

⊛

Columbia University Press books are printed on permanent and
durable acid-free paper.

This book is printed on paper with recycled content.
Printed in the United States of America

c 10 9 8 7 6 5 4 3 2 1

Designed by Lisa Hamm

References to Internet Web sites (URLs) were accurate at the time of writing. Neither the author nor Columbia University Press is responsible for
URLs that may have expired or changed since the manuscript was prepared.

For Alison

CONTENTS

INTRODUCTION

WRITE WHAT YOU KNOW. I am a New Yorker who directly experienced the searing effects of 9/11. As the towers burned and collapsed, I watched in horror from Greenwich Village. I could only imagine the suffering of those inside the burning towers. Though I was to learn in time of many whose loved ones died that day, the shadow was not far from my own life. My wife, who has severe asthma, was caught in the first flush of debris that was lifted that day by strong westerly winds into Brooklyn. Since then she once nearly died from her worsened condition. I myself suffered only mildly. My personal knowledge of the individual and collective trauma on 9/11 is mostly vicarious. But from the moment I watched the towers burn and collapse as I stood there on University Place between 12th and 13th streets outside the Newsbar I felt a mission to study this disaster.

I am a history professor at John Jay College of the City University of New York. For years before 9/11 I taught courses and published several books on the new terrorism and apocalyptic violence, intellectual experiences that shaped my creation in the late fall of 2001 of a Center on Terrorism at John Jay. My college, where fire and police officers gain their higher degrees because of its special mission in criminal justice, lost sixty-eight alumni on September 11th. Some of my former students died that day. Many of my subsequent students were among those who survived and served on the scene to save many lives and then dive into the monumental and, in the end, essentially fruitless task of working on the belching, burning pile to find survivors (only two Port Authority policemen stuck in an unusual cavity and a few civilians pinned under debris at the edges of the disaster were found still alive, and all of those were found on September 12th).

And I am a psychoanalyst with a practice in Greenwich Village. My patients then—and some still—mulled over their pained reactions to 9/11 in their dreams and in their lives. That first afternoon a patient slogged through the tsunami waves of debris from her office in Lower Manhattan to make a session. She was covered with that awful dust. It was a remarkable moment of psychotherapy in the midst of chaos.

This book tells the New York story of the World Trade Center disaster through the words and experiences of survivors and witnesses. The period I cover extends from September 11th until the fires stopped burning at Ground Zero (with some concluding reflections on the effects of 9/11 in the past decade up to the death of Osama bin Laden on May 1, 2011). Those 100 days reshaped America. New York City was the crucible of the disaster, which was ultimately a local and particular event.[1] My focus is on the human perspective on things. Many respondents enter into my narrative. They are men and women, young and old, black and white, and of several ethnic backgrounds. My respondents are ordinary people who stumbled on an extraordinary event. In their stories, carefully listened to, lies what I feel is the best history possible of the World Trade Center disaster. There are other important aspects of 9/11. Washington was also attacked, and a plane went down in Pennsylvania. Two wars have been fought in its wake, one in Iraq that included my youngest son in the army. There have been serious consequences in terms of domestic surveillance. The culture of fear after 9/11 that became such an integral part of our cultural landscape has led to many radical changes in our institutions. My story, however, told through the survivors, is an attempt to explain where the world we live in came from.

I am deeply grateful to my respondents who allowed me to draw on their wisdom in making this book. All their names have been changed to protect their anonymity, and the original records of my contacts with them have been long since destroyed and for the most part even forgotten by me. I found my respondents in several ways. The main characters whose lives I probe in great detail came to me from what in anthropology is called "respondent-driven samples" (RDS).[2] From my own contacts a handful of potential respondents led me to others they knew whose experiences were relevant for the questions I was asking about the disaster. The pool of respondents who agreed to be interviewed came to understand my goals and purposes, and they in turn recommended others they knew whom they personally contacted for me, and so on, until I felt I had interviewed widely and deeply enough to write this book.

My interview method drew on familiar traditions in qualitative research from psychoanalysis, social psychology, and anthropology. In my interviews I tried to learn specific things. I believe strongly that, as Robert Jay Lifton has put it, we take nothing naked from the world. It is all reshaped and given meanings in the self. A robust interview method must somehow capture those meanings as well as answer the questions I deem worthy of exploring in my respondents. I worked from a memorized protocol, tape-recorded the interview, and sometimes needed to prod a respondent toward subjects that I was interested in but that might not otherwise have occurred to him or her. At the same time, the interview process was entirely open-ended. It mattered less that I "covered" my protocol than that I learned deeply about a given topic from a specific respondent who might be especially articulate and psychologically insightful, able to address shared themes of larger significance. Besides, my method involved two long interviews with each subject (and sometimes many more). Although many have contributed to the approaches I took in my method, I learned most from Robert Jay Lifton, my friend and long-time mentor, who helped me write my protocol and advised on the course of my research from the very beginning. Lifton followed my work closely through the long years of analyzing my data and writing this book, listening to my endless discussions of it, and commenting wisely on many of my most important presentations about it. There is no question my study was only possible using the psychosocial research method that Lifton has developed in his wide-ranging studies.[3]

The emotional intensity of the interview process itself, as well as the fact that I was a participant-observer in my study, turned aspects of my scholarly research into something close to psychotherapy. My main characters, whom I call "respondents," were in many ways more accurately partners in mutual exploration of an event and process that affected both of our lives. Those who shared their experiences with me were certainly not "subjects," a term that would objectify them, nor simply random people I interviewed the way a journalist might in chasing down a story. My relationship with those who contributed to my work was much deeper. I was always moved by their stories, sometimes to tears. I often dreamed of towers burning, or other such 9/11 scenes, the night before most interviews, as though to mobilize the full range of my psychological resources for the encounter I faced the next day. I also got to know most of my respondents well from my interviews. In fact, I often had the curious and unexpected experience of many respondents asking me to take them into psychotherapy at the end of our interviews. I demurred for ethical reasons, as the point of research is not to build up one's practice, though of course I made sure to refer each to another therapist with whom I followed up on their progress. The only exception I made was an especially troubled woman whose story I ended up not using in my book (except for one brief passage). I agreed to take her into therapy at a nominal charge that was far below my normal fee.

Other survivors and witnesses contributed to my study. I draw on some of the interviews that are now archived in the Columbia University Oral History Office under the general auspices of Mary Marshall Clark and am grateful for her help in making these interviews available to me. I learned from the 500 or so interviews with firemen after 9/11 that a *New York Times* lawsuit forced into public view.[4] I have examined the 9/11 Digital Archives, not to mention many of the thousands and thousands of photographs from 9/11. I learned from and am grateful for the fascinating interviews Helen Whitney carried out for her PBS documentary for the first anniversary, "Faith and Doubt at Ground Zero." I also personally interviewed a group of Jewish hidden children in Chicago and a cohort of women in New York who got pregnant after 9/11, and others who shared their stories with me came into my line of vision more serendipitously. Many of my students over the years who were survivors, especially the first responders, gave me more than they could ever know in class discussion.

Finally, and very important, my patients in my psychotherapy practice provided a seemingly endless and recurring source of information about the unconscious meanings of 9/11. I had no idea at first that I would draw on what I learned from my patients in my study. In this sense, I made it up as I went along. I never crossed the line into changing the course of psychotherapy into research without consent. But I did learn from my patients and in several places, especially in one chapter, draw extensively on their stories and insights (changing their names, of course, and obscuring details to make them anonymous). I am hardly a remote Freudian therapist. My orientation is self psychological (I wrote Heinz Kohut's biography[5]), and I believe empathy defines the ground of therapeutic healing. I involve myself in the process, sit face to face with my patients, and often share relevant details about my own life. That is my style. Besides, almost all of them knew about my research. In the early months and years after 9/11, I was publishing pieces regularly, including in the *New York Times*, being interviewed on television, and giving scholarly talks that were widely noted. It would have been impossible to be unknown, even if I had been so inclined. Some of my patients were more interested in the specifics of the research and my preliminary findings than others, but nearly every one expressed the feeling at one time or another that my work meant I understood an important aspect of their experience. It may well be that my clinical data is biased, because it was precisely my well-known interest in 9/11 that elicited dreams, associations, and fantasies of the event from my patients in order to please me. It is difficult to address such concerns in dealing with clinical material, because there are no controls. It is not scientific in that sense. On the other hand, such data can be illuminating and invaluable in providing insight into otherwise inaccessible levels of the human response to the disaster. Just living through 9/11 and coming to psychotherapy on a regular basis meant my patients became de facto respondents.

What this book contributes to the literature on September 11, 2001, is context. Although 9/11 has been overwritten, its most important aspects have not been studied. We are all familiar, to the point of numbness, with images of the planes flying into the towers or of scared people fleeing the cloud of debris. We know all too well the heroic tales of firemen and many of the sad stories of survivors. We have lived ad nauseam with the political manipulation of 9/11. But all the images and tales are disparate, scattered, ungrounded. At least much is preserved, including the personal memories of many millions throughout the world who will remember the details of their experiences that day for the rest of their lives. But we lack an overall interpretation of 9/11 that binds the stories into a cohesive whole. That interpretation must provide some sense of the similarities but also the important differences between the experiences of those in various parts of the city; an idea of what it meant to watch it all on television; how one's personal past shaped meanings on that day; why it was a public event of such dramatic proportions; and what it meant when a day became a week and a week became a month and the months dragged on in the wake of the World Trade Center disaster.

This book describes the events of that day and its reverberations through-out the fall of 2001. I try to explain the meanings of traumatic experience throughout the city, and by reflecting on what was seen on television, to cap-ture what 9/11 meant to many within and without the city. The World Trade Center disaster was the first television event of its kind watched in real time on high-quality television monitors. I grapple with the historical and psy-chological meanings of the disaster. Part of that imbedded analysis explores themes in comparative history, from familiar disasters such as earthquakes and floods to events such as the bombing of Hiroshima. And throughout I locate myself in the text. This is a very personal book. I talk of my family, of my own past at times, of what I experienced talking with my informants, and of things I have learned from a lifetime of reading that seem relevant for understanding 9/11. It would be false to the event and to my method of investigation to stake out an objective stance at a remove from the despair, the trauma, and the death of those 100 days. At the same time, I try to avoid self-indulgence. I am not writing autobiography. I let my wonderfully articulate and compelling informants tell the story.

The book begins by reminding readers of what actually happened that day and in the long weeks and months until the end of 2001. I then provide a detailed account of the disaster in its enormous complexity, followed by some reflections on the form of the dying, an "apocalyptic interlude," thoughts on the language of trauma (or "Traumasong"), and some of what I feel are the ambiguous meanings of the way most Americans experienced the disaster through television. I then examine the way a day of terror became an organic process of fear throughout that fall. In a final section I examine some con-ceptual and historical issues of the last ten years that have come to define our enduring encounter with 9/11.

Two themes dominate my work. The first is what I call "zones of sadness," a term I borrow from my colleague Michael Flynn.[6] On September 11, 2001, it mattered where you were in relation to the death, even though the trauma of 9/11 was psychologically ubiquitous and universally shared in what is called the "illusion of centrality." The zones of sadness, however, were real spaces in the city, moving outward from Ground Zero north into Manhattan, east into Brooklyn, south into Staten Island, and west into New Jersey. The zones move outward in concentric circles of topography and experience, in ways analo-gous to the violence that radiates out from Ground Zero of a nuclear bomb. Survivors in zone 1 directly experienced death and all the exquisite details of the disaster. Witnesses in zone 2 saw the disaster unfold but without the immediacy of the chaos, the towers falling, or most of all, the people falling or jumping to their death. Participants in zone 3 saw nothing except perhaps the towers burning from a great distance but were caught up in the New York City experience of the terror, the evacuation of most office buildings, the sight of debris-covered survivors wandering glassy-eyed up the West Side Highway or on other thoroughfares. Finally, onlookers in zone 4 throughout the city and the world watched the disaster on television, some in real time but everyone in the days and weeks that followed with a compulsivity that intensified their experience but also numbed them to meaning. The further out one was, in other words, the greater the numbing, or lack of feeling, and at the far end of television, which also circled back into everyone's life, the remoteness fed the psychologically unproductive, even dangerous, experience of rage that proved to be so politically responsive to manipulation.

My discussion of the traumatic meanings of 9/11 in this context of the zones of sadness does not try formally to locate my analysis in the academic or psychoanalytic literature on trauma, to address questions of "adult onset," for example, or issues in the transmission of trauma through subsequent generations. I know well and have learned much from this literature and its concerns, especially with the experience of the survivor (which I do discuss), and it informs my work in many subtle ways. My project, however, is more experiential and phenomenological and always seeks to address the larger meanings of the disaster itself. I did my interviews in the immediate wake of 9/11. Everything was fluid and changing, as I was myself psychologically. I try to capture that sense of raw immediacy in the book and place it in the context of an overall narrative of the disaster in American life, rather than connect my work more directly with the many, and often very interesting, scholarly debates over the meanings of trauma. That said, I do hope my work contributes to the important research on trauma that deeply engages so many of my colleagues in the academy and in psychoanalysis.

I did not begin my research with the idea of the zones as an organizing principle. It emerged empirically from my work. I kept being struck as I read and analyzed my interviews with the different quality of experience of those in physically varying spaces of New York City. As a result of this process in the way my research unfolded, there is a definite imbalance in the texture of my data. Survivors and witnesses are overrepresented, whereas I have fewer stories and less in-depth material about the experience of participants and onlookers. I adopted various strategies to compensate for this imbalance in my interviews, including some additional interviews later on and much further research, but it would be false to pretend I had all my ideas clearly in my head when I began and then systematically studied the disaster to test my hypotheses. My work was, instead, much messier. I was in and of the events I describe, confused about their meanings in the moment, as were most New Yorkers, and the clarity I have now at the great distance of ten years was not there at the outset.

The second theme of this book explores the apocalyptic meanings of 9/11. The World Trade Center disaster was not an apocalyptic, or world-ending, event. Several thousand people died and the human and political repercussions were enormous. The disaster changed the course of American history in profound ways. But as with other disasters and extreme historical events from Hiroshima or the Holocaust to Katrina, the Indonesian tsunami, the oil spill in the Gulf, or the multiple tragedies in Japan in the spring of 2011, New York City has already begun to recover. Ground Zero after a decade is a construction site (even if the rebuilding and the memorial have proven to be politically contentious and delayed). Lower Manhattan, including Wall Street, is thriving. In this and many other ways, those directly caught up in the death may live the rest of their lives suffering in traumatic memory while the community at large has moved on. Such disjunction between personal and collective experience can be wrenchingly tragic for survivors, no matter how much 9/11 is honored and memorialized.

But the way New York, and the country at large to a degree, *experienced* the disaster was something altogether different. It was not a matter of plain old ordinary death, as Kurt Vonnegut might put it. The disaster seemed for those up close to be the end of the world. Many caught in the cloud of dust were convinced it was detritus from the explosion of a nuclear weapon. Witnesses from afar saw a mushroom cloud from the collapsing towers, when in fact it was much more like the shape of a cone. In the wake of 9/11 were malevolent threats like that of anthrax that felt unending and ultimate for many. A Middle Eastern war began within weeks. And so on. Such stray pieces of data that I explore in detail suggest that contemporary humans have as an integral dimension of their mindset a kind of preexisting nuclear template that this disaster was peculiarly able to evoke. What 9/11 was and how it felt were quite different. One cannot understand the effects of the disaster on the soul of the country except in this context.

There have been many stages in the history of our understanding and experience of 9/11. For years survivors could barely talk about it, and others never stopped talking. Politicians wrapped themselves in its mantle. Movies (mostly quite bad ones) were made about the disaster and a shelf of (some) good novels has appeared over the years about the day. A conspiracy movement around 9/11 has waxed and waned in relation to larger events, especially the two wars we got ourselves into after 9/11. Many began frankly to forget the details of the disaster as the years passed and as other needs pressed in on individual and collective lives. In some ways that can be disturbing. The events of 9/11 are beginning to enter history. It moves away from us. Yet that very distance may yield deeper understanding as we gain perspective. Perhaps now during the ten-year anniversary we have sufficient distance to begin to capture how the World Trade Center disaster that was the length of a movie (102 minutes) became a transformative historical event in the next 100 days.

UNTIL THE FIRES STOPPED BURNING

THE EVENT

THE DAY DAWNS bright and clear, with the weather as lovely as it has ever been in New York City. The crispness is almost piercing. On the news that morning the cheerful weatherman reports "severe clarity" for the day.

8:46 A.M. American Airlines Flight 11, going 466 mph and loaded with about 10,000 gallons of jet fuel, strikes World Trade Center 1, the north tower, between the ninety-third and ninety-ninth floors on its north side. The wings tilt left but the plane strikes the building precisely in the middle. Mohammed Atta, the pilot and operational commander of the attacks, unfortunately steers well. No one survives above the ninety-third floor. The plane plows into the central core of the building and cuts most of the lines for the ninety-nine elevators, which crash into the basement, leaving the shafts empty spaces to tunnel burning diesel fuel.

9:03 A.M. United Airlines Flight 175, piloted by Marwan al-Shehhi, hits World Trade Center 2, the south tower, between the seventy-seventh and eighty-fifth floors. It is flying at 545 mph and is also loaded with about 10,000 gallons of jet fuel. Both planes are flying at well over safe speeds, but United Flight 175 is especially unstable as it roars into its target. In fact, the United plane comes close to falling apart from the vibration caused by being flown at high speed at such a low altitude, where the air is thicker. The plane banks to the left at the last moment because it is about to miss the building altogether. The large difference between the air speeds of the two planes accounts for the greater damage inflicted by United Flight 175 and is the reason for the south tower, though it is struck second, falling first. Kinetic energy, or the energy of motion of any object, varies with the square of its velocity. This translates into an important difference in terms of the disaster: United Flight 175, though traveling only about 25 percent faster than the first plane, releases about 50 percent more energy on impact.

One striking fact of the attack on the two towers of the World Trade Center is that the terrorists strike the towers from opposite sides. It is not surprising that American Flight 11, traveling south from Boston, crashes into the north face of WTC 2. That merely follows the trajectory of the flight after the hijacking. But United Flight 175 goes to great lengths to fly down the Hudson River, south of Manhattan, before beginning a long U-turn back toward the city in order to hit the south tower on its south face. The clear suggestion is that the plan is to knock the towers into each other.

9:37 A.M. American Airlines Flight 77, piloted by Hani Hanjour, crashes into the Pentagon. After it is hijacked from Dulles International Airport and is five miles west-southwest of the Pentagon, the plane makes a 330-degree turn. At the end of the turn, it descends rapidly on its path toward the Pentagon and downtown Washington. Hani Hanjour advances the throttles to maximum power. Flying very low and at 530 miles per hour, the wings of the plane clip five street lampposts and hit a portable generator before striking the Pentagon wall at the first-floor level. The plane crashes into the western side of the Pentagon, killing all fifty-three passengers, five hijackers, six crew members, and 125 people in the building.

9:59 A.M. World Trade Center 2 collapses, less than an hour after being hit. No one, not even Osama bin Laden, predicts such an event. The building just suddenly buckles and falls in on itself, spreading debris in a vast mountain of dust that envelopes Lower Manhattan.

10:03 A.M. United Airlines Flight 93, piloted by Ziad Jarrah, crashes in a field in Shanksville, Pennsylvania, about 80 miles southeast of Pittsburgh. Of the four planes hijacked on 9/11, Flight 93 is the only one not to reach its target—either the White House or Congress—because of a passenger revolt that ends in storming the cockpit. It seems that Jarrah, once he is aware that he is about to be overpowered, decides to crash the plane.

10:28 A.M. World Trade Center 1 collapses. For those watching, the collapse of the second tower is almost anticlimactic. It seems inevitable that after WTC 2 falls so will WTC 1. Many report that the dust storm from the second tower is darker, dirtier, and more ominous than that from the first.

When the towers collapse, 220 acres of cement and steel, 3,000 miles of electrical wiring, 425,000 cubic yards of concrete for the floors, 2.2 million square feet of aluminum cladding for the façades, 7,000 plumbing fixtures, 170 miles of connecting pipe, 40,000 doors, 45,000 windows, scores of thousands of computers, countless square miles of nylon carpeting and drapes, enough wire and polyvinyl chloride–insulated computer and telephone cables to reach the moon, millions of pieces of paper and vast quantities of wood for desks and other office supplies from the felling of several forests, millions of pounds of plastic products, and many people are incinerated into a mountain of smoke and debris that fills the air. The solid inorganic pieces of steel and building material that survive settle into a pile estimated at 1.2 million tons standing some ten stories high. Mixed in the pile are the body parts of those who jumped or fell to their death and of those who were trapped inside when the buildings collapsed. Many victims, or at least most of their bodies (except for some of the firemen in their protective suits), are incinerated in the raging fires.

The collapse of the two World Trade Center towers destroys virtually an entire city, which burns for the next 100 days. An astonishing number of toxins are released into the air.[1]

- Somewhere between 400 and 1,000 tons of asbestos are released into the air, though that fails to account for the labyrinth of pipes and other utility conduits beyond the immediate vicinity of the towers.
- Between 200,000 and 400,000 pounds of lead from computers, batteries, pipes, and electric soldering connections are pulverized in the collapse. Lead does not disintegrate but can travel large distances and attach itself to other substances before settling into the ground. Even in small

amounts, lead causes serious damage to the central nervous system, and children can suffer brain damage and other deformities.

- Some 10 to 25 pounds of mercury are released from the 500,000 fluorescent lamps destroyed that day. To put that number in perspective, the mercury in twenty-five lamps can pollute a 20-acre lake. Mercury is an extremely toxic heavy metal that accumulates in the body.
- Dioxins and furans, two categories of large numbers of chemicals found especially in plastics, are released in quantities that are difficult even to measure. They continue to be released in the fires that burn for three months at the perfect temperature of about 1,000 degrees.
- More than 130,000 gallons of oil and insulating fluid from transformers and high-pressure voltage lines burn, along with another 200,000 gallons of diesel fuel in tanks in and around the complex, feeding the fires started by the 20,000 gallons of fuel on the two planes.
- All that burning diesel fuel releases large, though indeterminate, amounts of PCBs.
- Extremely toxic benzene and other volatile organic compounds found in plastics, resins, nylon, synthetic fibers, gasoline, rubber, lubricants, and dyes are in the air at Ground Zero at levels far above what is regarded as acceptable.

5:20 P.M. World Trade Center 7, across Vesey Street just to the north of the WTC complex, collapses. It sustains heavy damage on its south face from the collapse of both towers, especially WTC 1, and fires burn on various floors throughout the day. The ignition of fuel in the storage tanks for the Con Edison substation located in the basement of WTC 7 adds to the stress on the building. By the time of the collapse everyone is evacuated from the building.

8:00 P.M. President Bush speaks to the nation from the Oval Office. His face is drained of color, his tone somber, his mood dark. He tries to assure a frightened nation but also promises revenge. "Today," he says, "our fellow citizens, our way of life, our very freedom came under attack in a series of deliberate and deadly terrorist acts. . . . Thousands of lives were suddenly ended by evil. . . . None of us will ever forget this day, yet we go forward to defend freedom and all that is good and just in our world."

September 14. In the morning, Bush speaks at the National Cathedral and says: "We are here in the middle hour of our grief. . . . This world He created is of moral design. Grief and tragedy and hatred are only for a time. Goodness, remembrance and love have no end, and the Lord of life holds all who die and all who mourn." In the afternoon, he arrives by helicopter at Ground Zero amid the tightest security New York has ever seen. He walks onto the pile surrounded by thousands of grieving firemen, police officers, and others searching vainly for survivors, grabs a bullhorn, puts his arm around one of those firemen, and says: "I can hear you. The rest of the world hears you. And the people who knocked down the buildings hear you." By then his popularity has soared from its previous low of 50 percent approval in August to well over 90 percent approval.

September 25. An assistant to Tom Brokaw of NBC News opens a letter with white powder in it and handles a second letter with a sandy substance. The FBI is immediately called. Within days the woman develops symptoms of anthrax that were confirmed by the CDC in Atlanta. It turns out letters had been sent at the same time to ABC, CBS, and the *National Inquirer* in Boca Raton, Florida. A full-scale panic sets in. Headlines blare and the threat of biological warfare in the wake of 9/11 terrifies the entire nation. The number of suspicious specimens to be analyzed in New York reaches into the thousands, even though none were found for nearly three weeks after the initial mailing. The laboratory of the city's Department of Health on East 26th Street is quickly overwhelmed with thousands of mysterious white powders that need testing. The army even comes to help by setting up a mobile lab in the lobby of the building. Lab technicians work twenty-four hours a day but are still severely criticized for not processing the specimens quickly enough. In the end, five people die and seventeen are injured.

October 7. The war in Afghanistan, dubbed Operation Enduring Freedom, begins. At first it is overwhelmingly popular with most Americans as an appropriate response to the attacks on 9/11. Its stated goals are to capture Osama bin Laden, destroy al-Qaeda, and remove the Taliban regime that rules the country and provides support and safe haven for bin Laden and al-Qaeda.

November 16. On the same day that the United States begins to bomb Tora Bora, Bin Laden and his key followers, including Ayman Zawahiri, escape from their hideout with the help of local warlords. They use a path out of the mountains that is inexplicably not bombed by the U.S. Air Force. In the next few days some 600 al-Qaeda members follow their leader into Pakistan.

December 20. One hundred days after 9/11 a spokesman for the New York Fire Department, Robert Calise, announces that the fires at Ground Zero are officially considered extinguished, though he cautions that some small fires might still be uncovered.

PART 1
102 MINUTES OF DISASTER

Zones of Sadness

I saw the debris still falling from the sky. I saw the fire.
That was on top. And I saw people. There were people
on fire in the middle of the West Side Highway stumbling.
I saw one guy fall and roll around and I don't know
what happened to him after that.   SANFORD

And I looked up at the building. And I saw this man on the
side of the building, holding on. And then [he] just pushed
back and let go. And then I closed my eyes.   DEIRDRE

It's ridiculous to say this, but I mean it literally was like
a movie. Like we were being chased by this like amorphous
black cloud of like stuff. And you could see—I mean I kept
turning back to look and you could see it was like gaining.
I couldn't run fast enough.   HENRY

1

SURVIVORS: ZONE 1

NOTHING MATCHES the immediacy of experience in
the first zone of sadness. It was in that zone stretching from inside the towers to approximately Chambers Street to the north and Wall Street and the end of
Battery Park to the south, to the Hudson River to the
west and the East River to the east that survivors actually encountered death. This zone is approximate, for
many within a few blocks of the World Trade Center
had their view obscured by other buildings, and some
at quite a distance witnessed death directly. (People
standing on the shoreline of Hoboken, for example,
reported seeing people jump, though they could not
see them hit the ground.) What matters most about
the experience in this first zone, however, is that there
was nothing symbolic in what people saw, heard, and
felt. It took no act of imagination to enter into the
direct experience of the disaster. For everyone close

to the violence of the World Trade Center disaster it was shocking, abrupt, extreme, scary, completely out of context, and it almost always had a lasting effect. None of the survivors discussed in this chapter had any physical injuries as a result of their experiences that day, though it is often forgotten that quite a few people close to the burning and then collapsing towers, especially first responders and the thousands of people escaping from the inside, suffered injuries.[1] But they carried with them a different kind of pain and stories worth probing in some detail. It is from within the human experiences of survivors, and perhaps only in that context, that one can hope to understand the disaster.

THE DISASTER BEGINS

Only one video of the first plane flying into the north face of World Trade Center 1 is extant. Jules Naudet, a French filmmaker, took it. With his brother, Gedeon, he was shooting a documentary and was in Lower Manhattan a few blocks north of the WTC complex. Naudet was standing on the sidewalk facing south, taping an interview when American Airlines Flight 11 flew directly overhead. Instinctively, he raised his camera and captured the plane as it crashed into the building.

The initial moments of the disaster were utterly baffling. No one could understand what was happening. Sanford, a thirty-five-year-old stockbroker who worked in the World Financial Center across the West Side Highway, was late that morning and rushing to work as he passed between WTC 1 (the north tower) and the U.S. Custom House (WTC 6), which had an awning. He was caught off guard by the sudden chaos surrounding him. Perhaps because he was underneath the awning at that moment, he heard not the explosion of the first plane slamming into the north face of WTC 1 but instead a "rumbling and the ground shaking." He was aware of something falling from the sky. The first thing that occurred to him was that there had been a "construction accident, something falling off the roof." Whatever it was, he was startled to see that glass and other pieces of metal and debris were falling down and bouncing off the side of the building. All of that "slammed on the ground around me." It seemed to him in the moment "almost like scaffolding falling" or "like lumber just collapsing."

In his effort to understand what was happening, Sanford ran through in his mind a series of possible explanations for what was going on, including a construction accident that had involved scaffolding and lumber falling. The idea that a plane had hit WTC 1 was unimaginable to him. All he knew with certainty was that he was in danger of losing his life.

On the other side of the WTC complex, Henry, a thirty-two-year-old graduate student with a day job on the corner of West and Rector streets, got off at his stop on the N train near Broadway at about 8:40 A.M. and walked west toward his office. He was about to turn into the entrance of his building when he heard an explosion. A moment later a 6-foot-long piece of lamppost flew by in front of him. In an almost out-of-body experience, he was suddenly aware that he had nearly died. He smelled gas, then noticed a large airplane wheel to the side.

It was equally confusing for workers inside the towers. Miranda, an insurance executive in her mid-fifties, was at her desk on the sixty-seventh floor of WTC 2, the south tower, facing east when the first plane hit the north tower.[2] She could not remember hearing anything specific but happened to look out her window when she felt the building move and saw lots of paper and pieces of metal flying sideways. She immediately thought a bomb had exploded, as in 1993. Without a moment's reflection, she decided to leave the building as quickly as possible. She reached down to pick up her purse, but in her haste to move toward the door and escape she did not bother to take the few steps to retrieve her briefcase, which she had placed on the ledge near her desk. It was her immediate instinct to escape and to let nothing impede her progress to the door. In her interview Miranda relived the drama of the moment:

> And I grabbed my—and my pocketbook was at my feet, so I took that, but my briefcase I kept on the ledge. And I looked and I remember saying to myself, "You don't have time to bend down again," and I left it. And I ran out, 'cause outside of my office were all the cubes and in two rows is my group and I yelled, "We gotta get out of here." And then there's another girl who's in my group who's like two rows over and I just stood there saying, "Alex! Alex!" So she finally stood up and I said, "Come on."

At this point in the interview Miranda began to cry at the thought of all those who failed to respond as quickly as she did and who stayed in the office.

Deirdre, a thirty-three-year-old photographer working part time on the thirty-ninth floor of WTC 7, across Vesey Street to the north of WTC 1, with her partner Leticia had set up all the juices, coffee, and food for the training meeting at their company that was to start at 9 o'clock. She remembers looking at her watch at 8:44, because it had been amusing all week the way a number of the younger employees in the company kept coming late to the training sessions that they were required to attend. Some of the instructors had become very annoyed the previous day and had insisted that if anyone were late that morning, Tuesday, September 11th, there would be serious consequences.

With everything set up Deirdre and Leticia retired to a tiny room at the end of the hall to wait until 9 o'clock. At 8:46 A.M. Deirdre felt a rumble and thought to herself, "That felt like an earthquake." It was indistinct and muffled enough that Deirdre and Leticia dismissed the idea that anything serious had happened and continued their conversation. When they heard another rumble, Deirdre opened the door and saw people running about and looking very anxious. Somebody noticed her and gasped, "You need to get your things. We're being evacuated." Deirdre went back and told Leticia they had to leave. The two women quickly grabbed their things. Deirdre hastily stuffed her personal items into her backpack.

That first thought that it might be an earthquake was common for those who found themselves in the middle of zone 1. As Felicia, a twenty-six-year-old college student, walked into the Marriott lobby, she heard an explosion and felt the entire building shake. Her first thought was, "The subway's very loud this morning." She continued walking toward the doors that connected the hotel lobby with that of the World Trade Center. The building continued to shake. She thought, "Maybe it was an earthquake." She had never been in an earthquake, but the "walls were shaking, and things [were] fall[ing] down and [I was] just standing there." In that moment of terror and uncertainty, Felicia grasped for the only reasonable meaning available to her. It was not a bad theory in the moment, but its coherence was immediately undermined as people started screaming: "It's a bomb! It's a bomb! They're bombing us," which probably reflected in part memories of 1993. Felicia had no direct proof of a bomb. She had neither heard nor seen a bomb explode. But the mention of that possibility shattered the effectiveness of her earthquake theory. It also wiped out any logical route of escape. If it were a bomb, how could one know whether to go forward into the lobby of the World Trade Center, back into the Marriott lobby, or out into the street? Where were the bombs located? Who was setting them off? Of course, she also had no certainty in the moment that bombs were causing the havoc into which she had suddenly been placed. Her response was a kind of eternal negative. She stood frozen in place. She had no idea where to go. She was completely confused. "I just stood there screaming," she said with the self-reproach that is so typical of survivors looking back at their behavior during disasters. "I was not processing anything." Smoke began to pour out of the World Trade Center, debris was falling everywhere, everything was shaking. "There was a big cloud." she said, "and I remember thinking, 'Maybe it's a fire.'"

Shock

The sense of shock that overwhelmed Felicia quickly deepened for all those in zone 1 as scenes of death appeared everywhere, and immediately. Such radical encounters with death shift the self out of normal existence. All the predictable dimensions of life fall away. There is no longer anything that is familiar to guide decisions about where to go and how again to feel safe. The world itself is threatening.

Having survived the flying lamppost, Henry decided to walk up West Street (the West Side Highway) north to get closer to the WTC. He came across all kinds of debris, including human remains, even though he was then three blocks to the south of the complex. There were "pieces of bodies on West Street," he said in quiet despair. One was "essentially what was like a torso," a head lay near it on the ground, and "then one other large like piece of flesh." He then turned back south on West Street to the office building where he worked on Rector Street. By then most of his colleagues were out on the street, milling about, trying to figure out what was happening. Henry had the dissociated thought that he should go to work. Something bad had happened but it was now over and the most sensible thing for him to do was go to work. But that fleeting thought was quickly overtaken by the scene that was unfolding in front of him. Cars from both directions on West Street were being directed into Rector Street, passing directly in front of where he was standing. He noticed with horror that many of the cars passing in front of him had "blood and small pieces of flesh all over the side and, like, hood of their car." One guy stopped, "got out of his car, looked at the blood and I mean chunks of flesh on his windshield and just, like, looked at it kind of with a blank look on his face, and then, like, got back in his car. I mean, like, what do you do?" A cab driver got frustrated at how slowly the traffic was moving and started honking insistently. Henry got furious at his insolent disrespect. His annoyance at the cabbie became a substitute for all his feelings about the detritus of death he was looking at on the cars.

On the other side of the WTC complex, Sanford's vision was obscured by the awning and he could not see what was occurring ninety stories above him. Somebody authoritatively yelled that everyone—which at that point consisted of thirty to forty people—should get against the wall to escape the danger. Sanford at first agreed and flattened himself against the wall as he continued to witness the crashing of debris onto the area around him. Then he changed his mind, feeling the awning would provide very little protection if something large hit it. Perhaps his preliminary explanations for what he had stumbled onto were inadequate to the danger he faced. Standing there in the midst of such chaos, he decided, was definitely a mistake.

So without further thought Sanford started running. His "thoughts weren't to go back from where I came, but to get to my building, to get onto the walkway because I felt at least there's some kind of shield there." The topography he is referring to is the covered walkway, or North Bridge, that one entered from the northwest corner of the WTC Plaza that led over the West Side Highway (West Street) to the World Financial Center, where Sanford worked. His instinctive, if somewhat impulsive, idea of running in part grew out of the fact that he is an athletic young man and knew he could run well, but also seems to have come from an instinct to flee danger. As humans caught in situations of great danger, we generate large quantities of adrenaline. Sanford drew on that physical stimulus in his effort to run at top speed away from the danger he felt under that awning.

Once he got onto the walkway and was about halfway over the West Side Highway, he stopped to look back and saw a scene worse than that which turned Lot's wife into a pillar of salt. "I saw the debris still falling from the sky. I saw the fire. That was on top. And I saw people. There were people on fire in the middle of the West Side Highway stumbling. I saw one guy fall and roll around and I don't know what happened to him after that." The scene Sanford was witnessing was the horrific sight of people on fire who had apparently been inside the building by the elevators when the now-empty elevator shafts tunneled burning diesel fuel down ninety stories. People standing by the elevator doors, probably many of whom were clutching cups of coffee, were suddenly engulfed in flames as the burning fuel exploded into the lobby. Many of those on fire ran out onto the street in a desperate effort to escape the inferno inside.

Such scenes evoke the horror of Hiroshima. John Hersey, the first Westerner to report on the effects of the atomic bomb, described how there were

> hundreds and hundreds who were fleeing, and every one of them seemed
> to be hurt in some way. The eyebrows of some were burned off and skin

hung from their faces and hands. Others, because of pain, held their arms up as if carrying something in both hands. Some were vomiting as they walked. Many were naked or in shreds of clothing. On some undressed bodies, the burns had made patterns—of undershirt scraps and suspenders and, on the skin of some women (since white repelled the heat from the bomb and dark clothes absorbed it and conducted it to the skin), the shapes of flowers they had had on their kimonos. Many, although injured themselves, supported relatives who were worse off. Almost all had their heads bowed, looked straight ahead, were silent, and showed no expression whatever.[3]

That lack of expression on the faces of survivors, often called the "thousand-mile stare," reflects what Robert Jay Lifton calls "psychic numbing." He argues it is the survivor's most significant defense strategy in the moment of radical death encounters. Such numbing shuts down feeling and is a kind of affective anesthesia. In the moment, such a numbing is highly adaptive. It helps fight through the weirdness of everyone around you dying. Such a disaster syndrome leaves the survivor stunned and dazed, unable to focus, shocked and unresponsive. It cuts out the severely threatening outside world. As Lifton shrewdly notes, such numbing is a form of symbolic death to protect against actual or psychic death.[4]

All survivors abide by the dictum "Don't dare to feel." Such complete closing off is what allowed those in Nazi camps to cope with the extreme situations, the death and suffering, and the physical deprivations. They became walking corpses, "damned souls wandering in the half-world," as Elie Wiesel put it. This is the state of "death in life" that forms the title of Lifton's book on Hiroshima, a "state of such radically impaired existence that one no longer feels related to the activities and moral standards of the life process."[5]

One dangerous consequence of such numbing is subsequent psychosomatic symptoms of withdrawal from social life, nightmares and flashbacks, insomnia, depression and anxiety disorders, general fatigue, and social and sexual dysfunctions that we now label as part of a syndrome called "posttraumatic stress disorder" in the sanitized language of contemporary psychiatry. The body keeps the score, as Bessel van der Kolk has put it.[6] The survivor becomes entrapped by what is felt to be a continuous threat of death that lives on in the survivor.[7]

Chaos

Confusion reigned after the initial attack, as escape became the central task of survivors. Some wandered, dazed, down hundreds of stairs in dark buildings. Miranda, after rushing out of her office in WTC 2 at the first sign of fire in the opposite tower, got onto the express elevator down to the forty-fourth floor, the "Sky Lobby." The system of ninety-nine regular and seven freight elevators in each of the two World Trade Center towers was organized according to these express floors on the forty-fourth and seventy-eighth floors, which allowed for quick access for those in the higher floors of the towers without overloading the elevators going to the lower floors. When Miranda and her colleagues arrived at the express floor they found complete chaos. The security officials were not letting anyone onto the express elevators but were directing everybody to take the stairways down. At first Miranda got into one line entering the stairway, but when it was not moving she shifted into another line, grabbing her friends to go with her. One of those friends was in the advanced stages of a high-risk pregnancy (though she had a healthy baby the following February), a fact that added drama to the chaotic scene. On the stairs, moving in single file, Miranda felt worried by the crowding and the slow pace, but she was not at that point crying or panicking. She did note that everybody was scared and trying to use their cell phones, which were not working, which added to the fear and sense of isolation. One very powerful image that stayed with her was that of an obese man who had stopped to rest on one of the landings where the stairs turned. "He was standing and the sweat was dripping and I remember saying, 'Do you need help?' The man replied that he just needed to rest." Miranda and the rest of the people passing down the stairways left him there, but the image of him in such distress and her inability to help in any way—plus the dread that he may have died in the collapse of the towers—continues to haunt her.

Early in the descent from the stairs below the forty-fifth floor, Miranda heard the announcement on the public address system requesting people to return to their offices because the "problem is in Building 1." It was sound advice, based on established procedures during emergencies, for the engineering supervisors in WTC 2 to announce on the public address system that people in the building should return to their offices. One of the worst things that can happen in high-rise fires is for large numbers of people in surrounding office buildings to exit onto the street and impede the work of firemen and other first responders. On 9/11, however, it was tragically bad advice and caused the death of untold numbers of people who failed to exit the buildings because of the advice they heard over the public address system. Not Miranda. She turned to her friends and said defiantly, largely because of her experience in 1993, "I'm getting the fuck out of here. You guys can do what you want." The egress of people on the stairs was still orderly at that point, but it became somewhat complicated below the Sky Lobby, because some people turned to go back up the stairs to the forty-fifth floor to take the express elevators back to their offices.

Miranda's apparently rational, forceful response to the announcement on the public address system belied her true confusion in the moment. Her actual state of mind becomes clearer in the mixed sequence of events that she reported. In her first interview, she reported her determined response to the announcement on the forty-fifth floor, but in her second interview she returned to this topic and remembered she only heard the public address announcement when she was much further down the stairs. Again, as with Sanford, Miranda confused some details in the sequence of events as a result of her traumatic memory.

The intervening event that seemed to have led to Miranda's dissociation and confused memories occurred when the second plane hit the south tower as she was somewhere in the twenties on her way down. The sound was horrendous, the building shook violently, and very soon smoke filled the stairways. It was both confusing and terrifying. There was no way for Miranda or the thousands of people trapped in those stairways to understand what had just happened, though she must have guessed that whatever caused the fire in the north tower—and because of her 1993 experience she assumed it was a bomb—must have also now hit her own, south tower. She had the clear image in her mind that those who walked back up to their offices returned to their certain death, especially those who took the express elevators when the second plane hit. Miranda recounts the absolute terror she felt trapped in the stairway without cell phone service, feeling the building shake and the ground tremble beneath her feet: "But then we were crying and screaming, 'cause then we knew. Like we didn't know, but like you just felt like every time you made a zigzag [that is, the 180-degree turns on the stairways between each floor], I mean I just had visions of being blocked in, 'cause that's what it felt like. It felt like you were just going to see chunks of cement, that ... because of the sound and feeling."

From this point on, everything for Miranda is confused and largely disassociated. Her account of her experiences on the stairs in both interviews contradicted themselves. Where she was on the stairs changed in her various accounts, and she seemed unable to reconstruct her narrative from that point in only the most general way. She assumed she would die, though she kept walking steadily along with the rest of the workers, many of whom were crying hysterically. She reached the bottom of some stairway, having become separated from her friends, though she does not remember how or when, and found a huge iron gate, rather like the kind she has on the back door of her house. Her first thought was that she was trapped, which caused her, in her own words, to lose it. After some fiddling with the knob, however, she was able to open the door onto another stairway that led her into another part of building she had never been in before. She had no idea what floor she was on, but after some stumbling about she found herself on the open stairway leading to the lobby where the elevator bank was located.

In these lobbies of both towers the scene was chaotic. The panic increased as the journey down ended. Everyone started moving faster. Two women told some reporters for *The Guardian* immediately after leaving the building, "There were so many [people] running down the stairs; running over each other and screaming and pushing and trying to get out. And that was before the tower came down. That was before I learned that my traders and friends were still up there, on the ninety-second story, and I don't reckon I'll ever see them again." Another woman told the reporters that it was an accident that she hadn't arrived at her office. She said, "I heard an explosion as I was going into the building, and everyone was running over each other down the stairwell."[8] Other survivors interviewed in the large study of the evacuation of the building led by Robyn Gershon of Columbia University confirmed this chaos and also reported a telling detail: Women who had not already kicked off their shoes nearly all did so in that final exit from the stairs into the lobby (and on the escalators, which of course were not operating).[9] That image of hundreds of shoes collected on the stairs and escalators is often remembered by survivors as evoking the room in the museum at Auschwitz, in turn re-created on a smaller scale in an exhibit in the Holocaust Museum in Washington, D.C., with the thousands of shoes from victims that have been piled high behind a protective glass.

THE SECOND PLANE

The crash of the second plane into the south tower instantly created renewed panic in survivors in zone 1, while at the same time clarifying the nature of what was unfolding. Theories of earthquakes, bombs, construction accidents, and fires faded away. No one doubted any longer that we were under attack by terrorists. Henry, standing on Rector Street, watched the second plane fly directly overhead just above the buildings where he stood and a second later crash into the south tower. "That was probably the most terrified I've ever been in my life. It was absolute terror, because at that point, as soon as I saw the second plane, the first thing that registered in my head was, 'Somebody's doing this on purpose. Somebody's flying planes into . . . crashing planes into Manhattan.'" He felt, "We are under siege here . . . like a war." Everyone around him went crazy at that point. "I mean people just started screaming and running all directions." It was as though there was a collective feeling that we were under attack, that it was all "intentional and not an accident at all."

Felicia stood frozen in place after the initial attack, screaming in the Marriott Hotel lobby. Out of nowhere a man came up from behind her and grabbed her hand. She was so confused and he acted with such authority that she placed her trust in his apparent wisdom. He led her quickly back through the Marriott lobby and out onto the street, never letting go of her hand. On the street it was at first much more dangerous than it had been in the lobby, because there was so much debris falling from the sky, large and small pieces of the building that were crashing down onto the cars and the cabs lined up in front of the Marriott Hotel entrance. She thought, "Maybe we should get in a cab," but the man never stopped his rapid walking holding her hand. They got to the corner, at which point he left her to go in a different direction. This mysterious figure who probably saved Felicia's life disappeared forever into the morning. By then she knew her only hope for her own safety was to keep running. Her goal now was to get to her boyfriend's apartment in Battery Park. Dave became her beacon. "I ran across the West Side Highway. And there was debris bouncing off the cars, and those were big, huge pieces, like they almost looked like they were flopping when they were coming down, maybe just because—I don't even know what they were of, just the building, I guess." She could not believe she was not getting hit or cut as she ran.

She called her stepfather to tell him she was okay, though he had been asleep and had no idea what was going on and was therefore confused. Felicia, however, was unable to reach Dave. In fact, he had woken up earlier when he heard the racket. After looking outside at the dangerous scene that was unfolding, he left the apartment quickly to try and find Felicia. He ran all the way out of Battery Park and across the West Side Highway and into the Marriott lobby. As he stood there trying to find his girlfriend, somebody passed him "basically without a face." He decided to leave and return to the apartment, where he guessed Felicia might return. Luckily, they happened to find each other on the outskirts of Battery Park. She told him of the bomb, of being frozen and afraid, and of the escape with the man. At that point Dave happened to have a cell phone call from a friend who got through. His friend explained it was not a bomb but that a plane had accidentally hit the north tower (this was the prevailing theory in those early minutes). He told this to Felicia, who found the news enormously satisfying, much more reassuring than her earthquake theory or her idea about a bomb. An accident can be dramatic and deadly but passes, posing no long-term threat to life itself. "That [the news that it was an accident] was comforting, extremely comforting."

Felicia, however, was not entirely convinced, suspecting that Dave might not be telling her the truth, and in any event was still in a state of high anxiety. "We sat down on the curb because I was crying hysterically." All kinds of strange ideas ran through her head, including that she had gotten cut running across the West Side Highway and was seriously injured, even though she could not see or feel anything wrong with her body. Dave kept trying to reassure her: "It's just a plane. It's fine. It's fine. It's fine."

At that point Felicia heard the roar of the second plane flying extremely low. It was astonishingly loud and got louder as the engines were revved to a deafening roar. She did not actually see that second plane hit, but everything changed in that moment of impact. She cannot remember the details of what happened from then on. Like Miranda on the stairs of the south tower, Felicia seems to have dissociated in the moment. It was all a blur. Dave later told her that he saw the plane hit but Felicia did not, perhaps because she was crying. But she did feel an altogether new kind of fear. The benign explanations for what was going on were now themselves shattered. This was an attack. They were newly threatened. Dave at first wanted to go back and help people, but Felicia was adamant: "You're staying with me." He therefore took her hand and led her away. For a second time in less than half an hour, Felicia was being led numbly away from violence by a man, though this one she knew and loved and could trust without question.

ESCAPES

Then began the Odyssean journey of those attempting to flee the danger in the immediate vicinity of the WTC complex. Sanford, for example, had first thought of jumping into the Hudson River as he watched the second plane strike the south tower. He assumed that the impact of such a large plane crashing into one of the towers, something he had only a second or two to ponder, would surely knock the building over. His thought was that if the towers did in fact fall over, there would be debris everywhere and the whole area would be one of great danger. As he said to himself, "If this building comes down this way and debris is raining, I'm going to jump in the water." Interestingly, that impulse to jump into the water to escape a raging inferno was exactly what prompted many people in Hiroshima after the bomb dropped to jump into some of the many rivers in the city. In Hiroshima, as Lifton describes, "Some jumped into the rivers to escape heat and fire, others were pushed into the water by the pressure of crowds at the river banks; a considerable number drowned." There is perhaps something primal about returning to water in the midst of great danger. On 9/11 the Hudson River was immediately to the west of Ground Zero. It offered an appealing escape for some, and many others, like Sanford, considered jumping into it.

Instead, his instincts took over and he said to himself, "I've gotta get to Brooklyn." Sanford was then living with his girlfriend, who worked at the courthouse just on the other side of the Brooklyn Bridge. On the bridge he discovered, to his great astonishment, that people were moving in *both* directions. Most were fleeing Manhattan. All traffic had been stopped and pedestrians were flooding the upper walkway and both sides of the car lanes on the road below. The vast majority of people were moving toward Brooklyn (a religious woman among my respondents said she felt she was crossing the River Jordan), but others were going in the opposite direction, as though they were "watching a movie. They thought it was cool. You know, not that they're saying, 'This is great,' but you could see that they were just amazed and enticed and they were just staring and—you know, I guess they felt like they were far enough away that it was safe. And I saw that all the way, even on the Brooklyn Bridge. They were stopping and watching it like it was the fourth of July. And there were also people crying all around me, just freaking out." This extraordinary contrast is worth noting. In one direction people filled with fear, crying, and desperate to escape, were moving east across the bridge toward what they felt was safety in Brooklyn. Others who felt little or no fear and were intrigued by the disaster, onlookers who were curious to find out what was going on, were moving west across the bridge toward the scene of destruction.[10]

Miranda, meanwhile, after stumbling out of the south tower at last, found herself somewhere on the plaza to the south of the tower, though she was confused then, and later, about where she was exactly, because of the chaos and confusion of the moment. She still had absolutely no idea of what was going on, nor of what had occurred as she walked down the stairs. At first in the bright sun she was confused by all the pieces of metal and paper that littered the land. Then she saw an identifiable body part and realized that what she assumed were pieces of meat from a butcher shop that must have blown up were in fact body parts. "Holy heavens," she said to herself, "it was pieces of people." She also became aware that stuff was falling from the sky, including people. She never looked up, out of fear and the intense desire she felt to escape, but could see "stuff falling" in front of her. She was running now "just bent over."

Eventually she got about a block away, where a police officer was motioning to everybody to run. He was, in fact, screaming, which alerted her to the danger. So she ran as fast as she was capable of moving, until she came to the far end of Battery Park near the ferry. At that point she finally turned around to look at the burning buildings. She was able to talk to some people milling about and learned that planes had hit the towers and a terrorist attack was under way. She bought five bottles of water as she stood there, using some to wash herself. She found a man whose BlackBerry was working and managed to get him to have his wife call her mother and tell her that she was okay. Knowing that she had gotten word through to her family, Miranda relaxed for the moment.

Others took to the water as their escape route in the general chaos that reigned after the second plane hit the south tower. The many and varied boats in the harbor, from Staten Island ferries to private charters, in the end evacuated some 300,000 New Yorkers that day. As elsewhere, the points of embarkation were mostly scenes of chaos. Tom Sullivan and his crew on the FDNY fireboat the *John D. McKean* arrived at the pier near the World Trade Center, but because it was low tide the boat was 10 feet below where people were standing. Most took no mind of the distance and simply jumped into the boat. Several broke their legs on landing. Some mothers dropped their children for the crew to catch and then jumped themselves. Two missed the boat altogether and crew members had to jump into the water to save them. Patrick Harris, the captain of a charter boat, was also docked off the World Trade Center. His first mate, Josh, was frantic because he had been unable to find his wife, who was eight months pregnant. Suddenly she came walking toward the boat with blood all over her legs. Josh panicked at first, but it turned out she had been walking near where bodies fell and splashed blood on her. Bert Szostok, an equity broker, went to Pier 11, the Wall Street ferry, to find a boat out of Manhattan. He found a crowd of people pushing and shoving and beginning to panic, though the ferry he got on was only half full. It seemed everyone was waiting for their regular ferry.[11]

COLLAPSE OF THE TOWERS

Then the south tower collapsed and that ominous dark cloud, that blob of debris, roared through the valleys of the city. Miranda stood in place, watching the cloud approach, transfixed, screaming. She knew she had to run and escape, though it was not clear to her where she could go. She dropped her bottles of water. She remembers a great deal of screaming that created a noise even louder than the "muffled sound" of the falling towers. Somehow in her fear as the cloud approached her she fell with her arms outstretched. She held onto her pocketbook but was aware of people walking over her arms. She kept telling herself, "You've gotta get up" but found it incredibly difficult to move. Finally, she managed to stand up, but in the process her glasses came flying off and were lost.

She began to follow the crowd aimlessly, lost and confused. She says she "went sideways a little bit first, 'cause I remember I climbed a fence," but she wasn't clear whether she was running east, west, or south. There was some kind of "cement thing" and "some trees, little bushes and then there was a little fence and we climbed over the fence and then you're right at the water," though, again, it is not clear where exactly she was when she reached the water. She was aware that people were jumping into the water at that point to escape. Miranda stood there screaming and thinking, "The whole island's gonna collapse. Maybe if I'm in the water, somebody will find me."

At that point, a man grabbed her and ordered her to run. "Just run, run!" She obeyed and even followed him, though the smoke was so bad that she remained uncertain where she was. She dove into a space behind the Maritime Building. She was at that point with a number of other people and they went up to the door and were banging on it to try and get the policeman inside to open up the door and let them in. This "rent-a-cop," as she called him, shook his head "no" and refused to open the door; it must have been against the rules. She then found herself in front of the building and saw some bushes. She decided to dive into one because she thought that she might be better able to breathe if she were hiding in the bushes. Lying there all by herself, she took her driver's license out of her pocketbook and put it in the pocket of her pants. Her reasoning was that if she were to die and they found her, they would be able to identify her.

This extraordinary sequence of Miranda's dazed escape and throwing herself into the bushes evokes a scene in Hiroshima on August 6, 1945, described by John Hersey from his interviews with survivors the following year. A Mrs. Hatsuyo Nakamura, a tailor's widow, in a desperate effort to get away from the destruction at the center of the city, fled with her children to Asano Park, which was filled with trees of all varieties that had not been blown away or burned. After the atomic bomb fell on the unsuspecting city early that morning at 8:15 A.M., hauntingly close to the time when the first plane hit the north tower (8:46 A.M.), the park became a haven for many survivors who assumed that if the Americans returned they would bomb buildings, not parks. Asano was also felt to be a haven because it was filled with green foliage that symbolized life in the midst of death, because the rock formations in the park were exquisitely Japanese and evoked images of normality, and, Hersey adds, because of an "atavistic urge to hide under leaves." Mrs. Nakamura settled in a bamboo grove near the river. Many, in their great thirst, drank from the salt water and became desperately ill for the rest of the day.[12]

Henry, fit and alert, grabbed three co-workers standing on Rector Street and said, "Let's get out of here." His impulse to escape was similar to the spontaneous action that prompted Sanford to run toward the Hudson River as pieces of debris fell from the sky or Miranda to flee south after her harrowing escape from the south tower. Henry and his colleagues walked quickly south on West Street, away from the WTC complex. They got as far as the entrance to the Battery Tunnel (some six blocks south of the WTC complex) when they stopped to turn and watch the burning towers. Henry tried to call his parents from his cell phone but was unsuccessful and could not find a pay phone. This task focused his attention. He also felt less confused and lost because by this time the reports on the little radio he always carried with him tuned to the twenty-four-hour AM station, 10/10 WINS News, were more complete. He understood that we were under attack and that two planes had been flown into the World Trade Center. He was also able to be the source of knowledge for all those around him. Henry was the interpreter, and everyone looked to him.

Suddenly the south tower collapsed. All those around Henry were struck dumb with fear. "People started panicking again, obviously, because I mean the building's coming down and like you don't know which way, how it's going to fall." It looked as though the building was falling straight down but he could not be sure. Would it or the other tower fall on top of him? There was little time to stay with those thoughts because very soon the great cloud of dust and debris began to come toward him, moving fast (at close to 50 miles per hour). It was a blob of terror. Everyone was "screaming and running." The cloud was an awful color, "very dark," kind of "charcoal." Henry continued:

So we could see the cloud coming down and then we started running and I mean people were—I mean they were freaking out at that point. I mean it was screaming and some people—you could see them like freeze up from fear, like where they just like couldn't run. You know, people just deal with it differently, you know, and so we turned, went down one block, we turned left and then turned right. And I kept . . . so it's ridiculous to say this, but I mean it literally was like a movie. Like we were being chased by this like amorphous black cloud of like stuff. And you could see—I mean I kept turning back to look and you could see it was like gaining. I couldn't run fast enough. So we turned the corner and it was like—it was coming around the corners. I mean we turned left and then when we turned right again and looked back and I could see it coming around that corner. It was like coming from all directions. And we're like six blocks away at this point and at some point I just couldn't run any faster and I basically just put my shirt up like this and it came like right over the top of us.

Henry ducked into a subway entrance to escape but of course the cloud followed him. He had trouble breathing and could see nothing. He felt trapped and therefore came out of the subway. At least he was then in the open air. Still listening to his radio, Henry learned (and shared with his companions) that the Pentagon had been hit. "It was just total chaos at that point." After consultation with his colleagues, they decided the "safest place for us probably was one of the other boroughs" and the closest at hand was Brooklyn. They therefore walked toward the Brooklyn Bridge by heading toward the FDR and walking north. The air was terrible because, as they learned later, the second tower had collapsed by then and added its debris to that created by the collapse of the first tower. Henry was reluctant to cross the bridge, fearing it might be the target of an attack but reasoned that risk was still less than staying in Manhattan. Within an hour Henry found his way back to his apartment in Astoria, Queens.

Deirdre reached the ground floor of WTC 7 about half an hour after the disaster began. As she was searching for an exit there was a scream that sent shivers down her spine. By that point, however, many people were milling about and a security guard was telling them that it was safe to continue walking. Deirdre was not convinced. In the lobby area, which was all glass and faced the twin towers, there was a gaping hole with flames darting about, presumably from diesel fuel that had spilled onto the side of the building. "Stuff," she said, "is flying and it's hitting the glass front of 7. Things were flying and hitting and people are getting nervous and we're all coming down the stairway and we've got to go around and they're trying to move us away from the front of the building and around this way to a loading dock." Deirdre and Leticia were clutching each other's hands as they continued to move toward an exit.

By the time Deirdre finally emerged from her building both towers were burning. She and Leticia stopped to rest for a second. She took comfort in the fact that they were okay and had escaped the chaos inside the lobby of her building. At that point she turned toward the north tower that directly faced her. "And I looked up at the building and I saw this man on the side of the building holding on and then just pushed back and let go, and then I closed my eyes and I looked down and I grabbed—went to grab for Leticia's hand and she had turned around to do something else." In complete shock Deirdre told Leticia, "People are jumping from the building." As she turned to pick up her backpack she looked again and "there was another man just did a swan dive out of the building. And people were crying and screaming." Leticia wanted to stop and rest. Deirdre, however, was appalled at what people around her were doing, for they were "running into these bodegas like real close to us and grabbing little disposable cameras and standing around and taking photographs." Deirdre could not believe it. She also felt it was incredibly dangerous where she was standing and grabbed Leticia and said, "Let's just keep walking away from this building." She felt the whole building might blow up. But whatever was going to happen, Deirdre was very clear that, "It doesn't look like this is a good place to be. I just want to be far away. Maybe we can get cell service if we walk further. We can call the people we need to call."

At that point Deirdre learned from a man who was standing near them about the second plane hitting the other tower. That knowledge further confirmed her sense of the extreme danger she was in. She did manage to convince Leticia to leave with her and they started to walk north, away from the disaster. Deirdre noticed with some surprise that her backpack was still open from when she had quickly picked up her stuff on the thirty-ninth floor of World Trade Center 7; she was even still clinging to some papers that had been on her desk. "I still had all of the stupid papers that I was clinging to. And we stopped to put all my stuff in my backpack and Leticia wanted to use the pay phone to call her boyfriend. Deirdre insisted that that was not a good idea. For one thing she was keenly aware that as she and Leticia were moving north a large number of people were moving in the opposite direction, that is, toward the disaster. "Everyone was crying. There were so many people with kids just moving towards the buildings. So many people in general and people running in and buying these little cameras and taking pictures and I just thought—and I'm a photographer and that was the last thing I wanted to do right then."

Deirdre came upon three women with babies walking toward the building. All around them were people with their cameras taking pictures. People in cars were getting as close as they could, opening their doors to watch the disaster. Deirdre, however, was particularly appalled at the sight of these three women with their babies going in the wrong direction. She had met the Three Fates. One was holding her infant in her arms; the other two had the babies in their strollers. Deirdre confronted the woman with the baby in her arms, looking her directly in the eye: "What are you doing?" The woman looked at her in a numbed way, ignored her, and returned her gaze toward the burning towers as she continued to walk with her baby and two friends toward the disaster. Later, that image of the woman with the baby in her arms and the two in strollers walking in the wrong direction haunted Deirdre. She dreamed about her constantly. Her thought was that the woman and the baby must have died when the towers collapsed, even though she had no way of knowing what actually happened.

Deirdre continued to walk up Greenwich Street as far as the Tribeca Grill, 375 Greenwich Street, at the corner of Franklin Street, where she stopped and put her stuff together more efficiently. She tied her shoes and got some of her papers in better order in her backpack; she seemed unable to order the disarray. She was at that point out of the immediate range of the unfolding disaster, and her intention was to continue walking north toward Greenwich Village in the hopes that she could get far enough away to feel safe.

As Deirdre and Leticia stood outside the Tribeca Grill, the first tower collapsed. She grabbed her friend's hand and said, "Leticia, the tower's gone." It happened at that moment that someone among the hundreds of people on the street screamed that an airplane had hit the Pentagon. "So now we're really getting nervous. There were people talking—you were getting sound bites as you walked through the streets. People were screaming that we're being attacked, we're being attacked, there's another plane on the way." It was all confusing and very disorienting for Deirdre and Leticia. They did continue their journey north. They were not running but kept walking "at a good pace." At some point along the way they stopped to use a pay phone because Leticia was adamant about calling her family. Neither of their cell phones worked and everyone around them kept asking them whether their phones were working and, if so, whether they could borrow them. One person who asked to use Deirdre's phone said, "I need to call my boyfriend who's on the 101st floor of Tower 1." So, despite Deirdre's objections, they got into a long line at one pay phone. While on line a man in front of them was complained, "It's the United States government's fault and, you know, this is why this is happening." Another man behind them said he was never going to work in that building again, that he would quit his job, and while he was saying this he was crying. One lady got off the phone in front of them and said, "Another plane is on its way."

At that point everyone dispersed and Deirdre and Leticia kept walking north. They tried to stay in the shadow of the buildings so that they would be less visible in case of an attack. Both women were disoriented. In retrospect, Deirdre felt her disorientation was surprising, because she had walked in the area many times and knew the streets and landmarks around the World Trade Center, not to mention the West and East villages, very well. On that day, however, Deirdre was not even clear which direction she was walking, let alone where she was going. Something inside of her, however, must have kept her walking north, and eventually she made it to either 9th or 10th Street, turned east, and managed to work her way over to Second Avenue and her boyfriend's apartment.

The 102 minutes of disaster were over for survivors in zone 1.

I was sort of in a liminal place between observer and participant, you know, because I wasn't close enough to have been afraid for my life or had been hit by ash or had run from a building and all that, but I wasn't far enough, you know, Connecticut or whatever, [not to be affected] directly. KYLE

2

WITNESSES: ZONE 2

IN THE SECOND ZONE OF SADNESS witnesses saw the disaster unfold but could not see people actually dying. This zone is defined geographically as that space north of Chambers Street in Manhattan as far as 14th Street (and further north in the southern views from some skyscrapers), west along the New Jersey shore across from Lower Manhattan, south along Staten Island, and east as far as Brooklyn on the shore from Brooklyn Heights to about Bay Ridge. Again, a precise geographical definition of zone 2 is impossible. The twin towers were so huge and so dominated the skyline of Lower Manhattan that they were visible burning from great distances within the city. In defining this zone, however, I am seeking to delimit an area in which the images of the burning and then collapsing towers was within immediate visual range, though just beyond being able to see actual death. This is the zone in which I found myself, and even as I watched things happen I found it difficult to stay with the horror that I imagined was going on inside the burning towers and then the sadness of the collapsing towers that I knew had crushed untold numbers of people. As I stood on University Place and 13th Street I began to monitor this disjunction between feeling and imagination that distance fostered.

Witnesses were one step removed. Their relation to the death was symbolic and imaginative, rather than actual. That absence of visual engagement had significant psychological consequences. None of their other senses was stimulated. Witnesses heard nothing (except perhaps sirens where they stood), smelled nothing, could touch nothing. The absence of sensory input required witnesses to take a huge leap of imagination to enter into the experience of those who suffered and died. Some important qualifications must be noted. The initial plume of dust and debris from the collapse of the first tower settled in a swath of Brooklyn stretching from Carroll Gardens to Park Slope because at that moment the westerly winds were unusually strong. That meant many tens of thousands of people in Brooklyn who were very far removed from the early stages of the disaster were suddenly and dramatically facing it. Many other witnesses in the second zone of sadness responded empathically to the experience of those trapped in the burning towers and then their collapse. For some of these witnesses watching the disaster unfold revived earlier trauma, and that became the focus of their concerns. Others watched it unfold before their eyes but could not see people dying and therefore found it difficult to react in the moment. They did not encounter death, or face it. They were safe as they watched the horror and knew at some level that it would not touch them. This made all the difference.

The most pained gaze might have been that of Rosemary, a sixty-four-year-old administrative assistant with a large firm in the city. She was sitting at her desk in midtown and knew something horrible had happened when her supervisor, Valerie, who worked at the firm's offices on the ninety-first floor of the north tower, failed to answer her phone in the conference call scheduled for 9:00 A.M. Rosemary heard quickly about the first plane, though it was of course minimized by those in her office as nothing more than a relatively small accident. She, however, suspected something much worse, in part stirred by knowledge of the World Trade Center itself. When she had worked in her company's offices for several years before 9/11, she hated every minute of it and often wondered if one of the many helicopters or small planes flying up and down the Hudson with reckless abandon would crash into the upper floors of one of the towers. She had no way of imagining the scale of what had actually happened a few minutes earlier, but she felt that even a small plane could have done significant damage. Besides, why had Valerie not answered the phone?

Rosemary quickly left her ninth-floor office with an obstructed view and took the elevator in her midtown building to the thirty-fifth-floor cafeteria, which had expansive glass windows facing south and a clear view of the World Trace Center. She stared in disbelief at the gaping hole in the northern face of the north tower at exactly the place where she had once worked and where she knew Valerie had been that morning. That was the "whole awful moment" when she "looked downtown and realized what was happening." It occurred to her that the plane hit at the desk where she would have been sitting. By this time quite a few of the company's employees had gathered to watch the tragedy unfold downtown. Everyone was stunned and was keenly aware that their entire staff had most likely been killed when the first plane struck the north tower. At one point Rosemary gathered with some ten or twelve of her colleagues, trying to figure out if there was anything that they could do. The company had already begun setting up phone banks and lining up various services, but this group of mid-level employees felt helpless in the face of the unfolding tragedy. Rosemary and the others kept asking, "Well, what can we do?" Rosemary asked them if they could have a moment of prayer and tried to send some energy toward anyone from the towers who might be trying to escape. As she comments: "This was before the buildings collapsed, and I pictured them trying to get down the stairwells like they did with the bombing [the 1993 bombing]. But everybody was really good about that and we held hands. (*Laughs*.) Right in the middle of a Fortune 500 company we're standing there holding hands and somebody said, 'Well, we could pray if that's what you want.' And so for about a minute we all stood there holding hands and kind of collecting ourselves. It was a great gift to me."

COMPULSIVE WATCHING

Eric, an investment banker in his early forties, recounted his experiences on 9/11 in remarkably detailed and precise ways, reflecting his obsessive tendencies. It seemed that if he were able to remember every minute of what he went through, some of the anxiety he was feeling at the time of my interview with him a little over two weeks after the event could be dispelled. He knew, for example, that he had exited from his local Seventh Avenue (red line) train at the Franklin Street subway stop at 8:54, or eight minutes after the first plane struck the north tower. When he looked up he saw the smoke pouring out of the top of the north tower. He could see nothing more detailed than the smoke, but that was quite dramatic for him. He stressed that he was probably a mile away from the building itself and that he did not see anybody falling or jumping to their death. This keenly intelligent and rational man was struck by the absence of flames. It was incongruous that there would be such a huge black hole in the building and so much smoke but no visible fire. Those around him seemed only mildly interested. He happened to be standing next to two workmen from Verizon who were joking about the fact that, "They just leased this building to some guy for ninety-nine years. I'll bet the Port Authority's really happy about that!"[1]

Eric decided that whatever had happened he would find out about it later but that it was time for him to get to work. Such a practical thought was unimaginable for anyone close to the disaster, with its chaotic scenes of death. Eric began to walk toward his office, which was three blocks west from the subway stop. As he got to Greenwich Street, where the building in which he worked was located, he came upon a large number of people in the street looking up at the towers. His building holds several thousand people and there were easily many hundreds on the street looking up at the twin towers. "Just as I was standing there looking at it, the second tower exploded. And I say 'exploded' because from our angle we couldn't see the plane." He was astonished at the sight of the huge fireball created by the explosion and the way it came crashing down the side of the building. A woman he worked with who was standing next to him asked, "My God, what is that?" and was extremely distraught. At that point in the interview Eric had to choke back tears as he recalled what he told the woman: "Well, this is obviously a terrorist attack, because, you know, one building, you know, it's a calamitous event, but two buildings, that's no accident." At that point Eric ran into another person he knew coming out of his building and asked him for further information. He learned that the planes that had struck were commercial jets, which of course confirmed his quick reasoning that the attack on the towers had to be terrorism.

Eric's immediate response was to call his wife. Reaching her became his determined mission in the next hour or so. She and their son were his lifeline.

He could survive if he could find them. Otherwise, it seems, his fragile self, held together metaphorically by Scotch tape, might unravel. Eric tried his cell phone but, as with so many people that day, could not make a call. He therefore went into his office building to find a phone. The guards told him he had to leave because they were evacuating the building, but he was able to convince them that he had to come in for a few minutes in order to find a phone and reach his wife. They agreed, and he was able to call his wife. She, however, had her phone turned off because, as he figured, she was on her way to work. He was only able to leave a message.

Eric was close to panic. He began walking back toward the subway stop at Franklin Street, figuring that if he could take a train at this point it would be the wisest course of action because the trains would probably become congested later on.[2] He also reasoned that if he started walking it would take him forever to get home because he lived in the nineties on the Upper East Side. In his style of meticulous recounting, he reported getting off the express Seventh Avenue train on 96th Street, trying again to call his wife and without success, and getting on the cross-town bus to the Upper East Side. As the bus approached the park, however, it seemed that police blockades were preventing traffic from going through. The bus driver was at first reluctant to let him off but Eric was insistent about needing to find his son. He said, "I'm trying to go get my son. I was just by the World Trade Center. I want to see my son. Let me off the bus." The driver relented and opened the door.

As Eric walked across the park toward home, he ran into a man with a radio and confirmed the news of another plane crashing into the Pentagon. His reaction, curiously, was one of relief. His reasoning was that, the "amount of work it takes to get two planes crashing into both World Trade Center towers in and of itself is a miraculous feat. To have gotten one to crash into the Pentagon is, well, I can't imagine that there could be much more that they could be hoping to accomplish today." Eric's reasoning was comforting for him—and it was quite an accurate assessment of what had occurred and the future possibilities for destruction. As he walked he turned south to look at Ground Zero. What he saw was a huge plume of smoke next to the still-standing north tower. He was confused but figured that because he was at such a great distance from the sight, the second tower must have been obscured by the angle at which he was viewing the World Trade Center. In any event he turned his gaze away from the site and returned to trying to locate his wife and son. He eventually found them in the park's playground.

THE SPREADING FEAR

Serena, a Hispanic woman in her forties, was in her midtown Catholic school classroom on the morning of 9/11 when a nun passed by her room crying loudly. Serena was confused but realized she needed to find out what was going on, so she left her assistant with the children and went downstairs, where there was a television. She quickly learned about the attacks and was overwhelmed by the ensuing scene at the school. Parents were streaming in, anxious to the point of hysteria, to pick up their children. Serena herself began to get very nervous because her own five-year-old daughter, Karrie, was in a school located on the Lower East Side, at 12th Street and Avenue B. Serena was also four months pregnant. She began to panic about whether her daughter was safe after she discovered that because the phone lines were overloaded there was no way for her to get in touch with her daughter's school. Serena told her principal that she simply had to leave.

The school was on the West Side, in Hell's Kitchen. Serena ran east on 42nd Street. As she passed through Times Square she saw some additional scenes of the disaster on the large screen in the middle of Times Square. She found the scene "surreal." Absolutely everyone in Times Square was "at a standstill, staring up at the screen." As she watched, the second plane hit the south tower. She was now even more terrified and proceeded on her journey in even greater haste, alternately running and walking fast the entire way to her daughter's school. The further south she got, the more desolate the neighborhoods became. Everyone was moving in the opposite direction. The desolation made her feel even more terrified. All she could think of was "My baby, my baby, my baby," though she also found herself wondering, "What kind of world am I bringing my baby, my second child into?"

Serena found her daughter was perfectly fine in her school and waiting for her. She did, however, immediately begin asking about the twin towers. Serena tried to reassure her, though her reassurances must have been rather lame, given the state in which Serena found herself. The mother and child then walked north to her own neighborhood near the Manhattan Bridge on the East Side. As they got closer to Canal Street, they began to run into people covered with ash and discovered that the south tower had collapsed. Serena was shaken at that news and found it increasingly difficult to explain things to Karrie. She did say that there was smoke and the buildings fell down and everyone got dirty.

When she returned home Serena discovered that the disaster had literally come to her front door. Right in front of her apartment building was a large parking lot for a nearby store. Because of its strategic location the fire and the police departments had turned the parking lot into one of their staging areas. As they walked up many firemen and police officers were crying and hugging each other. Karrie was completely confused and Serena could not explain what had happened or understand events well enough to modify them to relieve her daughter's anxieties. It took Serena some time inside and in front of the television before she could piece together what had happened. By then she and Karrie were traumatized and in a state of shock that was to last for many weeks.

THE NUMBED RESPONSE OF A PSYCHOANALYST

For some witnesses the moral and psychological meanings of the disaster were particularly difficult to absorb. Their gaze fell on the scene of destruction in Lower Manhattan with numbed awareness. It took time to react and feel. Only then was a nuanced emotional response possible.

Kevin, for example, is a psychoanalyst who lives in Greenwich Village and has had a therapy practice there for the last forty years.[3] At the time of the interview he was seventy-one years old. He is well known in the field, having written a number of respected articles and several books. He also is an artist and during the interview referred to a painting of a maple tree that is in the waiting room of his office.

His experiences on the morning of 9/11 were oddly removed from the traumatic events of the day, especially given his later very strong emotional response. On the actual morning, however, and even throughout the day he busied himself with his daily tasks and seemed almost unaware and certainly numbed to the events that were literally swirling around him. Around 9:00 A.M. he heard from a friend that a plane had flown into the World Trade Center. Like many people, he assumed at first that it was an accident and went about his business, though it did occur to him that this "accident" accomplished what terrorists might have wanted to do. He left his house about fifteen minutes later because he was supposed to meet a friend in midtown. He found himself on Seventh Avenue and 11th Street and saw that both towers were on fire. He figured that the fire from the initial accident must have spread to the other tower and left it at that. By that time the sounds of sirens and the conversations of the throngs of people on the street swirled around him. But Kevin was in a hurry and entered the subway, which he took to midtown for his meeting over brunch. He went through all of that and still was without much reaction to what was happening at Ground Zero. After his lunch he went to a doctor's appointment in the Empire State Building and seemed not to notice any of the increasing anxiety that was spreading through all of New York. He finished his doctor's appointment and then heard that the towers had collapsed. But because he did not see them he had almost no reaction. One has to wonder whether he felt at some level that the disaster had not really happened if he did not see it. In his numbed state Kevin returned by subway to Greenwich Village, where he went to his office and dutifully began to see his patients beginning at 1:30. He notes in the interview without comment that all his patients came for their appointments that afternoon. One wonders what they talked about.

By the evening, Kevin returned home and was impressed with the scene outside St. Vincent's Hospital that he passed on his way from his office to his home. Floodlights lit up the hospital, but the gurneys on the street were empty, waiting in vain for the injured to be brought in. By then he realized that many people had died after the collapse of the towers, but he had very little context for understanding the significance of what had happened. He deliberately refused to watch TV in order to protect the authenticity of his own reaction. "I was not eager to watch TV and watched very little because I didn't want my emotional reactions defined by the commentators on television. I had a very strong feeling about that." The problem is that his lack of knowledge about the event left him in an emotional cocoon into which he had very quickly retreated.

In the days that followed—and Kevin makes a point of emphasizing that he saw all his patients for the rest of that first week and from then on—he began to be inundated through his patients with the more detailed stories of the events that occurred on 9/11. Kevin was forced to encounter such stories in ways that were particularly true for anyone who had a psychotherapy practice in the Village, because his patients were more likely to work in Lower Manhattan. Through his patients, Kevin heard stories of the reactions of people to the fire, of patients having witnessed people falling and jumping, and of their strong response to the heat and the flames surrounding the disaster.

These stories evoked Kevin's own childhood trauma, when he was severely burned at one and a half years old. His mother had been drawing a steam bath for him and he accidentally fell into the hot water without her immediate awareness because of the steam in the room. As a result the wounds from the burning water were made even more severe than they might otherwise have been. He was in a coma for two weeks and was given a 30,000 to 1 chance of surviving. As it turns out, of course, he did survive, because of the extensive ministrations of his mother. He went through numerous operations before he was four years old and subsequently had to undergo additional surgeries until he was about ten. As a result, he always felt somewhat deformed as a child. One arm was particularly badly scarred; the other arm was injured in many places. He felt scarred by this for life and despite the very loving care that his mother gave him had to deal as well with her massive guilt that the accident had occurred in the first place and then her response to him as being deformed.

Kevin's experiences of his patients talking to him caused this early trauma to come flooding back to him. As a therapist himself, he had gone through two long psychoanalyses and had had additional shorter-term experiences with therapy, but in none of his extensive psychotherapeutic work had he ever fully experienced the meanings of the early trauma associated with his burning. It was clearly distressing for him to have this experience, but he also found that it was healing to begin to talk about it openly, at least among colleagues and at meetings, seminars, and conferences. He noted specifically that he did not share these personal experiences with his patients, which reflects conventional wisdom about psychotherapy, but the specific ways in which the significance of the disaster entered into his consciousness remain quite remarkable for understanding the intersection of personal history with public disaster.

CONCLUSION

Kevin's reaction to the disaster and those of Serena are important examples of the ways in which the experiences within the various zones were moral and psychological and not solely determined by geographic distance from the scene of the disaster. Serena saw little but had to run into zone 1 to retrieve her daughter and then lived with part of the recovery team literally on her doorstep. Kevin watched the towers burn without any significant reaction and spent the day almost oblivious to what was unfolding a mile from his home. But as he took it in over the next few weeks he was to have a powerful emotional reaction. The meaning of the event, in other words, entered into people's consciousness in a variety of complex ways. Even those who for various personal reasons were far removed from letting themselves feel the significance of the event in the moment, it still had the potential to insert itself in traumatic ways into people's consciousness. The events of 9/11, for example, evoked Kevin's very early trauma that had never fully been resolved, if indeed anyone could be expected to work through completely such an awful trauma. Probably Rosemary more than anyone I encountered brought to her story a level of moral witnessing, a kind of spirituality that makes us feel and directly experience some of the pain of 9/11.

3

PARTICIPANTS: ZONE 3

PARTICIPANTS IN THE DISASTER were those New Yorkers who found themselves in what I am calling zone 3: Manhattan above about 14th Street (except for southern views from many skyscrapers in the 20s and 30s), all of the Bronx and Queens, most of Brooklyn east of the shoreline, Staten Island except for the shoreline, and the areas of New Jersey beyond the shoreline but within the metropolitan New York area. Most "participants" in this realm of experience saw little or nothing of what was unfolding in Lower Manhattan—except on television or from a very great distance—but were very much part of that day's chaos and trauma. The experience of participants was indirect and symbolic but equally present and palpable. It was in this sense contradictory. The disaster was unseen but felt. What entered into virtually everyone's imagination in this zone of sadness was the fear that the attacks would spread, that, for example, the Brooklyn Bridge would be bombed, that something terrible would happen in midtown, that chemical gas would be released, and so on. Others lived in terror at what they feared was the fate of loved ones near the disaster, fears that were greatly magnified by the failure of cell phones to work. In certain areas, especially in Manhattan from the 30s to the 60s and from Sixth to Madison avenues, bomb fears and threats emptied many buildings of workers, who then rushed north in the subway or on foot, or east across the bridges for what they felt was the safety of their homes in Queens and Brooklyn. At the same time, many others in this zone were nonchalant about the disaster, going on with their daily lives, having lunch, talking about other things. It is a very complex picture, and few generalizations easily capture the experience of participants. One can only enter into that complexity through their stories.

THE FLOW OF PEOPLE

The best general descriptions of the remarkable flow of people in the city that day have come from journalists. They were trying to get to the disaster, while others were streaming away from Ground Zero, and so taking note of the crowd movement was a part of almost all their accounts, particularly after the collapse of the towers. One reporting from a helicopter, Melinda Murphy, said that it looked like a scene after a major sports event with people streaming out of a stadium, multiplied times 10. All the streets heading north were filled with people escaping the scene of disaster. The Brooklyn, Manhattan, and Queensboro bridges were filled with people crossing into Brooklyn and Queens. The ferries going out of Battery Park toward Staten Island were overflowing with people, and the occasional boat leaving on the Hudson for New Jersey was weighted down with those trying to get to Jersey (it was particularly difficult to travel to New Jersey, because all the tunnels were closed to traffic).[1]

Marvin Scott of WPIX-TV found himself stranded on the New Jersey side of the ferry. He spotted a small powerboat that was pulling into a gas dock not far from where he was standing. He showed the driver his identification and begged to be taken on board for the return trip to Manhattan. Scott and a few others were on the boat by the time the man finished refueling and began preparation to drive back across the Hudson to Manhattan. At that point, a woman on the dock began desperately screaming that she needed to get a ride on the boat as well, because her daughter was in the Trade Center and she did not know if she was alive. The driver of the boat unfortunately shrugged her off, as his boat was already overloaded. As the boat pulled away from the dock, the woman was crying and screaming, leaving Scott filled with remorse—but he also did not give up his seat. Joe Collum of WWOR-TV in Secaucus, New Jersey, also desperately trying to find a way to get into Manhattan, came across a man standing near a yacht. Collum introduced himself and noted that it was extremely important to get him and his crew of five people across the Hudson and into the city. His cameraman had happened to withdraw $4,000 from the bank some time before, in preparation for their work, and Collum promptly offered the man $1,000 to take them across. He agreed, and they got in. The driver, with his hands trembling, managed to dock at a pier on 40th Street on the west side of Manhattan. He and his crew disembarked and paid the man the $1,000.[2]

Mary Murphy of WPIX-TV approached Manhattan from Queens. For the first time in her life she stood on the road hitchhiking. Most drivers passed her up, but finally an elderly man stopped in a rundown pickup and drove her to base of the 59th Street Bridge. He was unable to drive any further, but the bridge was open to pedestrian traffic. As Murphy approached the bridge, she saw thousands of people walking toward her and what they felt would be safety in Queens. Tim Scheld crossed the George Washington Bridge on his bicycle on the first leg of his long journey to Ground Zero. After he reached Manhattan at 178th Street, he found a large crowd of commuters in all kinds of vehicles, as well as on foot, gathered in the street trying to find a way to get back home to New Jersey. It was a chaotic scene that evoked a striking image for him: "It had the feel of the fall of Saigon, as those on foot descended on those cars and trucks, begging for a ride out of New York." Scheld found a huge array of people—"Blue-collar workers, men in business suits, women in heels, senior citizens carrying shopping bags"—all desperately searching for a way out of the city. Like homeless people, some would knock on the windows of cars and ask for help. Some climbed on the back of trucks and clamored into any empty seat in a cab. "A ride was a ride," as Scheld put it.[3]

AN UNDERWORLD OF EXPERIENCE

An underworld of experience existed in this zone of sadness. On the way to the subway Eric tried again to call his wife from a pay phone but could not reach her. He therefore sent her an email from his BlackBerry saying,

"I'm O.K. I'm on my way home." He then got onto the subway and ran into a woman who said she had been in one of the lower floors of the north tower and had managed to evacuate. Even she was unclear what was really happening at the site and could only vaguely fill him in. Eric, the banker who was desperately trying to connect with his wife on the Upper East Side, got on the local Seventh Avenue (red line) train at Franklin Street and traveled the four stops to 14th Street.[4] On that train he chatted with a number of people who had been coming from the area near the disaster itself. He found this conversation comforting. "The train I was on was a train that had come from further south, so they were people who were very much experienced [in] the moment and we were sort of half quiet, half talking." Eric realized that, "I enjoyed talking to these people. If I get on this express train [which comes in from Brooklyn and thus is likely to be filled with people who had no knowledge of the ongoing disaster], I'm going to be talking to people who, you know, they're literally coming from a physically different place and won't have had the same experience." Eric, in other words, had quickly developed a sense of community with the strangers on the local train in the four stops from Franklin to 14th streets. That fleeting sense of community relieved some of the fear he had experienced at watching the initial stages of the disaster. These very positive feelings filled him with a desire to maintain the connection. This spontaneous development of community between people is something often commented on by those who study disasters. In this situation with Eric the sequence was very rapid and soon to be disrupted but represented a moment in situ when the psychological and spiritual disruption caused by a disaster prompts people to reach out to others, pulling together in new and unfamiliar ways that bind themselves into a community.

Eric was to remember and even long for those feelings of connection on the local train, because when he arrived at 14th Street he got off the train to wait for the express 2 or 3 that would take him much more quickly to 96th Street. He immediately berated himself for his choice. "I was on a perfectly good train headed north away from danger. Fourteenth Street is not that close to danger, but if things are really going to get a lot worse, it's probably too close." He stood there on the platform and thought to himself that he had made "a really bad decision" purely out of habit. This keen sense of failed enactment in the moment of crisis, together with the sense of loss at the supportive group he had spontaneously found on the train, filled him with doubt and with self-criticism. In any event he was only on the platform for a few minutes before an express train came that he took all the way to 96th Street.

The tone on this new train was quite different from the earlier one. A woman who had been nowhere near the towers commented, "Gosh, I hope we don't overreact about all this." Eric felt instantly annoyed with this woman and frustrated with her point of view. It brought a radical disjunction into his experience ever since he had watched the second plane hit the south tower.

Andi Rosenthal, from the Columbia University Oral History Project, got into the elevator after leaving her office in the Jewish Museum, located just south of the World Trade Center complex (beginning her journey, in other words, from within zone 1). The elevator was packed. Somebody from the law firm that rented space in the building just above the museum put his arm on her shoulder, perhaps sensing her mounting anxiety, and said: "Don't fall apart now. You've got to keep yourself together. Fall apart all you want when you get home, but you are going to need every bit of sense that you have to get out of here. Take a deep breath and keep it together and when you get home, do whatever you want, but just keep your wits about you."[5] She never saw the man's face and thus had no idea who he was, but she found his advice enormously valuable. It helped keep her focused during what followed.

Rosenthal left the building "very calmly" and "very quickly," "almost as if it wasn't me anymore." Apparently not looking up or about, she noted, "I was just moving, nothing mattered, I just had to keep moving." She walked to the subway and found the platform mostly empty, something that shocked her. But her train came and she got on. One woman said, "Well, I was here in '93, when they tried to bring it down. Here we go again." But most of the people on the train were in their typical New York subway mode that preserves personal space and minimizes contact with others (especially eye contact). Rosenthal realized "they had been underground since Brooklyn and they probably had no idea." It was a "calm, regular subway" just like "any morning in New York." At the next stop nobody got off and Rosenthal suddenly felt, in what seems to have been a flash of paranoid fear, that everyone on the subway knew more than they were letting on. She asked herself, "What's happening in the subway that I don't know about?" At that point the conductor announced that the train would not make the Fulton Street stop. He was not alarmist. Her thought was that the more accurate announcement would have been "Due to the fact that the world is coming to an end over our heads, this train will not stop at Fulton."[6]

At this point Rosenthal's overactive imagination led her to wonder if they were planning to firebomb the subway, or drop explosives into it. Was she setting herself up to be trapped? As she says, "I don't like subways anyway. I'm a suburban girl." On the other hand, she wondered about the dangers on the street. What if the Empire State Building were bombed and she was in Grand Central? Would she be affected? Would she be far enough away when her East Side train (the 4 or 5) reached Grand Central Station? Would she be trapped? As these thoughts went through her head, a woman got on the train at the Brooklyn Bridge stop, fell to her knees, and started screaming and crying. That prompted the other passengers to take off their Walkmans and close their books. "The twin towers were on fire," the woman screamed, "They were attacked." People were shocked but remained calm. "It was a reaction beyond panic," as Rosenthal put it.[7]

After that she counted each stop as a marker of death cheated. "I'm not going to die at Canal [Street]. I'm not going to die at Bleecker." And so on until the train reached Grand Central Station. Then it stopped but the doors did not open. Over the intercom she could hear the conductors talking to each other. "This train's not going anywhere. The terminal is compromised. The terminal is in trouble." Rosenthal began to panic as she realized it was now 9:50 A.M. and then 9:57 A.M. and that her Metro-North train out of the terminal was at 10:10 A.M. and she might miss it. Finally, the doors were opened at 10:07 A.M. with an announcement that the last train leaving Grand Central would depart in three minutes from Gate 25. Rosenthal took off her heels and ran up the stairs and across the terminal to the track. "It was pathetic. It was like a bad movie," she said of herself. Bells were ringing to announce the departure of the train, which had been switched from the Stamford local to a New Haven local to accommodate more people. It was packed to the gills. Just as she made it the doors closed. At that point she fell apart and panicked and started banging on the doors, screaming, "Let me in. I have to get out of here. I have got to go home." Finally, the doors opened and she managed to squeeze in.[8]

Rosenthal remained in a state of fear. She held her breath through the tunnel and never felt so glad to see the Bronx as when the train emerged above ground. But most of the other people on the train were relaxed. Few had been downtown and had not really taken in what was going on. "It was a strangely jovial crowd on the train. Very much like, 'Oh, we'll get through it. Terrible thing. It's going to be all right,' and I was just shaken." Just then, however, someone who had a cell phone working reported that the towers had fallen and the Pentagon had been attacked. The mood changed.[9]

Blake Radcliffe, who wrote down his 9/11 experiences that very evening and later shared them with me, left his Brooklyn apartment in Park Slope with his wife, Constanza, at 9:05 A.M. They both worked in offices near each other in SoHo. Constanza usually began her day later than Blake, but today she had an early meeting. They walked together south on Flatbush toward the Bergen Street stop on the 2 and 3 trains. Walking in that direction, the city was behind them, so they never noticed the plume of black smoke in the sky. Nothing was untoward in the subway. No signs were posted and no one on the train seemed to be aware what was happening. No one knew that the train was heading toward the epicenter of the disaster. At Clark Street, however, the last stop in Brooklyn, an elderly woman got on and reported that a plane had rammed the World Trade Center in a terrorist attack. Some people looked up but then quickly averted their eyes as one does in response to weird ideas that are often heard on the subway. Blake himself began talking with Constanza in Spanish about what might be a terrorist attack going on above ground.

The ride through the tunnel was a torment, which in the best of times Blake finds claustrophobic. At Wall Street, the first in Manhattan, two businessmen got into their car and reported that two planes, not one, had struck the towers. Blake and everyone else on the train got so caught up in listening to the reports that they forgot to consider that their train was heading next to Fulton Street and then to Park Place, a subway stop across the street from the WTC complex. "Our sense of shock overrode that of danger. Preoccupied with the details of what happened, we did not realize where we were headed." At the next stop, Fulton Street, a woman entered the car and said the towers were on fire and that "two jumbo jets had punched holes in them." Again Blake failed to leave the train, though now the panic was spreading. As the train pulled away from the platform, a man with a cell phone started screaming, "They're bombing the whole country. They're bombing every city."

At Park Place the doors opened and the "sound of hundreds of sirens penetrated the distance between the underground platform and the street above." Blake and Constanza debated whether to leave. They decided at this point the wisest course of action was to remain on the train and escape from the scene of the disaster. Besides, Blake did not want his wife "to see the dead that I feared were in the streets above us." But neither was calm. Both felt disoriented and wanted to run but did not know where to go. At Chambers Street they switched from the express to the local train, which they took to Canal Street. In this moment of crisis, this educated, professional, and highly intelligent couple failed to remain on the express train that would have headed much more quickly north and away from the disaster and instead stuck to the familiar rhythms of their morning commute. Constanza's stop was Canal, so it was to Canal they went.

A JOURNEY THROUGH ZONES

The story of Felicia with her boyfriend Dave may represent the most interesting and dramatic meanings of zone 3. Felicia was an emotional wreck from her experience in the immediate vicinity of the disaster. Once out of danger, she and Dave fled south around the tip of Manhattan and then walked north on the FDR. They stopped occasionally to try to call their family and friends, sometimes getting through but mostly not and having to try again and again, leaving them both frustrated. The street was packed with frightened people, including Felicia. As they approached the Brooklyn Bridge, Dave wondered if they should cross into Brooklyn, but Felicia said absolutely not. It was "much too famous." Besides, by then she wanted to meet her roommate in midtown. She had had a phone call from her. A "nervous type," the roommate was completely hysterical and Felicia hoped to find her and return together to their Queens apartment. So Felicia and Dave trudged on. As they passed the United Nations, a woman panicked and said, "Don't walk past the UN. They're going to hit the UN. And I heard they're coming from Brooklyn now." A man in the crowd told the woman to shut up or she would make everyone crazy. Despite this outburst, Felicia was impressed with how calm everyone was, certainly more calm than she felt, especially since by then the highway was filled with army and National Guard jeeps, fire trucks, FBI, and police. She kept wondering, "Where are they all coming from?" It was like the movies, she said.

After 34th Street, Felicia and Dave veered west toward midtown. As they approached 42nd Street, Felicia was appalled at the scene. Everyone was out. There was an "excess of people." They were walking about, seeming to enjoy the beautiful weather, relaxed. People were having lunch in the restaurants and "doing their thing," while Felicia and Dave had just come from hell. People here, Felicia thought, "will never feel the same way as being down there." It was confusing. It was "very everyday, and not everyday."

Nothing could more accurately capture the differences between the zones of sadness. Felicia, who had been hysterical herself, had just come through probably the most searing experience of her life. She was still traumatized. In midtown, however, some were calm, eating their lunch while others, more frightened, milled about, confused but not terrified as those were who had more directly experienced the disaster. But for some with obvious predisposing trauma in the self—Felicia's roommate and to a degree herself—the news of the disaster set off loud psychological alarms and eliminated whatever safety she might have found in her distance from the scene of the violence.

Felicia, now with the roommate and Dave, then walked toward and over the Queensboro Bridge. Felicia wanted to run. She was sure the bridge would either be hit by a bomb or collapse from the weight of all the people on it. "I kept looking over at the side to see when the water would end and we would be like over the bridge. And I wanted to run so bad." She also felt alone in her terror. "It was weird that everybody was so orderly. I mean people spoke and some people were like still trying—everybody was trying on their phones, but nobody seemed as panicked as me. I just wanted to get home. I just wanted to get home and I wanted to run."

THE DISASTER FROM AFAR

Ivan Almonte, from the Columbia University Oral History Project, was born in the Dominican Republic in 1964. He was from a poor family and only managed to get through high school before emigrating to New York at 21 in the mid-1980's. He lived in the Bronx with his wife and three children. For many years he worked on the maintenance crew at the World Trade Center, something that he felt very proud about. He was not in the Trade Center that day but at home watching it all on TV. His wife, however, worked in the World Financial Center and had been down there that day. She saw people jumping and falling from the burning towers. As Almonte puts it, "She saw all those things, and she saw the tower collapsing behind her. She was running away, the tower collapsing. You can imagine how that thing could be for anybody being there." But his experience far from the disaster was much more remote than that of his wife. "We stayed home watching TV all day, all night. I couldn't sleep for two days. Then I was feeling OK. But now [December 10, 2001] is when I'm feeling more the thing." Rather like Kevin, Almonte only felt "more the thing" long after the event itself, when he had had time to process it and take it in.[10]

Almonte has a keen sense of the desolation in the city after 9/11. He was most struck by the complete emptiness in what normally would be a bustling city. "The street was no car running, everything was empty, no traffic from Manhattan to the Bronx, from Queens to Manhattan or to Manhattan, no traffic. So all the street was empty. It feel different. I mean, that day was gray, I mean gray color. Everything was gray, dark, a little bit dark. People feel very sad. Everybody feel very sad. It was horrible." The poignancy of this description in barely literate English captures the image of the landscape of the city even distant from Ground Zero. The city was empty and had the gray color of the landscape.[11]

Ellen, a psychoanalyst in her early fifties, never left her apartment or office. She watched the entire disaster unfold on television and was totally in shock. The only thing she did to gain a closer sense of reality was to walk up to the roof of her building at one point to look at the smoke rising into the sky from Ground Zero after the collapse of both towers. That brief moment brought home to her the reality of the disaster. Otherwise she sat immobilized in front of her TV and was, as she says, "vicariously traumatized." She was entirely alone except for occasional phone calls. On the afternoon of 9/11 she noticed outside of her apartment the extraordinary sight of a stream of people walking north through Central Park away from the disaster. What she was most struck by was how there was in all people a "deathly quiet, a sense of mourning." Everyone walked "with their head down," something she found extremely eerie. What is most telling about this detail of Ellen's experience is the silence that reigned among those survivors streaming north away from the disaster. Ellen was herself ensconced in her own silent world, alone in her apartment with the TV. It was a scene of mourning and death and eerie silence.

Cathryn Compton (my wife) is a preschool teacher. That morning she was preparing her classroom in Huggs Day School in Park Slope for the annual Open House with parents that immediately preceded the beginning of the year. She was anxious because the room had to be finished. "I'm very compulsive and such a perfectionist and I was driving myself crazy with the smallest of details." She felt the classroom needed to be in "perfect order" before inviting the parents in to see it. She knew parents could be harsh critics. Her assistant, Beth, was scrubbing "tiny blue chairs," while she was labeling each child's cubby with his or her name. This year they had chosen a dinosaur theme and had made the "cutest dinosaur name tags" for each individual child's cubby that "corresponded to their clothes cubby and the bulletin board." As they worked, a parent stopped by the room with her son, Jake, who would be in the class that year. The mother said gravely, "Did you hear that a plane hit one of the twin towers?" Cathryn gave her an "annoyed look" because the parent was obviously talking about something inappropriately in front of the child. She grabbed Jake's hand and led him away with the comment, "Hey, Jake, let's look around your new classroom." Cathryn did not, however, ponder what it might have meant that a plane had flown into one of the twin towers.

As she was showing Jake the classroom, she heard Lisa, another teacher, cry out from behind a curtain that separated the classroom from an area where seniors gathered occasionally to play bingo. (Huggs Day School is located in a Catholic school on President Street between Sixth and Seventh avenues.)

Cathryn left Jake with his mother to find out what was wrong with Lisa. There she found her colleague in front of an old TV with the image of the "tower with smoke billowing out like mad and in flames." Cathryn thought it must have been a "horrible accident" and wondered why a jet would be flying so low. She watched for a few minutes but then left to return to cleaning her classroom. She had to prepare for parents' night. But soon there were more cries from the next room, so she returned to the television. The second plane had struck. She was convinced "we were being attacked by terrorists" but thought, "What am I to do?" She once again returned to work and started cleaning the gerbil cage, which was quite disgusting.

As she worked, Beth was trying to reach her husband, who worked across the street from the World Trade Center. The call kept failing and Beth was getting hysterical. Cathryn, somewhat dissociated, stayed with her gerbils. There were then more wails from the other side of the curtain. The Pentagon had been struck. That broke through Cathryn's wall of denial. She stopped dead in her tracks. "I dropped the sponge and stared down at the gerbil cage that I had been so intent on cleaning. It finally dawned on me that we were under attack and we are all going to die. I started shaking uncontrollably. I felt terrified and paralyzed by my fear. I began to cry." Cathryn found an old rotary phone and tried repeatedly to call the Montessori School in Cobble Hill where our daughter, Alison, was in eighth grade. It was always busy. She tried to call me on my cell phone. She knew I was in Greenwich Village in my therapy office, about a mile from the World Trade Center, though she could not know I was standing quite safely on 13th Street watching the disaster unfold. My phone was also always busy.

Cathryn had "nuclear images swirling around in my head of Hiroshima and Nagasaki." After all, she said, "I live with a man who studies and researches and has written about all kinds of violence. Apocalyptic discussions are a frequent and regular topic at our house over dinner." Cathryn was immobilized. Her director advised her to leave Alison where she was, as that would be the safest place. But, she asked herself, how could she know? What if she remained at Huggs and they were all to die? That thought led, in turn, to the idea that, "If I was going to die then I would die with my child." Cathryn tried to get someone to give her a ride to Cobble Hill but to no avail. She also tried to get Lisa to go with her, but Lisa was hysterical because her husband worked on Wall Street and she had not reached him yet. Cathryn took off on foot for Cobble Hill.

She alternated between "running and walking and crying" as she made her way down the streets of Brooklyn. It was about two miles. Cars were stuck in traffic jams and she could hear the wail of sirens everywhere. The smell of smoke and the taste of the debris from the collapse of the first tower were heavy, which she noticed immediately because it affected her asthma. Cathryn was wheezing and coughing. The sky was "filled with smoke and bits of paper floating everywhere." She decided to hitchhike and was soon picked by up a nervous man who said he did not usually pick up hitchhikers. She said: "I don't usually hitchhike, but don't worry, I'm pretty safe. I'm a preschool teacher."

When she arrived her lungs were seriously taxed. She was huffing and puffing. The air was much worse than in Park Slope. Some people had masks on. At the school she was greeted by the dean, Jim Betts, who directed her to the teachers' lounge until she could pull herself together. There she sat with a small radio in the middle of the room, crying with other parents. The radio reported the sequence of events, the massive fires, the people jumping and falling, and of course the collapses. Cathryn did not know what to do. She was restless, anxious, and frightened. She could not sit still. She felt drained from all her crying. She began to wander the halls of the school and peered into some of the classrooms, where teachers were trying to continue as normally as possible with their day. In one classroom of three-year-olds the children were joyfully playing while the teacher walked around like a zombie.

Cathryn had had enough. She felt she would never really pull herself together and was tired of waiting. She found the dean and insisted on seeing Alison. He went into the classroom to fetch and send her out into the hall, where he made Cathryn wait. It was a huge relief to find Alison, whom she hugged "while tears streamed down my face." Alison was baffled by what she saw as her mother's hysterical state. Astonishingly, the teachers had told the students that the twin towers had been hit by planes and collapsed but that only six people died. Cathryn said it was a good deal worse, but she was vague. She told Alison she would return to take her home after school but that if they got separated she was not to take the subway. "Do not take the subway!" she said emphatically.

Cathryn then watched more from the roof playground of the school, but all that was visible was the plume of smoke. She wandered back, talked with more parents who were now coming in greater numbers to take their children out of school. She ran into Chris Kater-White, who had come to pick up her daughter, Gwen, a friend of Alison, and offered to give Cathryn a ride back to Park Slope. That decided it. Cathryn herself took Alison from the classroom. "We're going home," she said.

4

ONLOOKERS: ZONE 4

THE WORLD TRADE CENTER disaster was the first such catastrophe to be shown in real time on live television. Portions of earlier disasters and wars had appeared on television, as when CNN came of age with its live images of the bombing of Baghdad on January 16, 1991, or the live shots that were nevertheless still and static of the immediate aftermath of Timothy McVeigh's bomb that blew up the Murrah Federal Building in Oklahoma City on April 19, 1995, but since television came of age nothing on the scale of 9/11 had been captured live from almost the beginning, through its unfolding, and into the aftermath. Millions around the world watched it in real time. Others came to it later to confirm the horror of what they knew had happened. I had both experiences nearly simultaneously.

On 9/11 I stood on University Place between 12th and 13th streets just south of Union Square in Greenwich Village and watched the World Trade Center burn and collapse. I had been in my therapy office at 113 University Place writing after seeing an early patient when my brother called to tell me something awful had happened with planes flying into the twin towers. I rushed down to the street, where I had a direct line of sight to the World Trade Center complex. In fact, the very visibility of the towers from that vantage point had long served as a source of topographical reference for me, providing grounding in a large and sometimes intrusively busy city. By the time I got to the street the disaster was well under way. As I stood there and watched the towers burn, I felt scared, disoriented, and deeply confused. I had no idea what was going on. It occurred to me after about ten minutes that I could go into the very familiar Newsbar next to my office, a coffee shop and computer cafe with three television monitors. Two of the monitors were tuned to CNN and one to NBC, and that day the sound was turned up loud. It was crowded inside the Newsbar, but the monitors were placed high enough on the wall that I could easily see the screens from any angle. I stayed inside long enough to learn the basic facts of the attacks (to the extent they were known) and watch the fires burn; then I went back outside to watch the reality of the event. In another ten minutes or so, I returned to the television monitors to get the latest updates. Then I returned to the street, a pattern I was to repeat several times over the course of the next hour and a half, because new information was constantly being broadcast and new images were being shown, some new to me and others confirming what I saw from the street. I became aware of how odd it was to watch reality in what I would come to call the second zone of witnessing but simultaneously to seek out its virtual form. The researcher in me began to observe the different ways in which I experienced the disaster from the street and from television. Reality trumped television in terms of the more powerful emotions it evoked. When I saw the first tower collapse from the street, for example, I nearly fainted as I imagined the people inside being crushed to death. It was so unexpected and horrible. I immediately went inside the Newsbar to watch the collapse replayed to be sure what I had seen had actually happened. The television images helped me establish the certainty of what I had seen. At the same time, it was filtered, removed, and in a sense sanitized, out of the movies, more Spielberg than bin Laden. One cannot overestimate the difference between the experience and the image of the experience.

On Sunday, September 16, I talked with a friend from her home in Wisconsin, an upscale resort area on Lake Michigan where Chicago's upper middle class vacations. People are educated and informed. All had been glued to the TV since the previous Tuesday but not talking in public or even much in private. My friend reported an awed silence in the grocery store. That struck me as very strange. One of the most striking aspects of life in New York in the immediate wake of the disaster was the almost compulsive way people told each other their stories, where they were, what they saw, how they felt, their fears, their sadness. It quickly became conventional that an encounter with anyone had to begin with the simple question, "Did you lose anyone?" There was nonstop talking. It was healing but in its compulsivity expressive of the trauma everyone had experienced. New Yorkers had encountered the violence directly. They smelled the smoke, saw the towers collapse, and lived with the fear and chaos that ensued (and continued). People in Wisconsin had watched the disaster unfold on television but had no stories. They were mute. They had the experience, to paraphrase T. S. Eliot, but missed the meaning. Or, as Kyle put it, those who saw the disaster on television watched the movie, but New Yorkers were in the play.

I am calling the television experience of the World Trade Center disaster that of "Onlookers" who occupied a fourth and virtual zone of sadness. It is one that is full of its own complexities and confusions. There is a psychology and politics of television, but the most important distinction to remember at this point is that between those who saw the disaster unfold in real time and those who turned to television to gain knowledge of its meanings, knowing that the planes had hit or that the towers had burned and collapsed. In real time, experience was virtual but closer to the trauma. The shock of the key moments—the second plane hitting the south tower and its collapse, along with images of the giant plume of smoke and the people covered in ash—was equally powerful, whether watching from Iowa, the Upper East Side, Staten Island, or Paris or Jakarta. It was a fearful day, and the reaction of millions to the disaster tells us much about the enormous power of television in our lives. But even in real time, television provides a powerful filter. The death is literally screened off. The viewer can stand up, walk away, return at will. He or she knows that the danger is not at hand. Informed and mostly older white men who come across as fatherly and reassuring provide commentary that is soothing, precisely because it explains what is happening. And perhaps most of all there is replay. The frightening image is immediately and repeatedly played back with more and deepening commentary. Though repetition in general intensifies experience and in this case therefore the fear, replay of the key moments in the disaster with intelligent commentary made it all fit into a pattern that became increasingly comprehensible.

We are meaning-hungry animals. To watch 9/11 on television was to place the disaster in a context that gave it meaning. That brought comfort, though not without costs.

WHAT WAS ON?

I have long questioned many of the stories I have heard anecdotally and read in the scientific literature about what people saw that day on television. Many conflated what they read about later, saw in isolated form (as, for example, the single image of the man falling in the *New York Times* on Wednesday, September 12), saw later in documentaries, or perhaps most of all, heard about from others with what they saw on television on 9/11.[1] Witnessing the horror of hundreds of people falling or jumping from the great heights of the twin towers defined the experience of death immersion for those in the first zone of sadness. But were those images on television? Much of the scientific literature takes it for granted that images of people falling or jumping to their death were shown on television. Conway F. Saylor and his colleagues, for example, in writing about the exposure of children to the violence of 9/11, write, "Unfortunately, children watching any major station following the terrorist attacks of September 11 had repeated access to images such as people burned, bleeding, and injured; adults screaming and running for their lives; and people leaping to their death from the burning World Trade Center." And Jennifer Ahern et al. in a widely quoted article in *Psychiatry* note, "This particular image [of people jumping or falling from the towers] was shown on television only on the first few days after the event. . . ."[2]

But was that really true? The "first few days" would be a long time indeed and would take the story up to Friday, September 14. Some producers at the networks may well have realized in the very early moments of the disaster that some of the feeds they were getting showed people falling or jumping to their death. Some of those images may have made their way onto the screen of local and national channels. Jennifer Nislou, a colleague whose experience was not unusual, reported to me that she saw no one falling to their death on TV during the day but in the evening of September 11 at a bar in Park Slope happened to look up at the monitor and saw a video of someone jumping to their death. The image was not repeated and was the only time she saw such a thing on television.

By all accounts of those inside the media, especially the networks, however, it is quite clear such images were pulled quickly. At ABC, for example, it is a long-standing policy not to show anyone at the moment of his or her death. Sometimes this policy is compromised by broadcasting images of a still photograph, but whenever possible, cameramen are instructed to pull away from showing someone's death. It was therefore a logical extension of this policy for David Westin, the president of ABC, to instruct his cinematographers from the outset not to show anyone falling or jumping to their death. Westin also got on the phone with the other network CEOs, who agreed to the same policy, as well as to pool their video. That pooling of video meant that any network had access to the same images and that by default the ABC policy on showing death dominated the coverage.

Such a policy about showing death does not exist with European and other television networks around the world. They have always been and remain much more graphic in this regard than anything seen on American television. These international networks may have broadcast from their cinematographers in New York a steady stream of images of people leaning out windows and then falling or jumping to their death, though the international significance of CNN meant that for many people around the world American standards prevailed. Images of people dying on 9/11 subsequently made their way onto the Internet and into the content of various documentaries and in this way became part of the iconic story of the disaster. On that morning, in other words, there was a quite remarkable contrast between what all Americans and many others in the world saw, as opposed to those viewing separate feeds.

The only question that remains is whether images of people dying appeared on some television sets for some of the first hour of the disaster. Local New York affiliates may have shown more than their more restrictive national networks, and one can only guess about what may have appeared on the Internet. (The disaster was the first major event logged in real time in cyberspace, though broadband was not then nearly as universal as it is now.) It is definitely fair to say that those graphic photographs that were later posted on the Internet eventually entered the public consciousness. But it is worth asking what onlookers saw that morning in real time as the disaster unfolded, as opposed to what they may have seen days, weeks, or months later.

I have watched the complete archival video of both CNN and ABC coverage of the disaster.[3] Neither shows clearly people jumping or falling to their death, and none of the commentators on either network notice the very few cases in which, and only with retrospective knowledge, one can imagine an object falling from the building could be a person falling or jumping. The CNN video is especially indistinct. CNN was using a feed mounted on a helicopter that stayed far away and flew at odd angles. Their early reporting was awkward and inadequate and the images unclear; it was only at 9:35 that they got Aaron Brown on the air from the balcony of an apartment quite far to the north of the WTC complex. That camera view showed nothing of the actual scene, and the only alternative shots were from the distant, shaky helicopter. Until 9:45—a full hour into the disaster—CNN even left the data on the bottom of the screen that gave the football scores from the Giants game the evening before and the stock market prices. The camera angle was so bad they missed the images of the second plane crashing into the south tower. For more than five minutes their reporters continued to speculate that a small plane with navigation problems had hit the south tower. CNN also never once throughout the disaster had a reporter who was actually on the scene.

The ABC coverage, in contrast, is much more complete. It is visually superior and, most of all, the reporting was much more informed. Its tapes have been carefully preserved and are regarded as the best available visual representation of the unfolding disaster. (They were used by the National Institute of Standards and Technology in its authoritative report determining the causes for the collapse of the WTC towers.)

The most remarkable moment in the ABC's coverage, however, was in connection with the collapse of the south tower (the first to come down) at 9:59 A.M. A sequence surrounding that occasioned so much commentary and soul searching that it is worth quoting directly from what was broadcast.[4] Peter Jennings was the main reporter covering the disaster and he was in contact with many other reporters on the ground, especially Don Dahler.

JENNINGS: The FBI Special Operations Center is now in control ... there would be additional....

[*The south tower starts falling onscreen, though it is a split screen. On the right is the scene at the Pentagon; on the left, in full view, is the south tower as falls down.*]

DAHLER: When we have a situation like this, they immediately get on the line to the CIA and various intelligence agencies trying to get a sense of who might have been planning something, but right now the first order of business is to protect against a second attack, third attack, the feeling is normally when you have this kind of situation, there will be more attacks almost immediately.

JENNINGS: Let's go to the trade tower again because, John, we now have a ... what do we have? We don't....

DAHLER: It looks like a new large plume of smoke.

JENNINGS: Now it may be that something fell off the building. It may be that something has fallen. We actually don't know to be perfectly honest. But that is what you're looking at, is the current, that's the scene at this moment at the World Trade Center right now. Don Dahler from ABC's Good Morning America is down in the general vicinity. Don, can you tell us what has just happened?

DAHLER: Yes, Peter. I'm four blocks north of the World Trade Center. The second building that was hit by the planes has just completely collapsed. The entire building has just collapsed, as if a demolition scene has been set off. It fell down by itself and it is not there anymore. The building's collapsed.

JENNINGS: The whole side has collapsed?

DAHLER: The whole building has collapsed.

JENNINGS: The whole building has collapsed?

DAHLER: The building has collapsed.

JENNINGS: That's the southern tower you're talking about?

DAHLER: Exactly. The second building that we witnessed the airplane hit. The top half had been full engulfed in flames. It just collapsed. There is panic on the streets. Thousands of people running up Church Street, which is what I'm looking out on, trying to get away. But the entire—the fire got through the top half of the building, at least half of it, I couldn't see below that. It started with a gigantic rumble, closing in on itself and collapsed with a huge boom of smoke and dust.

JENNINGS: We're talking about massive casualties here at the moment and we have . . . hoo. . . .

During the first part of this conversation the viewer has seen the collapse of the tower in real time. Then, while Jennings is still looking at the monitor, they show it again while Dahler, reporting from the street, is talking. Jennings still cannot take in what he has seen now twice on the monitor. It is an extraordinary moment of dissociation. Jennings cannot see what he is looking at. He was by that point a seasoned reporter with a great deal of war reporting from Vietnam. Somehow this is different, more startling, beyond comprehension. He loses his presence as the confident and authoritative commentator, making sense of the unfolding disaster for America, and becomes the terrified observer unable even to report what is right before his eyes. He at first talked about the top part falling off, then is quiet when Dahler believes that perhaps only the top part fell, and is merely muttering and silent as he tries to understand what has just happened.

That Peter Jennings could have been so completely flummoxed in the moment points to something about the nature of the psychological experience of watching the disaster on television. Jennings had watched many people die and reported on grim scenes of violence and human suffering in his many years as a reporter. He was neither squeamish nor inexperienced. But the coldness of the image on the monitor makes it intrinsically remote from reality. It has the feel of a comic book (which is why Hollywood has discovered in recent years that movies of comic books work well on the large screen). That psychological remove protects the viewer but also fosters various forms of dissociation, as was the case with Peter Jennings. If Jennings was so frightened and confused by what was before his very eyes—twice viewed and still the words not spoken—one can more broadly empathize with the distortions of what ordinary Americans experienced that day.

It is extremely important that Don Dahler, who is on the scene and not watching events on television, is reporting what is actually going on. Dahler is saying what Jennings cannot hear, that the top of the building imploded on itself and its weight caused the rest of the building to collapse. This contrast between what Dahler and Jennings see in front of their eyes illustrates dramatically what television is, and is not, all about.

Jennings further compounds his confusion by commenting gratuitously that for a building to implode like that there must have been some kind of destruction or bomb going off at the base of the building.[5] He is clearly groping for some kind of meaning structure within which to make sense of what he is watching. Dahler meanwhile specifically says there was no additional explosion at the base of the building (and he is standing blocks away).

It is worth noting parenthetically that Aaron Brown was equally unable to see what was before his eyes, which in his case was not on a TV monitor but in front of him from the apartment balcony. As he watches the south tower collapse, Brown talks about how there has just been a huge explosion with billowing smoke rising. The building has completely collapsed when Brown says, "I can't see that second tower" that is "ensconced in smoke." Then Brown adds his own comment: "It looks almost like a mushroom cloud," he says, when that was not at all the case.

To return to ABC, for the entire thirty minutes after the collapse of the first tower at 9:59, and before the second tower came down at 10:29, Jennings never considers the obvious possibility that if one tower collapsed, the other might do the same. In all the reporting in that time he never explores such a possibility.[6] He is forced to consider the possibility when a reporter on the ground says there is evidence that the northwest corner of the north tower, the one still standing at this point, is beginning to buckle. Even then Jennings fails to put into words the clear implication of such a buckling.

By 10:25 the fires in the north tower seem to have enveloped much more evenly the whole upper portion of the building. As one commentator tells Jennings, the fire also seemed to be moving down the building. The site is made even more ominous at this point, largely because we already know that the south tower has fallen, and a reporter on the ground has told us that now the north tower is buckling on one side, and because the wind has calmed and the plume of dark sooty smoke is now going directly upward into the sky.

At 10:29 the second tower goes down. Jennings is quiet and then says, "Oh my God." Now he knows. It is striking that in all this coverage of the disaster there have been very few shots from ground level. It is surprising that the only visual image has been the unchanging view from the camera in the helicopter.

After the north tower collapses, something of a mushroom cloud is created over its top. The reason there was nothing like this over the south tower is that the winds, which had picked up at that moment, were so strong that they blew the smoke off sharply at an angle. When the north tower collapsed, on the other hand, the winds had died down enough so that the smoke hung in the air. One does not want to overemphasize the extent to which the image presents itself as a nuclear cloud. It would probably be more accurate to say that there is, at least for a few minutes, the shape of the cloud into something that might be imagined as a mushroom cloud.

Jennings's confusions serve as a metaphor for all Americans watching the disaster unfold. It is difficult to imagine a more sensitive, intelligent, and deeply experienced reporter. His failings therefore help us understand something profound about the nature of this still-new medium of television. In the moment on television the disaster made little sense and in some crucial ways was made more baffling than it was, even with the context and commentary. Jennings's inability to see the south tower collapse before his eyes, for example, was not the experience of anyone on the street watching, just as it was quite apparent on the street that the north tower would soon suffer the fate of its twin, something Jennings remains unaware of until it actually occurs. Yet virtual reality feels certain, as I discovered going in and out of the Newsbar to find out the truth that the monitors could reveal, only to realize I was much the wiser alone on the street with this huge event unfolding before my eyes. Television is sometimes a mysterious medium.

Reflections

5

THE DYING

THE DYING ON 9/11 came in strange and mysterious forms. It was not about whole bodies that reach a natural end and those we commemorate in funeral rituals usually consecrated by religious traditions. On 9/11 in New York it was all more radically disjointed, more inhumane and contrary to nature, more filled with confusion and contradiction.

The deaths that day were varied. Felicia's boyfriend, Dave, saw a woman in the Marriott lobby with her face burned off, and another witness, who worked on the seventy-eighth floor of the north tower, passed a woman on the stairs without skin. She was "like a boiled potato that loses its skin. She was all raw meat." Marcella Palmer, a reporter, noticed that to the side of her car on the West Side Highway an arm lay on the sidewalk.[1] Some died because they were hit by falling debris. A large number were incinerated. But by far the most painful dimension of the World Trade Center disaster is the issue of those who jumped or fell to their death from the upper reaches of the towers, where the planes hit, commonly referred to as "jumpers." The nomenclature itself is in question. In common parlance, a "jumper" is someone who comes to work in the morning planning to commit suicide and then jumps out of the window of a tall building or onto a busy highway from a pedestrian bridge, as a result of some traumatic event. The term "jumper" implies intentionality and forethought. The depression that precedes the suicide tends to diminish our empathy for such a death. It is a gross death, highly dramatic, and leaves a big mess. There is intense shame associated with a family whose loved one becomes a "jumper."

We need a new language to describe those who fell, jumped, or were accidentally pushed to their death from the Trade Center towers. For one thing, an indeterminate number did not jump; they were literally blown out of the building by the terrific force of the planes flying into them. Henry, three blocks to the south of the World Trade Center complex, saw a human head hurtling down the street past his feet and other body parts around him because when American Airlines Flight 11, piloted by Mohammed Atta, flew into the north tower, the force of the impact was so great that it punctured holes on the opposite side and threw bodies three to four blocks in the air.

Henry mused about those who jumped or fell to their death. "It's not like a suicide, like you're depressed and you decide to take your life and it's probably a horrific thing, but it's like forced suicide. You don't . . . like how do you make . . . how do you—you don't like . . . like those people, they were either going to burn to death alive or they were going to have to jump." Henry's hesitations and pauses while he searched for words suggest the pain it caused him to formulate his feelings about those who jumped or fell to their death from the towers. After making his point about forced suicides, Henry associated to the fact that he had learned recently that just the week before (that is, three weeks after 9/11), they had found two bodies on the roof of his nineteen-story building four blocks south of the World Trade Center complex. As he reported this information, I could see the lines in his face deepen. It is not as though Henry has never thought about death. His doctoral dissertation that he was just finishing at the time of the interview was on serial killers. He did wonder in the context of his 9/11 experiences what drew him to such a topic. He is constantly surprised at how people wonder about the motivations of serial killers when he tells them of his work. In fact, people always ask the same questions. It is boring for him to field the questions. Even his dissertation now troubles him.

"I kind of wish I wasn't studying that. I almost feel that I have—for some reason I have to, or something."

The Marriott Hotel was a twenty-two-story steel-framed building with 825 rooms due west of the south tower and extending south from the north tower. The hotel was connected to both towers, and many (as did Felicia) went through the hotel to get to and from work. The lobby of the Marriott was also used as a staging area for firemen during the disaster. Some firemen explored the roof as the towers burned and later reported between thirty and forty bodies on it. Presumably, these victims flew out of the north tower from the south, but they could just as easily have been blown out of the west side of the south tower when the second plane struck it on the southeast corner sixteen minutes later. One also cannot exclude the possibility that they were the bodies of people who jumped or fell from either tower. In any event, one can only guess, because the Marriott was cut in half and destroyed by the collapse of the south tower at 9:59 A.M.

Many more bodies also flew out of the north tower, onto the roof of the forty-seven-story Deutsche Bank just to the south of the complex. The building was so severely damaged by the disaster that it was condemned and is now being torn down. Among other problems, the water system in the building that was activated by the fires left serious mold throughout the structure. Many people who remained in the building during the disaster were killed in the maelstrom of the collapsing towers, especially WTC 2, the south tower, which came down first. Many of those dead were recovered, as were the bodies on the roof. But even after several searches following 9/11 to recover bodies and body parts, as late as April 2006, 300 additional body fragments were found on the roof of the Deutsche Bank. It is astonishing, and unconscionable, that human remains would be allowed to lie uncollected on that roof for nearly five years while teeming workers below rebuilt at Ground Zero.

Other witnesses as well provide indirect evidence that the ferocious burst of energy as the planes struck the towers threw victims out the opposite side. An attorney caked in dust and staggering up Church Street reported to a British journalist that day, "Then the plane came by right in front of my face and into the trade center. Next thing I saw, there were people either jumping out of the window or else blown out into mid-air. I don't know, just flying people coming out of a building on fire."[2]

Many, in turn, surely fell out of one of the 22-inch-wide windows that they reached through the smoke, perhaps fumbling along the wall. Most windows had been broken by people hurling desks or chairs at them in a desperate effort to breathe fresh air. One can only imagine the confusion bordering on hallucination caused by the intense sooty smoke from burning diesel fuel and the fires it ignited. Still others may have been pushed out the windows in the crush of people struggling for air, piling on top of each other and gasping to breathe, scenes that are clearly visible in the photographs. Others probably recoiled from the intense heat and flames, perhaps falling accidentally to their death. Mike Sheehan, a reporter with WNYW-TV in New York, described a young woman he watched climb out of a broken window and dangle at the edge until "smoke and flames gushed out of the window next to her," forcing her to make the tragic decision to jump.[3] Or did the flames push her into the air?

The images of people huddled at the narrow windows above the fires in the towers, leaning out to gulp in air, has now, nearly a decade later, become almost iconic. For some families those images have provided a measure of comfort about their lost loved ones. Mike Rambousek, for example, is sure he can identify his son, Luke, in the picture of one of the upper windows of WTC 1, the north tower. Both Rambouseks worked in the World Trade Center complex. Mike was on the subway going to work when the disaster happened, which is why he survived. His son had gotten there earlier and was trapped where the plane hit. To be able to identify his son in this way meant for Mike that Luke became more real and his death easier to accept, even though he was never able to determine whether Luke was pushed out to his death, jumped to escape the fire and heat, or was incinerated.[4]

Nevertheless, most of those who jumped or fell from the towers appear to have made a conscious choice to die rather than perish from smoke, heat, or fire. Their deaths seemed willed. In the famous photograph that appeared in the *New York Times* on Wednesday, September 12, a man falls head first in his white shirt, dress pants, and black leather shoes. His left leg is half-cocked the way one often lies in sleep. His arms are straight by his side, his body perfectly aligned with the giant steel columns of the tower itself. He looks like a bullet gaining speed as it rushes to the ground, even though other pictures from different angles of this emblematic "falling man" show that in fact he was tumbling out of control. In some pictures, couples fall together holding hands. In another a man purposefully flattens his body with arms and legs extended, falling against the wind, as though to make himself a corporeal parachute. Several photographs show people pushing away from the building, as though there will be safety at last in the cool breeze. Some still wear their ties that flap in the wind; others are shirtless, in what must have been an attempt to get cool.

One witness told a reporter on the scene, "Can you imagine the smoke and the heat. People don't want to burn to death. I saw about fifteen fall or jump. First, there was one; about two or three minutes later there was another. I had tears in my eyes, I felt the emotions. I'm shocked."[5] A young fireman standing on West Street counted nineteen people falling to their death in less than a minute. The remarkable documentary by the Naudet brothers, shot from within WTC 1, the north tower, captures the regular and heartbreaking sound of bodies falling onto the awning of the circular driveway facing west. Those bodies broke apart, whereas those that hit the ground splattered. The rain of death was so intense it was dangerous to those below. Several firemen died because they were struck by falling bodies, the first at 9:30 A.M. at the intersection of West and Liberty streets. Nor is that the only piece of evidence for such tragedy. Amy Eddings, a reporter for WNYC in New York, saw a man on the street bleeding from a head wound. She asked what had happened and whether he had been hit by debris. The paramedics tending to the man didn't answer, but a passerby said, "No, it was the people." In the immediate wake of the disaster, one of the last victims found was a Cantor Fitzgerald employee, dead but miraculously intact, sitting upright, beneath all the debris, his tie still on. Where did he come from?[6]

A patient was deeply traumatized by the sight of people jumping or falling. It took months before he was able to return to any degree of normality in his life. He had been near the towers and had counted forty to fifty people falling or jumping. The patient noted a curious gender difference in the falling bodies. The men, he said, would try to keep their feet down to land on their feet somehow. The women went head over heels falling in an uncontrolled way, before hitting the ground with a thud that sounded "like cracking eggs." Remembering that sound unhinged him.

Andi Rosenthal, interviewed in the Columbia University Oral History Project, reported how the falling bodies mixed with the paper—colloquially called "silver rain"—and filled the sky. "I looked up, and the papers were still flying, and it [the tower] was still burning. I could see people falling, even though they were tiny, because they were falling faster than the paper, but the paper just floated on the wind, and the people just fell straight down."[7]

Rose Arce, a producer for CNN in New York, observed the disaster from an apartment building she had entered a couple of blocks away. The noise of sirens and the screams of people below filled the air. She was impressed with how close the building seemed, and by the appearance of everybody at the windows waving their shirts madly. She kept wondering whether any of these people could be rescued. As she watched, a man came out of one of the towers and stood on a ledge. He was helping others behind him push people off. As people came to the edge, they began to jump. Byron Pitts of CBS was watching what appeared to be sheets coming down from the building. A detective standing next to him thought that the people trapped inside were sending messages to tell us where they were. Pitts recalled Columbine at that point and how some of the kids outside the building had written on a sheet where they were hiding. That thought was briefly reassuring. Then, as he looked more closely, he saw that it was not sheets that were falling but people jumping out of the building. Joe Torres, a reporter for WABC in New York, found himself shouting at the falling bodies as he watched helplessly with his cameramen recording the scene. "Don't jump! Stop jumping!" he said. After he watched the third body fall from the sky, he turned away, unable to watch anymore.[8]

Niko Winstrall of Fox News saw people, looking like specks, hanging from the windows and waving their arms. People were free-falling one by one down the side of the building. He found himself crying uncontrollably. He was particularly captured by the image of a man falling backward, "dressed in a business suit, his hands outstretched and his tie billowing in the wind. He looked like he was parachuting, but the parachute never opened. I looked around at the people on the ground, and they, too, were in tears." Tom Flynn of CBS News says that he must have seen fifty people fall from the north tower. He was surprised at the way the falling bodies would suddenly emerge from the thick black smoke, as though emerging from the clouds. Robert Ginnane, a cameraman for Fox News, captured about fifteen people jumping to their deaths. After a short while, however, he could no longer continue videotaping and turned his camera off. Carl Glogg, another cameraman for Fox News, on the other hand, just kept shooting. He is not clear what happens to him in such situations, but he is aware that he removes himself from the scene.[9]

One visual sequence captures a strikingly beautiful woman with bright red hair in a dark shirt and white pants standing on a broken beam at the very gash in the north face of the north tower where the first plane struck. She holds onto the bent fragment of a beam and seems to be peering down at the street, pondering her fate. Then she jumps and in the next shot she is falling with her back parallel to the ground, her hands held tightly behind her neck, her legs together and pointed up, almost like a ballet dancer or someone in a yoga class.

To grasp fully and empathically the experience of a jump from 100 stories one must understand two facts. First, one can determine fairly accurately how long it took to fall before hitting the ground. The towers were 1,368 feet tall (WTC 1) and 1,362 (WTC 2). By Galileo's calculations a body falls at the rate of 32 feet/second squared. That translates to between nine and ten seconds. Second, those who jumped to their death were entirely conscious during the fall. Anyone who has ever parachuted, especially for sport, can confirm there are often long periods of free fall that can even be exhilarating before pulling the cord. One wonders what those falling from the World Trade Center towers were thinking.

HISTORICAL EXPERIENCES OF JUMPING TO DEATH IN DISASTER

It is rare for people to jump or fall from a burning building. In most cases, those trapped inside seek safe pockets of air to wait for rescue, or find exits that they attempt to use to escape an inferno. Two historical precedents to 9/11, however, are instructive for understanding the peculiar experience of September 11. In 1904 the *General Slocum,* a passenger ship that ferried people to and from different parts of the harbor, burned to the waterline. The disaster, in which 1,030 people perished, occurred when the ship was carrying mostly women and children from a church group bound for a picnic on Long Island. The ship caught fire in the East River. The fire spread quickly, while the captain foolishly (and tragically) failed to run the ship aground on shore. As was customary then, few knew how to swim and the lifejackets were worthless. Filled with rotting cork and metal, they had not been tested or used in seventeen years. Women who threw their children into the water with lifejackets on watched in horror as they sank before their eyes. Those who stayed on board were burned to death. Nearly everyone who jumped off the ship in a desperate attempt to avoid burning to death died in the frigid waters.

There are obvious similarities between 9/11 and the *General Slocum* disaster. Both cases involved an unsuccessful rescue operation, victims jumping to escape a fire, great difficulty in recovering bodies, creation of a special morgue, concern about the mental health impact of the disaster, and creation of a special relief fund. The public response to the two disasters was also similar, including relatives searching for victims throughout hospitals, crowds lining up to view the hulk of the ship and the WTC site, and mass funerals. The key difference—and in historical comparisons it is the differences that are most telling—was in those jumping from the flaming ship hurling themselves into water. To jump in that case was entirely understandable, even mandated by some human reflex imbedded in our DNA.[10]

A second historical example of people jumping from a fire to their death is that of the Triangle Waist Company on March 25, 1911. In that blaze, which is believed to have started in a bin of rags beneath a cutter's table on the eighth floor, young immigrant workers jumped to their death from windows on the ninth floor because all three exits were locked to prevent workers from straying away from their tasks. A young reporter, William Gunn Shepherd, happened to be on the street across from the fire. He filed an account of the disaster the next day in the *New York World* that had a profound effect on American politics.

> At 4:35 o'clock yesterday afternoon, fire, springing from a source that may never be positively identified, was discovered in the rear of the eighth floor of the ten-story building at the northwest corner of Washington Place and Greene Street, the first of three floors occupied as a factory by the Triangle Waist Company. At two o'clock this morning Chief Croker estimated the total dead as 154. More than a third of those who lost their lives did so in jumping from windows. The firemen who answered the first of the four alarms turned in found thirty bodies on the pavements of Washington Place and Greene Street.
>
> It was the most appalling horror since the Slocum disaster and the Iroquois Theater fire in Chicago. Every available ambulance in Manhattan was called upon to cart the dead to the morgue, bodies charred to unrecognizable blackness or reddened to a sickly hue—as was to be seen by shoulders or limbs protruding through flame-eaten clothing. Men and women, boys and girls were of the dead that littered the street; that is actually the condition—the streets were littered.[11]

One of the most striking aspects of the Triangle Waist Company disaster is that, despite Shepherd's report, it was never made clear precisely how many of the victims actually died by jumping. The authorities did not even compile a reliable list of the dead. The explanation for this failure is partly a class issue; that is, in the official and bureaucratic disdain for poor immigrant workers. But there may also have been an unconscious inability of officials to face the issue of determining the number of those who jumped from the windows to escape the inferno inside. The aftermath of the WTC disaster clarifies such deeper confusions.

NUMBERS MATTER

One of the most peculiar and troubling aspects of the World Trade Center disaster is that we do not have a firm grasp of how many people jumped or fell to their death from the burning towers that day. It seems to be a subject residing in that murky area that those who study death call "middle knowledge." Jim Dwyer and his colleagues at the *New York Times* pored over available photographs and could only document with certainty approximately fifty people who fell or jumped. The National Institute of Standards and Technology (NIST) estimated that at least 111 people fell or jumped from the towers on 9/11, though the parameters they used to arrive at such a figure are unclear. A team at *USA Today*, using a different and more flexible method of reading the visual evidence, estimated there must have been 200 such victims.[12]

By quite a different calculation and what is admittedly an indirect set of assumptions, I suspect the number of those who jumped or fell to their death may be significantly higher than any of the existing estimates, and may amount to many hundreds. There were 2,752 people who died in the WTC disaster as of early 2010 (not counting the nineteen hijackers), though it is anyone's guess how many undocumented and/or illegal aliens died anonymous deaths that day. Robert Shaler, the head of the DNA analysis team for the city, reports that many families who suspect they lost someone never came forward to provide DNA samples because of their own illegal status. We must also determine whether to count as victims of 9/11 those who have died—and will continue to die—of diseases from their exposure to the toxic air at Ground Zero during the clean-up. Consequently, we can only reasonably talk of the 2,752 official victims. Of those, 1,628, or 59%, have been identified by DNA analysis or by recovery of the body (fewer than 300 bodies were intact and only twelve could be identified by sight). Out of the total number of casualties, 1,124, or 41%, have not been identified. Some 20,000 body parts were recovered. In some cases, these amounted to a fingernail, in other cases as much as an entire leg; in one case, more than 200 pieces were matched to a single person. Most of the 1,123 unidentified victims were almost certainly vaporized in the collapse of the towers and will probably never be identified, though one must recognize that a body can be consumed by fire and yet leave several pounds of ash and that even cremated bodies can leave chunks of skeleton intact that may someday, with advances in DNA analysis, make identification possible (which is why those 20,000 body parts are being carefully stored).[13]

No qualitative description of these retrieved body parts is available, so there is no way of determining from the forensic evidence what percentage of the remains might have come from falling bodies that broke apart or were burned fragments that may have remained after the collapse of the towers. One has to proceed with great caution. But with many possible exceptions, it is not unreasonable to guess that most of those who have not been identified were actually in the buildings and were incinerated, whereas a great many of those who have been identified left sufficient evidence in the form of body parts precisely because they jumped or fell to their death. It seems obvious that many of the victims (though an indeterminate number) who left a sizable body part must have fallen or jumped, though those in charge of the remains have not provided the data that would allow one to make a more informed guess on this issue. There are some important exceptions to keep in mind. Many of the firemen in their protective suits were crushed but readily identified; those from the upper floors may have escaped incineration because they landed at the top of the pile; some, perhaps many, people below the fires who were crushed by the collapsing towers might have been severely dismembered but not incinerated; and some were trapped in protective pockets in the stairwells. It is impossible to know how many fell into these categories (except for the firemen).

There are other things to consider. The visual images of those jumping or falling that proliferated on European television later and everywhere on the internet were taken for the most part by people with handheld cameras at the site. Most of these images were from the north and west sides of the north tower. These faces of WTC 1 were the easiest to reach by reporters and photographers arriving at the scene from midtown and elsewhere in Manhattan and the safest during the unfolding disaster (especially the west between the World Financial Center and Battery Park City). It is definitely the case that most of those who jumped or fell to their death were in the north tower. The plane that flew into WTC 1 hit the north face between the ninety-fourth and the ninety-ninth floors and cut the internal columns, destroyed the elevators, wiped out all the exits, and concentrated the heat and smoke in a relatively few floors. No one survived in WTC 1 at or above where the plane hit. Victims either jumped or fell or were vaporized somewhat later. Those in the south tower had sixteen minutes to peer out their windows at the other tower on fire, and at the astonishing sight of people falling or jumping, before themselves rushing to the stairs and elevators to escape, leaving far fewer—but also an unknown number—of people in the upper reaches of the south tower when the second plane struck it at a lower level (seventy-eighth to the eighty-fourth floors).

The other six faces of the towers were for the most part out of sight of a camera but the scene of much horror. Those in WTC 2 saw the south face of WTC 1 and the falling bodies, prompting rapid evacuation—though, as Miranda noted, the command over the PA system in the south tower to return to their offices turned many back from their escape route and to certain death. Ron Breitweiser, who failed to rush out, called his wife, Kristen, from the south tower just before it was hit and he died. "Sweets," he says in his one and only call before he died, "I'm okay. I'm okay. Don't worry. . . . It's not my building. But, Sweets, you don't understand. It is really bad. I am sitting here looking and people are jumping out of the windows. Right across from me. I can see them. And they are just jumping."[14] Paramedic David Rivera arrived at the World Trade Center very early and found himself on the plaza between the towers, that is, the south face of WTC 1 and the north face of WTC 2. He started counting how often people were falling or jumping. He estimated a death every three seconds. John Palacia, producer for ABC in New York, watched people falling out of the sky and noted that the number of people jumping was so extensive that it seemed as though people were waiting in line for their turn. Patrick Harris, the captain of a charter boat, saw lots of people falling or jumping from the south side of the south tower. "And there were a lot of them," he reported, "a lot of them. Two or three were in the air at any given time." The smaller people were flipped in the wind "like a leaf" but most just "plummeted straight down."[15]

The images of broken bodies and rivers of blood all around the site of the World Trade Center seem lifted from the Book of Revelation. But in a cruel fate that compounded the insult the scene is also one that has entirely vanished, buried in the collapse of the towers that covered it all in a small mountain of dust and debris, confusing families who lost loved ones and complicating the culture's understanding of 9/11.

THE SACREDNESS OF THE BODY

Thomas Lynch, an articulate undertaker and poet, tells two stories from among his many experiences with corpses. One man he remembers well, about twenty, died in 1974. His twin-engine plane had crashed into the side of a mountain and burned, and it was several days before the body was recovered.

Once Lynch acquired the body in his funeral parlor, he had to add chemicals to prevent further putrefaction. The black pouch holding the body was then put inside a special metal box that fitted inside the wooden casket. Over the casket, was a spray of carnation and a ribbon that read "our beloved son." It was all as planned. But early in the morning before the funeral, the boy's father visited Lynch and insisted he see the burnt and broken body of his son. He refused to bury his son without first seeing him. Lynch opened the various containers holding the body. The smell was offensive and the sight horrendous. But the stricken father expressed deep gratitude and welcomed the sight of what he called his darling boy.[16]

A second story Lynch relates concerns the mother of an adolescent girl who had been kidnapped from her car in her town's park. The girl and her boyfriend had been necking when a drifter forced the pair out of the car. The man tied the boy to a tree and then took the girl into the woods, where he raped and killed her. He dug a shallow trench and threw the body into it. It was months before the severely decomposed body was found. The mother came to Lynch determined to see the body, against the advice of her pastor, her parents, her former spouse, and all of her friends. Even Lynch himself advised against viewing the body. But since she persisted, he had no choice but to open up the coffin and show the mother her daughter. The body was badly decomposed and only a remote approximation of what the adolescent girl had been. But what the mother saw through the almost unrecognizable corpse, the smell of rotten flesh, and the skull beneath the skin, was her lovely daughter. The mother was able to find her daughter's ankle tattoo and just enough of the shape and size of the corpse to feel secure that it was her daughter's body. Secure in that knowledge, the mother was able to instruct Lynch to put the body in the wooden box, say some prayers and lamentations, and allow the cremation to proceed. The ashes were placed in the family plot.[17]

Lynch emphasizes in these stories the significance of the corporeal presence in the mourning process. As he says, "We cannot take leave of what we do not have." In events like 9/11 or the Holocaust, the absence of bodies makes it difficult to properly mourn or even understand the loss. The victims in such cases not only die, Lynch emphasizes, but disappear. "There's the terrible fact of the matter, *we will not get them back to let them go again,* to wake and weep over them, to look upon their ordinary loveliness once more, to focus all uncertainties on the awful certainty of a body in a box in a familiar room, borne on shoulders, processed through town, as if the borderless country of grief could be handled and contained, as if it had a manageable size and shape and weight and matter, as if it could be mapped and measured."[18]

THE BODY REMAINS

Whatever death takes away, Lynch notes, it leaves the body. The dead may be silent but speak to us in different ways. In the law, the body is so important that the tradition is that no conviction can be obtained unless the body is found. There are, of course, some exceptions to this principle, and a number of murder convictions have been obtained even without the corpse. But the idea is you cannot convict someone unless you can find evidence of the crime. All the mourning rituals sanctified by religion focus on the body at the center of such experiences, and it can fairly be said that the absence of the body radically impairs the mourning process. Mourning requires a significant imaginative leap. To be left with only memories and nothing corporeal is to require the survivor to fall back on an imagined life and seriously compromise, or impair, the ability of the survivor to grasp fully the meaning of what has been lost. Most religions of the world furthermore assume that the body is the case or shell in which the spirit dwells. Although there is a widespread belief that the spirit moves into a different realm after death, the body that held that spirit is definitely revered, and hardly meaningless and without sanctity.

Christianity has a fairly loose set of rules dealing with how the body should be handled after death. It may be embalmed; in fact it usually is. Cremation is generally allowed, though Catholics are stricter about this than Protestants, and there are no set protocols for the burial and mourning process. These loose attitudes toward the body in Christianity derive from a tradition that tends to degrade the body in life and privilege the soul. In Judaism, on the other hand, there is a firm belief that humans were created in God's image. This has led to a feeling that autopsies should be discouraged and certainly bodies should not be embalmed or cremated, because doing so fails to honor the natural decomposition of the body. There is no question this traditional idea has been given new meaning after the Holocaust.

As with that radically transformative moment in Jewish history, 9/11 brought dismembered bodies and unnatural dying. It is a tenet of Judaism that when someone dies the body must be escorted from the moment of death to burial (the ritual of the shmira). Psalms are customarily chanted during this process. A corollary of this ritual is that the entire body must be together upon burial. Terrorism in Israel has profoundly disrupted the ability to gather the body together, which is why after any attack one sees a volunteer task force, organized by fervently Orthodox Jews, called Zaka, combing the streets for even the smallest body parts of victims. After the towers collapsed, there was a vast number of often minute body parts. But those were precious. After the disaster, a Jewish group in the city emerged very quickly to do the best that was humanly possible under the circumstances to carry out the familiar ritual. They called themselves the Shomrim, or guardians, conducting the shmira. From very soon after the disaster volunteers gathered at the city morgue on 30th Street and First Avenue next to Bellevue Hospital for four-hour shifts of prayer as the vans with body parts arrived from Ground Zero, on the rationale that whatever was being recovered had to include substantial parts of Jewish bodies. Normally the shmira lasts twenty-four to forty-eight hours until burial. But since a quick burial was impossible, this shmira lasted seven months. At least one member of the Shomrim remained at the morgue to pray every minute of the day until May of 2002, as Uri Heilman did on September 21, 2001: "The site where the dead were kept was bustling with activity when I arrived, even in the pouring rain at four in the morning. New York police officers and state troopers stood guard as police, firemen, FBI agents, federal investigators, and other officials made their way in and out of the cordoned-off area. I picked up my clergy tags from the previous volunteer and entered the scene."[19]

The atmosphere at the morgue conveyed the sense that death was not only everywhere but bizarre, unnatural, indecent, and absurd. One participant, Francis J. Balducci of the New York Police Department, has noted how the morgue was set up like an assembly line in the rear of the facility. In the garage and the loading dock, a triage area with up to six tables was designated where the remains were examined initially by medical officials and their assistants. After that the remains were brought further into the building, where they were weighed and photographed. If a hand or fingers was spotted, the remains were sent to an autopsy room where Balducci and the others in his "Hand Crew" went to work.

Most of the remains that came to the morgue arrived in panel trucks. But if the remains were thought to belong to a member of an emergency service, they were delivered by ambulance. The arrival of an ambulance was the signal for the formation of an honor guard. In the early days after 9/11 these ceremonies were very dignified. After a while, however, it became ridiculous and even something of a charade. On one bitterly cold night in late October,

Balducci and his peers were ordered to stand at attention and salute a fireman's helmet as it was marched by on the possibility, however remote, that it may have contained traces of the fireman's DNA.[20]

Eight or so simple white trucks were each draped with the American flag, each containing bags filled with countless body parts of the unidentified dead–victims of being in the wrong place at the fatally wrong time. A small American flag bound to the pole of the tent in which forensic investigators waited for the next truck to come in was drenched by the lashing rain, and even the flags adorning the trucks were curled up inside themselves.

ABRAHAM LINCOLN

As Americans we have one remarkable experience of public grief *with* the body. On the evening of Good Friday, April 14, 1865, during a performance of *Our American Cousin* in Ford's theatre in Washington, D.C., John Wilkes Booth, a kind of early modern terrorist, snuck into the presidential box and fired a bullet into the brain of Abraham Lincoln from just behind his left ear. The president instantly lost consciousness as Mary Todd Lincoln cradled his bleeding head in her lap and cried out for help. Charles Augustus Leale, a doctor who was in the audience, got to the box quickly. He found Lincoln breathing slowly, paralyzed, and without a pulse. Dr. Leale lay Lincoln on the floor and cut away his collar and shirt, then found the blood clot at the back of his head. He removed it and stuck the little finger of his left hand into the hole as far as it would go. Bleeding started, which brought some life back to Lincoln. At this point Charles Sabin Taft, another doctor, joined Teale in the box to work on Lincoln. The two twenty-three-year-old doctors carried out an improvised version of CPR. Leale managed to force air into Lincoln's lungs by breathing directly into his mouth while Taft raised and lowered his arms. Suddenly, Lincoln's lungs began working and the heart started pumping more regularly, though Leale was sure even then that the wound was mortal. By that time numerous people had gathered. The two young doctors, now joined by two others who had been in the audience, Dr. Africanus F. A. King and Dr. Charles A. Gatch, wanted to move Lincoln to a proper bed. Twenty-five men, including soldiers, the four doctors, and some bystanders bore Lincoln shirtless with a coat thrown over his chest in slow motion across 10th Street to the Petersen house. The cortege stopped periodically while Leale removed more clots from Lincoln's head to let the blood flow more freely. At last the procession moved up the stoop of William Petersen's home and into the room where Lincoln would be laid to rest. He would die at 7:22 A.M. the next morning.

The country immediately went into mourning. People put on black and donned other badges of grief, expressing their sadness. "Lincoln's death," wrote Walt Whitman, in New York City that Saturday, "— black, black, black— as you look toward the sky—long broad black like great serpents slowly undulating in every direction—New York is distinguished for its countless gay flags—every house seems to have a flag staff—on all these the colors were at half mast." Lincoln's assassination on Good Friday and death the next morning touched deep chords in a Christian nation rent by a bloody civil war in which over 600,000 died and at least three times that number were maimed. Just five days earlier, on Sunday, April 9, Robert E. Lee had surrendered the remains of his straggling army to Ulysses S. Grant at the Appomattox Court House. The bloody battles were finally over and victory complete. The South was vanquished, along with its institution of slavery. For that entire Holy Week people had been celebrating in Washington and throughout the country. Now suddenly the great hero of the war, the man whose steely resolve and wise humanity had kept the Northern effort focused, had been martyred. The great religious orators of the day and most ordinary citizens quickly drew the parallel between the deaths of Christ and Lincoln. People flocked to church the next day, Easter Sunday—it has been estimated that a greater percentage of the population attended church that day than had ever been the case (or has been since)—to hear sermons across the land describe the martyred president as someone who, like Jesus, had died for our sins, with the implication of course that in some way he would surely rise again. There were some ironies in these sermons that were mostly passed over. Lincoln was a deeply spiritual man but unchurched and mostly disdainful of preacherly self-righteous rhetoric and arrogance. He was also in a theater watching a light comedy on Good Friday, when he was killed. But no matter. Lincoln in that moment of his death became a newly martyred Jesus.

An important part of the sanctification of Lincoln in death and imagined resurrection was the amazing attention given his body over the next eighteen days in twelve separate funerals and viewings of the embalmed corpse by hundreds of thousands of people in cities across the land. But what now seems an elaborate public ritual of mythic proportions that could only have been planned by the gods in fact took shape rather chaotically. Mary Todd Lincoln, after her husband died, returned to the White House in a state of collapse, sobbing and at times hysterical. She refused to go into her room or the bedroom of Lincoln but chose instead one without memories, a sitting room that had been fitted so that the president could do some writing. After an autopsy and embalming in a room near where Mary wailed, Lincoln remained in state until Wednesday while those in charge frantically tried to decide a course of action. The first and most important question was where to bury Lincoln. Until Wednesday no decision was made. As early as Sunday, enterprising citizens in Springfield, Illinois, eager for the civic recognition and perhaps future business hoped to convince Lincoln's widow to bury him in the only town he had ever really considered home. He expressed his genuine affection for Springfield on his departure, February 11, 1861: "My friends, no one, not in my situation, can appreciate my feeling of sadness at this parting. To this place, and the kindness of these people, I owe everything. Here I have lived a quarter of a century, and have passed from a young to an old man. Here my children have been born, and one is buried." It was not an unreasonable argument that Springfield should be the site of burial. A delegation was quickly gathered, headed by Governor Richard Oglesby, and on Monday went to the White House to petition Robert Lincoln to choose Springfield as the final resting place for the martyred president.

Robert conveyed the request to his mother. She hesitated. Mary had long detested Springfield, a small, gossipy town where she had spent nearly two decades maligned by many as the odd and often troubled wife of the great man. She considered other choices. One was Chicago, her first choice, but that was distant and without any direct link to Lincoln himself. Another possibility was the crypt underneath the U.S. Capitol rotunda that had been prepared for George Washington but then never used. But Mary was also mindful of her husband's specific wish conveyed to her a few weeks before his death that he be buried in "some quiet place." She recalled that he had told her in 1860 he thought the newly laid-out green, rolling Oak Ridge Cemetery just outside Springfield as one of the most beautiful spots he had ever seen. She gave in, though only after three days of doubt and uncertainty.

Now concrete plans could be made. It seemed from the outset that irrespective of where he would finally be buried Lincoln's funeral rituals would be a vast public event. Inevitably, it all began in Washington. On Monday night Lincoln was laid out in the East Room in a gigantic coffin. Carpenters worked though the night on Sunday and Monday to complete a catafalque wrapped in black cloth with black satin rosettes. In the East Room itself crepe hung over the mirrors and paintings. Lincoln lay in state in an open coffin that has been wonderfully described by the Kunhardts:

The fifteen-hundred dollar coffin, which had been ready since late Sunday afternoon after marathon work by the undertaker for more than twenty-four hours, was the last glorious word in funeral trappings. The wood of the shoulder-flare style coffin was walnut but not an inch of it showed, for it was entirely covered with the finest black broadcloth. It was six feet six inches long on the outside and must have been a tight fit on the inside for its six-foot-four-inch tenant, the white satin lining being quilted and lav-ishly stuffed to make the resting place a soft one.

Inside the walnut case was an extra heavy lining of lead. On each side were four massive silver handles and on the center of the lid there was a shield outlined in silver tacks. . . .[21]

The body lay in the East Room for three days, and there, with only Robert representing the family because Mary was so distraught, a funeral was held on April 19.

During all this time special trains and carriages poured people into Washington to attend whatever they could of the various rituals unfolding in the capital, from the White House funeral to the public funeral in the Capitol rotunda the next day, where the casket was also open for public viewing. About 60,000 people gathered to watch and participate in the procession on Wednesday from the White House to the Capitol rotunda. It was an amazing scene, including dignitaries and exotic special guests along with grieving thousands with black crepe on their left arms and, if they could obtain one, a tintype of the president hanging around their necks. Many seemed dazed, as though it was a member of their own family who had died. In truly mythic religious fashion, some saw in the bright blue sky a new star born.

After two more days of public viewing in the Capitol, the body began its twelve-day journey to Springfield. The route was deliberately chosen to repeat (with Chicago substituting for Pittsburgh as the only important exception) Lincoln's twelve-day journey to Washington in February of 1861—but in the opposite direction. Then Lincoln moved ponderously across the country, traveling 1,904 miles via eighteen railroads, stopping along the way to give numerous impromptu speeches from the back of the train in places as obscure as Tolono, Illinois; London, Ohio; and Batavia, New York, along with more extended and formal speeches in Indianapolis, Pittsburgh, Cleveland, Buffalo, Albany, New York City, Trenton, Philadelphia, and Harrisburg. It was a remarkable passage and one filled with tension: By February of 1861 secession was absolute. A new Confederate States of America then existed, with its own constitution and its duly elected president, Jefferson Davis, traveling on his own train from his home in Mississippi, which he left on February 12 for his inauguration in Montgomery, Alabama (the first capital of the CSA), on February 18. Two presidents traveled from west to east along parallel train lines to their respective capitals. It was a haunting symbol of the total political disarray in the country and was to prefigure the great violence to come. Now four years later the South lay in ruins as the body of Lincoln wended its way home.

On Friday, April 21, Lincoln's body was removed from the Capitol to a train to begin its 1,700-mile trip to Springfield. In a bizarre twist, he was to be joined on the journey by the remains of his deceased son, Willie, who had died on February 20, 1862. Once Mary had decided to bury her husband in Springfield, she resolved to make it the site of all the deceased in the family. The Lincolns' first son, Eddie, died on February 1, 1850, and was buried in Hutchinson's Cemetery in Springfield. Now Willie was disinterred from Georgetown's Oak Hill Cemetery and placed on the train with his father. Willie had been the most talented and sensitive of the Lincoln sons and was always his father's favorite. His death at the age of twelve in the winter of 1862 coincided with one of the darkest periods of the war for the North. Mary even then went mad with grief and took to her bed for weeks; by the spring she was consulting mediums who called forth the ghost of her son. Lincoln's grief was less hysterical but his son's death left him in deep sorrow. Perhaps it was fitting that he was joined on his final journey with Willie. Mary, however, too distraught even to leave her bed for the White House funeral in the East Room, remained in Washington.

The twelve-day train ride witnessed an outpouring of mourning unlike anything in modern history. It was also captured on camera—the first such visually recorded funeral ritual—in ways that have indelibly imprinted it on the nation's memory. For the most part it was sad beyond anyone's imagination, but at times the excesses lent the rituals elements of absurdity. It was half circus and half heartbreak, as Lloyd Lewis once put it. At each of the major cities, where ten more funerals took place (two had already occurred in Washington), the train with eight black-draped coaches steamed into the depot past thousands of mourners on the tracks. An honor guard lifted the coffin from the car and carried it to the platform with a waiting hearse, itself a massive, canopied structure drawn by matched pairs of black horses topped by black plumes. Then began a long procession to the beat of muffled drums, cannon volleys in the distance, pealing church bells. In the crowd were masses of citizens, all dressed in black, paying their respects. Different cities brought their own variation to this template for the ceremonies. In New York City 75,000 people escorted Lincoln's hearse down Broadway. Cleveland erected its own outdoor pavilion. And in Chicago thirty-six girls dressed in white, each apparently symbolizing the virginal purity of the victorious states of the North, marched beside the hearse.

A crisis arose as Lincoln's body was still six days away from Springfield. Mary's instructions from the outset had been to place her husband's body (along with that of Willie) in the public receiving tomb at Oak Ridge Cemetery until she could go herself and chose an appropriate site on the grounds for the final burial. City leaders in Springfield, however, men who had never liked Mary, concluded very quickly that Oak Ridge was too far from the center of the town. They wanted it within the city limits, probably to promote tourism and enhance business. They quickly raised $53,000 and bought Mrs. Thomas Mather's big stone house next door to the home of Mary's sister and brother-in-law, the site now of the state Capitol. Working feverishly, a handsome vault was constructed in a matter of days. Mary got wind of the plans and wired in fury that they were to be abandoned immediately. The Springfield troublemakers, as she called them, refused to obey her and went ahead with the work on the Mather home. Finally, on May 1, just two days before Lincoln's body was due to arrive in Springfield, Mary sent a telegram that if her wishes in relation to her husband's remains were not obeyed she would remove them to Chicago in June. At that the Mather plan was finally and reluctantly abandoned, leaving bitter feelings toward Mary.

Lincoln's body, which finally arrived in Springfield on May 3, was beginning to smell. Embalming has its limits. Even then with the coffin not yet open the extent of the problem was not fully apparent. As in so many cities before this, the familiar ritual began. The coffin was lifted from the train and placed in a magnificent hearse built by the city of St. Louis especially for this purpose. It rode now in a large procession past old friends and neighbors to the old Capitol building in the center of the town and placed in the House of Representatives, which had been the site of Lincoln's "House Divided" speech in 1858. The coffin was taken to the second-floor hall and the door was closed to prepare the body for viewing. It was not a pleasant sight. Lincoln's face had turned completely black. Working frantically in the summer heat, Thomas Lynch, the courtesy undertaker, obtained a rouge chalk and amber and some brushes. He set about coloring Lincoln's features with thick coats. After half an hour, the body was presentable, the coffin was opened in the middle of an ornate catafalque, and the throngs were admitted for the viewing.

The sun beat down mercilessly for the final funeral the next day. A long procession marched the two miles to Oak Ridge Cemetery. General Joseph Hooker led the procession on a handsome horse as thousands followed in the heat and dust. The coffins of Lincoln and Willie were placed side by side in the lovely green cemetery. Methodist Bishop Matthew Simpson delivered the funeral oration and was at times so eloquent that people applauded. He also read aloud the Second Inaugural Address. A 250-voice choir sang a new hymn, "Rest Noble Martyr! Rest in Peace!" Mourners joined in the familiar words of the doxology. Simpson delivered the benediction as soldiers closed the great iron gate. The key to the tomb was handed to Robert Todd Lincoln, who in turn gave it to his cousin, John Todd Stuart. People slowly began to wend their way down the hill.

CONCLUSION

Disasters come in many shapes and sizes, and not all bring the sense of radical confusion that characterized 9/11. In a huge civil war, such as the one Americans fought to settle the questions of nationhood and human freedom, hundreds of thousands of soldiers died on battlefields across the land. The ground Lincoln walked on at Gettysburg in November of 1863 to give his famous speech squished in places from the soil haplessly thrown over the bodies after the battle the previous July. Lincoln's ringing phrases about a new nation conceived in liberty were repeatedly punctuated by "here" that marked the land itself, what Drew Gilpin Faust has called the "Republic of Suffering." It is not surprising that Lincoln's own death at the moment of victory came to symbolize all that suffering and that his heroic status helped a million citizens find a meaning in what they had gone through.

But it would have meant little without Lincoln's body. That is why it had to be viewed in that sarcophagus in all those cities as the train wended its way on its funeral journey. The contrast of what the country experienced with Lincoln's body and 9/11 is tragically as absolute as one finds in history. Families after 9/11 felt lucky to retrieve a body part that provided firm identification. The form of death on 9/11 violated all the norms that we desperately need to make loss make any sense at all.

As Thomas Lynch teaches us, we have a great deal of trouble constructing meaning after death without the body. The inadequacy of what was left us on 9/11 in that murky and belching pile profoundly influenced the shape of our political response to the disaster, not to mention the difficulties in finding common ground in the memorializing process. There is no simple answer to these dilemmas, though now, after a decade, we may be able to begin thinking about the form of dying on 9/11 and may be able to bring some cohesion and integrity to our public rituals and our collective stories.

6

APOCALYPTIC INTERLUDE

AS MUCH AS anything, the death in that smoke made 9/11 local and particular. In it were the burnt remains of fellow citizens floating in the air. New Yorkers breathed them into their lungs, literally taking in the victims, whose very molecules of blood and flesh joined the bodily processes of the living. This aspect of the World Trade Center disaster suggests echoes of Auschwitz, where the smoke of millions of burnt victims floated over the living dead. It is not at all that the World Trade Center disaster was like the Holocaust. Nothing in historical experience matches the unparalleled levels of genocidal destruction carried out by the Nazis. The World Trade Center disaster was small by contrast, and a direct comparison of it with the Holocaust demeans the memory of millions. But the experience of Auschwitz in particular, with its overworked crematoria in which some 3 million people were incinerated and approximately 100,000 a month were being burned by the summer of 1944, gives us as a kind of guidepost to grasp one dimension of the apocalyptic significance of 9/11. In this sense we begin to understand the death-drenched meanings of the World Trade Center disaster and at the same time honor the unrivalled significance of the Holocaust.

ASHES TO ASHES

Nearly everyone I talked with (including patients) understood why they had such a powerful response to the funereal smell in the air. Few, however, could bring that middle knowledge fully into awareness. As a result, their reactions were often erratic, even irrational, and they were left with deep confusions that involved self-blame, doubt, anger, helplessness, and depression. Some very personal experiences in my life have made me acutely aware of the significance of the funereal smell and incinerated remains of so many on 9/11. The trauma of my childhood was when my intensely idealized father died suddenly in 1960 just after I turned sixteen. We lived then in Tallahassee, Florida, where my father was president of Florida State University. Dad was being noticed nationally and was even under consideration for the presidency of the University of Chicago that was about to become available. On April 20, 1960, he flew to Chicago to give a talk at the Standard Club, which was the beginning of the interview process. I must have said goodbye, but I also have no memory of his leaving or of any parting ritual. That night after his speech he had a heart attack and died hours later in Billings Hospital of the University of Chicago. He was fifty-three. I know now how precarious his life had been. He had suffered an early heart attack when he was thirty-eight and, like so many in his time, smoked, ate badly, and never exercised. But to me he seemed an inexhaustible fount of energy and sparkling brilliance.

April 20, 1960, was a Wednesday. Various relatives and old friends showed up and camped out in our house and in nearby homes. The next three days were a blur of constant talk, eating and drinking all the time, and sitting in the living room greeting visitors, after which we would make jokes at their unctuous piety. There was a memorial service at the university and a funeral in our church with the governor as an honorary pallbearer. My mother was a blank screen of despair. She was on automatic pilot and made one crucial (and bad) decision. She decided my father's cremated remains should be spread in the Gulf of Mexico that washed up on the beach of our vacation cabin. Once the relatives were gone, she asked my brother and me to retrieve the ashes and dispose of them by the cabin. That home had been an important haven for my father. It never occurred to her that this spreading of the ashes should be a family affair, should be ritualized, and should involve her and my younger sister.

My brother and I drove to the funeral home and I went in to get the ashes. A man in a black suit, the perfect embodiment of a funeral director, had me sign a document and then handed me a round yellow can about the size of a 2-pound can of coffee. My brother and I drove the 40 miles to the coast with this can in the back seat, like a passenger. It was surreal. Once we arrived at the cabin, we walked to the shore and I walked into water up to my knees and stood there holding the can. I asked my brother if we should have some kind of ceremony. He impatiently said no. I did not disagree because I had nothing specific in mind and only sensed vaguely that this whole experience was not right. I opened the can. It was filled with ashes but also clumps of grayish white material. I have never been entirely sure what I expected, but I think it was finely ground, pure white dust. Instead, these "ashes" were too clumpy, too gray, too eerily evocative of something human and not the clean remains from a wood fire. I was momentarily paralyzed but brought to my senses by the annoyed voice of my brother to get on with it. So I spread the ashes on the water in something of a semicircle and watched as they fell slowly to the bottom of the sea.

THE APOCALYPTIC NARRATIVE

The examination of our apocalyptic experience of the World Trade Center disaster lies at the heart of this book. Nothing has more profound implications for the quality of contemporary life than the pervasive ways in which we feel the human condition is threatened. We are familiar with planes blowing up in the sky, with hijackings and dramatic scenes on the tarmac that sometimes end tragically, with crash landings in corn fields, even with fearsome midair collisions. In the same way we know of earthquakes, or floods, or lightning bolts that tear buildings apart. Such disasters can be understood because they fit into a meaning structure. It is not the number of deaths that is the psychological issue. Typhoons can take victims by the tens of thousands, as can earthquakes. A disaster has a human history of meaning that extends as far back as culture itself and is deeply imbedded in sacred texts, paintings, and mythic poetry. Kai Erikson makes the important point that modern human interaction with the environment often, if not usually, changes the apparently natural. An earthquake in Turkey happens in a decidedly *unnatural* way, precisely because thousands of flimsy buildings have been constructed on geological fault lines without regard to potential dangers, just as an earthquake that would have merely shaken a few buildings in San Francisco devastated Haiti in 2010 and took more than 230,000 lives. Hurricane Katrina devastated New Orleans largely because poorly tended dams were assigned the unnatural task of bottling up what Lincoln called the "father of all waters." Even with that qualification in mind, in a psychological sense we can think our way into the range of disasters that fill our landscape. We even impose a narrative structure on disasters. At the risk of anthropomorphic distortion, one might say we comprehend the horrific in predictable stages bordering on scenes; subplots and surprise turning points add complexity and texture to the drama; and character development even occurs, in the way victims and rescuers enact their roles. The familiarity may help contain the suffering. There is an almost infinite variety in the unfolding of these stories, but the one thing a disaster script always moves toward is a clear ending. We dig up the dead or recover body parts, cry, carry out burial rituals, rebuild, and move on. The disaster lives in traumatic memory for some but fades for the culture. Human life continues.

In the apocalyptic, on the other hand, there is no end, only traumatic beginnings that embrace a comprehensive vision of collective death, of vast suffering, of the very end of the world. Biological death is an expected and natural part of being human, and the knowledge of our own ending may be what most decisively distinguishes us from the higher primates. It could be said that we are born psychologically as humans in our pained awareness that we end, in large part because we can imagine our symbolic immortality through our children, our work, or kinds of continuities in communities. We are part of an endless chain of creation, which gives meaning to our own small life. But that meaning requires confidence in human existence, a certainty that we die but life continues. Apocalyptic destruction, however, breaks that connection between individual death but collective life. The absolute and final end of the world is without a meaning that has integrity, which explains the urgency of religious myths of the violent arrival of the messianic age or the bloody rivers and vast death that accompany the return of Jesus in the stories of Revelation.

Some are comforted by the idea of redemption for the faithful out of apocalypse. The existential dilemma for most thoughtful contemporary humans, however, is that such stories feel stale in the nuclear age, which threatens an entirely pointless apocalypse and makes us feel "meaninglessly doomed," as Robert Jay Lifton has put it.[1] The danger is ever with us. Before nuclear weapons we required God to be the agent of apocalypse. Only the divine could ultimately destroy. Now that august power lies in our own hands, and it is proliferating to include biological means of destruction and even the slow burn of environmental degradation. We are inevitably drawn to that power. We may even worship it, which explains our extraordinarily complex attraction for nuclear and other ultimate weapons. The awful dread draws us to it. It is God's power that we have made our own. It is a power that is both compelling and terrifying. Our profound ambivalence toward apocalypse lies within us at the margins of consciousness as a form, or a template, ready to be called forth by events like the World Trade Center disaster, which in the words of Bill Keller of the *New York Times* turned a "theoretical possibility into a felt danger."[2]

The peculiar workings of history have reversed the agency of annihilation. In a shift in consciousness of the first order of magnitude, we no longer need God to bring about the end of everything. The bomb and other chemical and biological technologies have thrust the power of ultimate destruction into human hands, first at the level of the state (from approximately 1945 to 1990) and increasingly with small groups of terrorists and other fanatics. It is seeping out. The apocalyptic shadow created by the mere presence of ultimate weapons in the world and the constant evocation of that shadow in the "entertainment" that streams into our lives on modern media create a psychological template that heightens the dread, despair, and expectation of absolute endings. We live with that apocalyptic shadow, indeed are defined by it spiritually and psychologically, and nothing in recent experience has evoked it more decisively than the destruction of the World Trade Center towers in an inferno of devastation wrought by a man and a group that seek, among other things, to annihilate American culture and make a purified Islam triumphant.

APOCALYPTIC OVERTONES OF THE EVENT ITSELF

The events of 9/11 were drenched in apocalyptic overtones, even at the highest levels. For example, there was much confusion in the U.S. military and among the political leadership about what to do about the crisis in the sky once it was clear that planes had been hijacked and the towers were hit. Only then did the FAA figure out what was happening. North American Aerospace Defense Command, or NORAD, had been downsized from a Cold War high of 750 jets under its command to monitor the possibility of a Soviet attack over the North Pole to fourteen jets in 2001. No jet was scrambled in time to prevent any of the hijacked planes from hitting their targets, even though the order was given (by Dick Cheney on his own authority, it seems) to shoot down any commercial plane that failed to respond to communication. But by about 11:00 A.M., the FAA had grounded all flights across America, while the military raised the threat preparation level to DEFCON 3, even though it was entirely a Cold War designation meant to respond to a nuclear attack. The only time this defense posture had been higher (DEFCON 2) was during the Cuban Missile Crisis. It was clear the United States was under attack on 9/11. What is important about this application of DEFCON 3 is that at the highest level—Dick Cheney and Donald Rumsfeld, while George Bush had still not returned to Washington—the leaders of government responded in apocalyptic terms to what they feared and probably assumed could be a nuclear attack. It was not just ordinary Americans who totalized their response to the disaster. Apocalyptic fears spread throughout government.[3]

The specifically nuclear associations to the World Trade Center disaster were strikingly common also among my respondents, though varied and highly personal. Miranda, for example, drifted into a kind of fugue state when the cloud from the collapse of the south tower overtook her. Even months later she had not sorted out her narrative. She first told me that once she got her license out of her pocketbook and into the pocket of her pants she passed out for several hours, aware that the ash from the collapse of the first towers had descended over her. She then contradicted herself in the second interview and remembered hearing the noise of the collapse of the second tower and noted that the ash that then descended on her was significantly darker and of different texture from the dust of the collapsed first tower. She was confused when she took her license out of her pocketbook. When I asked her about that specifically, she replied that she must have taken her license out of her pocketbook after the second building fell because the difference in the color of the cloud was so distinctly burned in her memory. The accuracy of her memory, of course, is not the point. What matters is that she was so overwhelmed by what she felt was surely a nuclear cloud that she lost awareness in the moment of what she was doing and later, in her interviews, could only evoke certain hyper-real images, such as the color of the second cloud. "Yeah, 'cause I thought—I remembered thinking like nuclear clouds. You know, you always see those pictures of the mushroom cloud and this was just a different color. So I took it [the license] out and put it in my pocket and then I stayed in the bush."

Miranda's odd behavior of jumping into the bushes as the cloud overtook her is not unusual in the midst of a severe crisis that is felt to be nuclear. In Hiroshima on August 6, 1945, many sought safety in fantasized corners of the city. In the late morning (the bomb was dropped at 8:15 A.M.), Mrs. Hatsuyo Nakamura, a tailor's widow, took her children to Asano Park, far enough from Ground Zero to seem safe, and filled with trees of all varieties that had not been blown away or burned (though that would begin shortly). The park became a haven for many survivors because they assumed if the Americans returned, they would bomb buildings, because the green foliage symbolized life in the midst of death, because the rock formations in the park were exquisitely Japanese and evoked images of normality, and, as John Hersey says in his 1946 coverage of the event, because of an "atavistic urge to hide under leaves." Mrs. Nakamura settled in a bamboo grove near the river, but in their great thirst, she and her children drank from the salt water and all got desperately ill for the rest of the day.[4]

In her traumatic dissociation, Miranda could not remember whether she was unconscious for three hours or for twenty minutes. This distinctive loss of time, so characteristic of trauma, seems intimately related to her association of the darker cloud from the collapse of the second building with a mushroom cloud. Such an extraordinary association, one that had nothing to do with the actual shape of the cloud after the collapse of the north tower, suggests dramatically the significance for Miranda of a preexisting idea of nuclear destruction with such an attack in which she had found herself. She, of course, brought to her experience a set of fears from 1993 (when she also worked in the World Trade Center), but Miranda also connects with a much deeper fear of nuclear attack.

It turned out that Miranda had lived with nuclear fears since her childhood. She was in the third grade when the Cuban Missile Crisis occurred in 1962. She remembers crying at night during the crisis. She recalls, "It was third grade, but I remember the drills at school. We went in the basement. Sometimes we went under the desks, which was really stupid. But we did. You had those little desks. I don't even know how the fat kids fit under them, but we had to go under the desks." Miranda's feeling is that now that she understands the lurking nuclear dangers in the world that are so closely tied to terrorism she might be able to limit her exposure to further disaster. As she puts it:

So nuclear? I'll be honest with you, when I read the newspaper even before 9/11, I even skipped those articles because I don't want to know. Before 9/11, I truly believed it is what it is. So I didn't want to read the articles. And I would click if I was watching the news to go to Seinfeld or something, 'cause what difference does it make, because, to me, that was something you had no control over. But post 9/11, now I know you can control some things. Like I feel I can control my risk. Some people call me stupid, but I feel I can control my risk … the nuclear thing….

Miranda's response to her nuclear dread and to her pervasive fears associated with 9/11 led her to narrow her existence enough that she eliminated as much contact with situations of danger as possible. She clearly was having a great deal of trouble returning to work, she started at any sounds of airplanes in the sky above us as we talked, and she tried to remove herself in all ways from the dangers of the world. This retreat into a cocoon in an attempt to protect herself from the evils of the world, especially those associated with nuclear destruction, led her to wonder at the very end of my interview why anybody would bring children into the world. This question of children and a future is somewhat abstract for Miranda, because she is past childbearing age. But she had where she planned to live all thought out. She planned to move to Iowa. She expects her aged and sick parents to die relatively soon, and her sister and her children who live down the street can manage for themselves in the future. She is concerned about her blind brother, who is in the care of her parents. Her plans when her parents die are to move with her brother to Iowa. She does not want to go to California, because it has earthquakes, nor anywhere near Colorado, because of all the military bases there, nor a place like Texas, because it has too many famous people (e.g., George Bush), and certainly not anywhere on the east coast, because of all its major cities that could be subject to nuclear attack. She figures that Iowa is about the only secure place in the United States.

Miranda's fears of a nuclear attack lurked very close to consciousness before 9/11. That dark cloud overtaking her, a cloud that she assumed to be nuclear, threw her into a dissociative state in which she lost consciousness. Her experience of having been overtaken by radiation was also the major cause of her highly disturbed condition six months after the disaster. Something irreparable broke in Miranda. Nor was she alone in this nuclear experience of 9/11. In fact, it was the norm.

Consider the case of Rosemary, who has never had a "great sense of security about the world anyway." All it takes, she noted sadly, "is one crazy guy with his finger on a trigger." On the other hand, although these fears had haunted her for much of her life, she also realized that, because nothing happened, she was able to move forward and push those fears into the background and lead her life. The unspoken point in this sequence, however, is that her apocalyptic fears lay close to the surface and ready to be powerfully evoked in the wake of 9/11.

Rosemary reported how startling it was when she first heard about the plane crashing into the Pentagon as she was watching the towers burn. It occurred to her, "Oh my God, oh my God, the country's under attack. We're at war." At that moment she felt her age and realized that she was the only one in her department who had any real memory of war. When Pearl Harbor occurred she assumes that her parents talked about it, though she was too young to remember those discussions, "but I certainly remember the war and certainly remember Hiroshima." She notes that many of her colleagues she was with on 9/11 remembered Vietnam, but because few had any knowledge of World War II they could not understand the "scale of massive destruction."

Rosemary's childhood experiences with nuclear threat, ones that extended well into her early adulthood, left an important imprint on her mind. She was ten years old when Hiroshima occurred in 1945 and brought to that event a level of understanding more insightful than that of the average schoolgirl in West Virginia. She worried then that the "world would end, that we'd blow it up with another atomic bomb before I had a chance to get married." She noted, laughing, that this fear was a symbolic expression of her underlying fear that the world would end before she could have sex.

At first the war fascinated the young girl in her remote corner of West Virginia. She learned all about the military. "I thought soldiers were wonderful. I knew all the ranks. I knew all the airplanes. I knew everything. That was just very fascinating to me." Nevertheless she began to understand the more brutal side of war from pictures in magazines that she saw of the destruction, especially some of what was happening to children in Italy. By the time she was old enough to take in these images of the war, the Allied forces were marching north through Italy. Images then published in magazines like *Life* found their way into her life. She was horrified at the images of "children who had been living in gutters and eating garbage and living like that." She was devastated and tried to understand how that could happen. "I mean I just really identified with those pictures." Then came the nuclear bomb and the existential crisis into which she was thrown. "It became a symbol to me of just irrational and unstoppable destruction."

Rosemay's keen moral sense of Hiroshima introducing irrational and unstoppable destruction into the world connects that first use of nuclear weapons with 9/11. The relatively small atomic bomb that fell on Hiroshima is no longer the historical irrelevance it seemed to many during the Cold War, with its massive build-up of nuclear weapons able to end life on Earth in one fell swoop. The tens of thousands of powerful weapons stockpiled by the United States and the Soviet Union, many of which had multiple war-heads that were vastly more powerful than the bomb dropped on Hiroshima, threatened human existence for more than half a century. We have pulled back from that brink (though proliferation may now pose an even greater danger of states using the weapons), but in an age of terror with groups such as Al-Qaeda aspiring to carry out massive but not exterminatory violence, Hiroshima becomes the model for what nuclear terrorism would look like. Sometime in the future a bomb that size could be acquired by Al-Qaeda or an entity like Al-Qaeda. We know that Osama bin Laden sought to buy uranium as early as his days in Sudan. Later, in Afghanistan, Ayman Zawahiri (Al-Qaeda's number 2 figure) experimented unsuccessfully with biological weapons. And in 2002, bin Laden sought and obtained from a radical cleric a fatwa to allow the use of nuclear weapons in pursuit of a jihad. There is no more likely target for such a weapon than New York City.

Hiroshima, as the first city actually attacked with a nuclear weapon, is the symbol of such destruction. In Hiroshima the bomb killed 95 percent of those within half a mile of Ground Zero, where the temperature reached 6,000 degrees Celsius, or 10,832 degrees Fahrenheit. In a city of 245,000, more than 100,000 died instantly, many completely incinerated or turned into shad-ows against the concrete. Another 100,000 were injured, many with grue-some injuries that led to death in stages from what was then an unknown condition, radiation sickness. Within two days came nausea, headache, diar-rhea, and fever, which lasted several days. A second stage set in about fifteen days later, the first symptom of which was hair falling out, then diarrhea, and a very high fever (as high as 106). A mysterious third stage came when the body struggled to stabilize itself after its severe traumas. For the rest of the *Hibakusha* (the surviving victims) who were further out from Ground Zero but still caught in the radiation, the suffering took more time. Most of all, there was a significant rise in cancer, especially leukemia, among survivors;

in 1950 it was estimated the rate was between ten and fifty times higher than normal. Exposed children were stunted in their growth and many suffered anemia, liver dysfunction, sexual problems, endocrine disorders, accelerated aging, and a general debilitation. The great (and reasonable) fear that *Hibakusha* harbored was that their radiation sickness would impair their genes and extend the suffering into future generations.[5]

Rosemary's feelings of dread about Hiroshima stayed with her throughout her adolescence, that is, well into the 1950's, as the Cold War led to the production of thousands of weapons and very intensive testing, that the world would end "before I got a chance to taste it." She grew up before the duck-and-cover drills of the 1950's and early 1960's, but she did experience air raid drills throughout her early school years during the war. She also had the curious experience of being fingerprinted. All children in her school were fingerprinted, presumably so they could be identified in the event of an attack. She reported a dream that she had from just before the Cuban Missile Crisis (when she was twenty-seven years old). In the dream she was on a hill with a friend and her children overlooking the town where they lived. An atomic bomb hit the town and exploded. She watched the mushroom cloud rise into the sky.

Rosemary experienced great fear during the Cuban Missile Crisis in 1962. In the very middle of that crisis she and her first husband were moving from Connecticut to Ridgewood, New Jersey. They were in two cars and put one child in each car so that if there were a war there might be a chance for at least one to survive. "So what do you do if you're on the Connecticut turnpike and all of a sudden they drop an atomic bomb—well, you hope you're under it and die. I mean, you know, just we were in our twenties and didn't quite know how to handle it, but I remember being scared then. I was really scared. When you have young children, you get a lot more scared."

These feelings about nuclear fear and startlingly keen understanding of what the Cuban Missile Crisis represented connected with Rosemary's personal crisis in her marriage. She had gotten married toward the end of her college experience in 1956. She had one baby right away and hoped to settle down but discovered that her husband, although a perfectly nice guy, had "never grown up. To this day he has not grown up." Rosemary then had a second child born in 1961 just before the Cuban Missile Crisis. The intensity of her fears about the end of the world sparked feelings in her personal life that her marriage and perhaps life itself was also ending. She found that right after the Cuban Missile Crisis she went into a serious depression. As she notes in the interview, there was some quality of a postpartum depression to her collapse, but to minimize the larger connections between the unraveling of her marriage, her feelings of hopelessness after the birth of her second child, and her feelings about the end of the world by nuclear war would be to misunderstand the many levels of her feelings and the synergy between them.

One very interesting detail in Rosemary's interview is that she had lived through a significant hurricane in 1960, when she and her husband were living in Connecticut. She had exactly the kind of ho-hum reaction to it that Deirdre experienced some thirty years later in California. Rosemary and her husband lived in 1960 a block away from the water, and the hurricane caused havoc in their area. The National Guard had been called up and was patrolling their street. There was water everywhere and they could hardly move about the town for three days. She and her family had to store water and go out to find food as best they could. But as she says, "It was no big deal. You just did it. And so I always did it. But—…once the Cuban Missile Crisis passed, I don't think I ever felt fear about that again." The point here is the radical difference in the way Rosemary—and humans in general—experience natural disasters as opposed to the apocalyptic fear of nuclear end represented in Rosemary's experience by the Cuban Missile Crisis. Natural disaster can create havoc, sometimes cause many deaths, and certainly disrupt lives on a large scale, though the hurricane of 1960 in Connecticut was not deadly and the disruption for Rosemary barely lasted three days. It was, as she notes, even something of an adventure. The contrast with the threat represented by the Cuban Missile Crisis is altogether different. That crisis threatened destruction on an absolute level. A nuclear war would not be an adventure but literally end human experience. Rosemary keenly understood that difference and felt the difference at very deep levels. It is not surprising that she collapsed after the Cuban Missile Crisis and went into such a deep depression that she had to be hospitalized for a while.

A week after 9/11 Rosemary's company, which had lost nearly 1,000 people in the World Trade Center disaster, sponsored a very large memorial service at St. Patrick's Cathedral in midtown Manhattan. "The place was totally filled with family and people who had worked at World Trade." There were so many mourners that they spilled out into the street and were directed to a nearby movie theater to watch the service on a big screen. Rosemary, who was able to get a seat in the cathedral, sat there in a pew and could feel the grief in the room. It was "as powerful as when you walk in where the kids have huge speakers and you can feel the sound. You could feel the grief in the cathedral, and all I could think was "Hiroshima." I think this grief is so—this grief is so big. This is the grief of all humankind, you know, that we've ever done to each other. This isn't just here, this isn't just us; this is just… (inaudible) I mean you're so humbled by it. It's so big." Rosemary, at this point, attempting to evoke an image that would adequately capture what she was trying to say, remembered an experience she had walking down a beach after a hurricane had hit it. "The whole beach had been wiped clean. There were no steps on houses. There were no—no little things lying around. There was no litter. The sand was absolutely white clean," leaving her with the thought, "Lord, Mother Nature sure did a house cleaning here." There was "just utter calm, beauty, and clean, clean, clean sand. It was so big. It was so big. It was so beyond anything in the normal human experience. And then that day in the cathedral was just … it was like another plane of existence that was just beyond anything—anything normal."

Rosemary continued her reflections on the absoluteness of the potential of destruction of nuclear war as a way of understanding what she had gone through in 9/11. There is nothing, no "standard path," one follows in life, she said. Anyone will have to deal with "issues of aging and issues of loss and issues of maybe disruption of having lived in a community and financial issues and stuff." It is natural to think about such things in the wake of something like the World Trade Center disaster. "You think about your family and all this stuff." But even in that context of pain and suffering,

there's a certain predictability. You think how your parents did it and you see how some older friends do it…. But this whole thing [the larger destruction evoked by 9/11] is like I don't know anybody who's ever been here before. I know what happened after the Second World War, when people saw destruction a lot worse, but somehow we were building a new world and I have a sense we're not building a new world now. I feel like we're watching the end of an epic of civilization, and that it's suddenly critically important to keep that kernel of humanness. It's not optional anymore. There's something that keeps human beings human and we'd better understand it and share it.

In this fascinating sequence, Rosemary makes the connections between 9/11 and nuclear destruction, noting in sensible and articulate ways the larger connections in the possibility of apocalyptic destruction, but in fascinating ways she locates the hope that lies embedded in understanding the deepest level of possible destruction. As she says, "It's not optional anymore. There's something that keeps human beings human and we'd better understand it and share it."

A MULTIPLICITY OF IMAGES

Jenna was the first person with medical training at the scene of the disaster. The policeman she was talking with at the NYU Hospital just east of the World Trade Center complex received over his radio, before the 9/11 calls that began quickly were routed through the system to her, the news that the first plane had hit the north tower.[6] She and he left immediately and soon found themselves in the midst of things. In time, Jenna heard a boom as the south tower began to fall, the "sound of things falling on top, like sheetrock falling on top of each other, like that loud sound at a construction site." She looked up then and all she could see was "dark dust and fumes coming out, pieces flying from everywhere." Jenna had her helmet on—"and it's pretty strong"—but she could feel the impact of debris hitting her head with great intensity, as though someone was "hitting my helmet with a hammer," which made her acutely aware of the danger that all the people around her were facing.

Eighteen minutes later she heard the "vroom" of the second (north) tower collapsing. She looked up to see this "big, dark" (she leaves her thought unfinished); "I mean it was huge, it was just coming." She thought to herself: "This is the end" (she meant of life on Earth). People were still running about in terror, cell phones and briefcases flying about. In front of her a large man, 6 foot 5, in his business suit, fell to his knees and yelled at the top of his lungs, "This is the end! Everybody repent! This is the end!" Jenna was astonished and came over to try and get him to flee to safety. "Get up," she said, "get up." But the man was in a dissociated state, "his eyes were blank." Jenna could hear the awful sounds. "Everything is turning dark and you see it coming down." Beside herself with frustration, Jenna, a petite woman, went behind the man on his knees and kicked him hard in the back. He fell forward, hitting the ground, and finally awoke from his trance. She was then able to herd him toward a subway entrance.

It was dark and ominous. She stumbled on two policemen who seemed to be the only other humans in the whole area. And she asked them, "Can you tell me what's going on?" Her thought was of "movies and the nuclear war, all that." She wondered, "What is it? This is the end?" She suspected a "bomb went up, the nuclear war." She quickly added that, "I have no concept of that" and that she only thought about it at all from "just seeing movies," which seems an unnecessary acknowledgment of humility. The source of Jenna's information about nuclear issues may well have been from movies and popular culture. She also had it just right. The bomb is the gold standard of the apocalypse and threatens the end as she was then experiencing it. She felt for sure that all of Manhattan had been attacked, but that thought took her immediately to the apocalyptic idea that, "This is the end. The end in my mind."

Tina, from the Columbia University Oral History Project, also thought the collapse of the second tower signified the nuclear end of the world. "I thought we were being bombed then. I thought, you know, just they were going to—get rid of New York." She thought, "Definitely. New York was getting blown up, that hell was on Earth. It was hell on Earth. It was like a horror show where like hell just came down into a cloud and just opened up and just dumped itself." There was so much dust and debris. She "felt like everybody was dead. It was like the end of the world." It reminded her of a scene from a Stephen King novel, or "something like that, or hell, just hell on Earth. She "thought everybody else had died and that I was still alive." There was nothing but devastation. She was the last survivor. "Just thought the world was over and I was about to die."

APOCALYPTIC ANTECEDENTS IN THE SELF

Renee, who is in her early thirties, lacked the life experiences, and therefore the sense of history, of Rosemary or even Miranda, but her imaginative musings on the apocalyptic meanings of the World Trade Center disaster extended very far. She was in elementary school during the late 1970's and early 1980's and went through duck-and-cover bomb drills. "We would either get underneath the desks and they'd sound that horrible siren and you'd have to march into the hall—and they'd have all the signs around. Like the fallout shelter signs and you'd do your little drill where you'd walk to the fallout shelter. How absurd is that, hiding in a basement when somebody drops a nuclear weapon?" Her insight and sensitivity to the meaning of the duck-and-cover drills led to nightmares about nuclear attacks. Her most startling recurring dream was of us getting bombed. Another recurring nightmare that Renee had as a child took place in the bedroom in her parent's house. In it she is lying in bed looking out of a big window in the room early in the morning.

What she sees is "like a World War II movie." Planes from the Air Force base nearby are doing maneuvers near the house. It was a scene of war and great danger, and seems clearly the adjunct of her more specifically nuclear dream.

Sanford, in turn, reported fantasies of apocalyptic destruction that had long preceded 9/11 and were clearly an integral part of the way he experienced the disaster itself. These fantasies emerged piecemeal, and in contradictory ways, in my interviews with him. But the more he talked about the fantasies, the clearer he became about the more murky areas of his personal narrative. In his first pass at explaining his childhood fantasies, for example, he reported that as a little kid, he used to have two daydreams. One was that a plane landing at Newark airport would land on the golf course near the airport where he frequently played. The second and more relevant fantasy that had occupied his imagination since childhood was that something would happen to the World Trade Center and it would simply fall over. "Just like some kind of accident or a bomb down below that would topple it. Like how could you build something with the wind down there and how could it be safe? And what do you do? Everything gets old. Like how do you take this building down if it gets, you know, old and it's no longer safe?" The crucial point that Sanford stressed several times about this fantasy of some kind of bomb toppling the Trade Center was that it had been active in his imagination for many years.

It was not until the second interview and further prodding on my part about these fantasies that Sanford in fact elaborated on them—and added another. His earliest sense of great danger was the idea of a meteor striking the Earth and destroying it. His idea was actually a good deal more localized, namely, that a meteor or asteroid would fall and level New York. It is worth noting that Sanford had this idea long before the Hollywood movie *Armageddon* put such an idea into concrete form. As he reflected on these three fantasies, Sanford realized that in fact they had been sequenced in his life, so that the idea of a meteor striking New York came from his early childhood or at least his adolescence, whereas the idea of a plane landing on the golf course had to come from his young adulthood, because he only started playing golf then, and that the idea of a bomb toppling the Trade Center almost certainly first came to him when he was in college (though before the attack on the Trade Center in 1993).

Sanford's nuclear fears fitted in explicitly with these concrete fantasies of destruction. He had long felt that there was a great danger of an atomic bomb exploding in New York. This specific fantasy developed in his mind in the late 1970's and was particularly powerful in the 1980's, a period of time that coincided with his adolescence and of course with the height of the Cold War. "That was another thing that I feared, was like just an atomic bomb coming our way and what would the—how would the United States stop that if, you know, it just launched a missile towards New York City or any other city in the United States? How do they stop that? Can they really shoot it down over the ocean? Or, you know, I don't have a full understanding of our defense."

Sanford's long-standing fear of nuclear attack that grew out of his childhood understanding of the dangers during the Cold War then got intertwined with his sense of the current dangers facing the United States. It is worth remembering that both his interviews were in the immediate wake of 9/11. As he says, "If that's what they're going to do, they would have done that first, not try and knock down the towers and stuff. But now as we're going to war with them, I don't know what kind of sophistication they have. And if we strike, all of a sudden is there going to be an atomic bomb going off here?" It is not clear whether Sanford was worried more about an atomic bomb being dropped on the city or some kind of dirty bomb, but there is no question that the most ominous threats that he feels facing New York after 9/11 are nuclear. Furthermore, such generalized fears had long existed in his experience and informed his sense of vulnerability that was so aroused by his experiences that day. He lived with an acute sense of the danger but also with the contradiction between our technological and military power and the puny but very real threats we face. "Yeah, like why? Well, what are they, crazy? What are they doing? Do they realize who they're up against? Do they realize the technology we have, the stealth fighters and do they have any clue? I then sometimes feel like—and, you know, you know what makes me feel helpless is when they keep talking about the fact that they're not one place and they're spread out all over the world."

Sanford had nightmares every night for weeks after 9/11 about his experiences that day. "I kept dreaming I was the people on fire in the street. That was me. I was watching myself on fire in the street, stumbling around, not feeling it, but just watching myself stumble around. And I keep dreaming about the plane hit, the plane hitting." As he recalled this powerful nightmare that relived in excruciating detail his experiences on 9/11, he added that, "last night I was dreaming that we just got bombed, missiles from planes and stuff, F-16's like just shooting, dropping bombs, you know." In other words, the traumatic dreams from the day extended in Sanford's imagination into dreams, into nightmares of anticipation of a military attack that suggests the use of nuclear weapons.

Sanford's personal life positioned him to respond acutely to the apocalyptic dimensions of the World Trade Center disaster. He noted that the shadow of death hung over his life in the months before 9/11. "I've lost, in the last six years I've lost the three dearest people to me, my grandmother first, then my grandfather, and then my mother and, ah, my mother was a surprise. That was last year, last November, and when I got the call I would just go numb." Sanford never explained the cause of his mother's death, but it was clear that she died suddenly and unexpectedly; the suggestion is that it was related to her alcoholism. A serious misreading of Sanford's narrative would interpret his sensitivity to apocalyptic issues in connection with the disaster as a mere projection of the inner turmoil associated with the recent deaths in his family, especially that of his mother. Such unidimensional psychologizing, unfortunately, is all too common in the observations of those with clinical backgrounds but unfamiliar with the subtlety and complexity of interpreting social phenomena. A much more relevant way of understanding the personal and the historical in this case, however, is to say that Sanford's personal experiences with death and the chaos of his childhood that included abandonment by his father opened him to the death-drenched, apocalyptic meanings of the disaster. That openness makes him an unusually valuable witness in understanding the apocalyptic meanings of the disaster.

THE RETURN OF THE APOCALYPTIC

After 9/11 many New Yorkers returned often to apocalyptic images to try and make sense out of their experiences. Serena felt she had periods of dissociation during which she felt she "lost it" while carrying out some mundane task. She also found it very difficult to concentrate. These typical symptoms of posttraumatic stress disorder were connected for her with broader fears of mass death and destruction. She began to fear future biological or chemical warfare. "All things seem possible," she said, reasoning that if terrorists could carry out such an attack as they did on 9/11, they could blow up tunnels or bridges or spread anthrax. It was impossible to know how far the malevolence could spread. She commented that, "You watch TV and you don't know what's—it was like what kind of world? I would picture bombs being thrown at us and just total devastation and then running away and living like we were in Jerusalem and all those places. I just pictured that." These exterminatory images of Serena were amorphous. She was very clear that she had no specific images of nuclear weapons as the basis of what form of destruction might come next for New York. Her image of destruction was simply of destruction on a vast and almost unimaginable scale. "You know, I just thought of just—in fact, I pictured New York just totally everything crumpled up."

After his return to the relative safety of his apartment, Henry found himself glued to the TV and radio for days. He barely slept, obsessively seeking out information so that he would not again be taken by surprise. His fear was that the next in the sequence of dangers was some kind of nuclear attack. "I didn't want to wake up and hear that like they had dropped, you know, an atomic bomb on, you know, some other place. Like at that point, anything is possible." He felt with some certainty that "the world is changed forever because of this." It completely altered his life but also that of the nation as a whole. "I was afraid." He dreaded what might happen next. "It seemed like everything was over. The whole thing was like very apocalyptic."

In the experience of the disaster Henry also had the thought that the cloud coming to envelope him might be nuclear. "I thought about that, but I dismissed it, not totally dismissed it, but for the most part dismissed it." Even in his greatest moment of fear, it seemed too preposterous to imagine someone getting hold of a nuclear bomb to attack New York City. But it was not impossible that such a plan was the next step in the sequence of horrors. "I mean if you hijack these planes and send them into buildings, I mean that could be a diversion for something larger."

"This," said Adam Cowes, an emergency worker at Ground Zero, "is what hell looks like, in case you'd ever stopped to wonder."[7]

7

TRAUMASONG[1]

DEEPLY IMBEDDED IN the survivor experience of my respondents, as part of their stories that touched their death encounters, was a psychological state that evoked poetic forms of language, a kind of "melodious tear," as Milton says in "Lycidas." It may be that the language of trauma is the state itself. Such songs of trauma, in my experience of interviewing survivors in depth, were not universal. Some survivors were so broken by their death encounters that their language remained inchoate and disjointed. Miranda's thoughts often trailed off. She hesitated, sucked in her breath as a substitute for words, and lived out her dissociation in the telling of her tale. Felicia left many sentences incomplete. Eric's compulsiveness shaped his language (and thoughts) into small particles neatly arranged in a linear order. He had to arrange his language with me in the same way he broke down his

9/11 experiences into manageable units. But Renee, Jenna, Henry, Melissa, Deirdre, Rosemary, and in fact most survivors I interviewed all surprised me when I examined their interviews later in what I can only describe as a kind of secondary analysis. For them it was precisely their death encounters that evoked the poetry that seemed imbedded in their souls. There is no question trauma can destroy language, as well as the cohesive self, but death encounters seem equally capable of bringing out a language of witness that is highly rhythmic and sometimes metrical, often stanzaic, and quite beautiful. Its often hidden structures wonderfully capture the inherent survivor yearning for transformative healing. I have no way of knowing from my limited sample what is generally true about trauma and language. It is enough to present my findings that suggest traumasong may be a much more universal experience than previously recognized.

In many respects, words failed us on 9/11 and for at least the first few weeks afterward. There was only the false witnessing of exhausted, bland, and uninformed television commentators. At best the anchors managed to repeat a few phrases endlessly as the images of the falling towers cascaded across the screen, redoing but not undoing history. The trauma spread. People spoke in clichés on the tortured path to healing through language. The attacks were "unbelievable" (the most common descriptor), "horrible," and "terrible." Such descriptors were usually accompanied by trite phrases, such as "Oh my God," or premature and therefore inappropriate questions, such as "How could they do this?" Language became more sorrowful plaint than meaningfully framed question.

The only coherence surrounding such clichéd utterances came with the hugging of friends and loved ones that usually accompanied initial encounters after the disaster. Kai Erikson, a shrewd observer, describes with a note of irony bordering on sarcasm the pervasive literature in the sociology of disasters about what has been called "altruistic communities," "postdisaster utopias," "communities of sufferers," or "therapeutic communities" that emerge after disasters, an idea that has been recently repeated by Rebecca Solnit in her study *A Paradise Built in Hell.*[2] Erikson, in his close studies over a lifetime, has never seen such a thing and clearly suggests the phenomenon may be more in the sentimentalized eye of the academic beholder than in the fact of what people actually construct after disaster. Certainly, there has been a tendency to sentimentalize things, and one should approach the study of disasters with great caution. Erikson, however, often came to the communities of suffering he describes so well in *A New Species of Trouble* long after the disasters themselves and in the context of helping disempowered communities recover from tragic abuse and neglect.[3] Without question people in New York City turned *briefly* to touch and help after the attacks. This new sense of community seems to have been a response to the shock of facing collective death. The relief in our own survival and rebirth of community joined New Yorkers in new ways. You could look someone in the eye on the subway. Not a single case of rape was reported in Manhattan for the two weeks following the disaster. The sense of euphoria did not last more than a week or two, but it was briefly authentic and powerful (after which it was powerfully manipulated by politicians and the survivor industry). Psychologically, in the fleeting moments after the disaster we reached for comfort in a fragmented world in which much meaning had been lost. Coherent and profound words themselves, let alone the more complicated stories that emerge when meaningful words find expression through witnessing, were far off.

But the expression of authentic experience in the form of poetry emerged in my interviews when respondents spoke about their direct death experiences with the World Trade Center disaster. It was in that context—even though I only realized it much later and in the context of analyzing my data and listening again to the interviews—that I came to feel that in the language my respondents used in their conversations with me they turned to rhythmic patterns forming poetry when they were most deeply describing scenes of death. It is striking how these poetic sections contrast with the more prosaic sections that came before and after the poetry. The person in trauma is often an infallible artist.

The psychological and linguistic principle is that ordered, rhythmic language is a way of healing the shattered self from the death encounter of the disaster. Trauma destroys meaning structures and leaves incoherence in its wake. The immediate survival strategy, as Robert Jay Lifton reported so well in his study of Hiroshima survivors, is a closing down of feeling, a numbing, that results in the zombielike quality and thousand-mile stare of the survivor.[4] Many reports describe such a state among Holocaust survivors as well. One can even see visual evidence of such numbing in the television shots on 9/11 of dust-covered survivors. For some, as with Miranda, who passed out for an indeterminate length of time, the closing down becomes a complete physical collapse. The self, however, struggles to heal and recover meaning. To repeat, for many the path to recovery from trauma remains a rocky road that is never repaved. But more commonly—and most especially in the context of an empathic interview situation—the telling of the tale becomes a process of finding comfort in the most elemental beat and rhythm of language, something we arbitrarily call poetry, as a way of distinguishing this primal security in beat from the more prosaic ordering of words in other modes of communication. The empathic context is crucial. One of the more convincing findings of contemporary psychoanalytic psychotherapy, an idea first articulated conceptually by Heinz Kohut in the 1970's and replicated since by innumerable clinicians, is that in the context of an empathic therapeutic encounter a patient becomes decidedly less pathological.[5] In the course of a good psychotherapy session, a venue in which a patient feels fully understood, the halting and broken language of personal trauma gradually fades and a new self that can sometimes create beautifully formed and expressive language emerges. As a therapist I find this a remarkable and sometimes inspiring process to witness. Often, a deep sadness accompanies the retelling of traumatic experiences or the detailed memories of chronic coldness and rejection by parents and caretakers. But if such telling of the tale is with another empathic listener, healing can result, and in that moment a very troubled patient becomes normal. The goal of therapy is to extend those moments outward into life.

The interview process for my research closely approximated that empathic therapeutic context, though while interviewing for this study I was not conscious of changes in language when my respondents told me of their traumatic encounters with death that day. I have since wondered why (especially since I am conscious of such a process during psychotherapy sessions with my patients) and can only guess that in a therapeutic context I am only listening carefully, while in the research context I am listening carefully but must also keep track of a number of things that occupy dimensions of my attention: Is the red light still on the recorder so that I can be sure it is taping properly? Where am I in my protocol and what are the next questions I want to ask? What kind of follow-up questions will help me understand better what my respondent is talking about? What time is it and have I covered what I need to in the hour and a half I have with this respondent? And so on.

Empathy is the oxygen of psychological life. We cannot breathe without it. Early investigators, such as Freud, thought it was the words that mattered. They missed the music. Anything that supports empathy supports healing, and my quasi-clinical, empathic method of interviewing 9/11 survivors revealed traumasong. Surprisingly, as respondents related their experiences that touched some aspect of their encounter with death, they slipped spontaneously into language that even can be scanned.

But what is poetry, and how does it relate to trauma? Poetry is, first, a way of writing or talking that contains meaning and feeling. Those meaning structures, expressed with just the right word imbedded in images and metaphors, evoke color, mood, fears, hopes, and most of all feelings across the widest imaginable spectrum of human experience. If prose explains, poetry evokes. Poetry can be allusive and obscure, but at its best it touches primal feelings, especially those touching death and its equivalents. There is, of course, a long tradition of love poetry that has inspired countless musical renditions and that defines much of our cultural heritage, but it is in relation to death that poetry finds its most compelling voice. To survive disaster on 9/11 often resulted in poetic forms of expression in the mutuality of the interview setting as respondents relived the experience in retelling their death encounters.

The other dimension of poetry is the fundamental significance of rhythm, or beat, which dwells within words themselves and is the most significant technique of order available to the poet. There are other poetic devices, such as rhyme, line division, stanzaic form, and overall structure, but, as Paul Fussell has put it, they are mere "projections and magnifications of the kind of formalizing repetition which meter embodies. They are meter writ large."[6] English poetry is for the most part accentual; that is, syllables are stressed in ways that can be quite formal. Classical Latin and Greek as well as modern Japanese poetry count syllables (as with the haiku) rather than stressing syllables in a determined pattern.

Fussell stresses meter per se, but the more universal dimension of poetry, given the wide forms of writing since T. S. Eliot and others, may be rhythm. It is impossible to imagine poetry without such meaningful patterns, though free verse, which is not always that free, inhabits a nebulous space between poetry and prose. Pure prose has a very specific function to communicate information and serve as the instrument of narrative. Prose connects humans in infinitely varied ways. But although it might be elegant and well shaped, psychologically prose is disconnected, removed, objectified. Poetry touches the soul. And although some poetic devices such as rhyme can seem to be essential markers, in fact all such tropes are epiphenomenal. What matters are the rhythmic patterns.

We are most familiar with the way such patterns express themselves in meter, which has been used in the history of poetry in remarkably diverse ways. The English language privileges the iambic pattern more than classical or modern romance languages because of its rising accented syllables. But our poetic tradition (including Old and Middle English) is also replete with anapest, trochee, dactyl, spondee, and pyrrhic patterns, whereas classical poetry devised other, more obscure and pedantic forms known now only to the most erudite scholars. Shakespeare created the dominant cadence of modern English poetry with nonrhyming lines of iambic pentameter, though the King James translation of the Bible, also written in the late Elizabethan period, equally defined the contours of beat in English ("The Lord is my Shepherd I shall not want,/ He maketh me to lie down in green pastures"). English poets in the nineteenth century (Alexander Pope and William Butler Yeats, for example) often invoked classical forms of meter that feel mostly stilted to contemporary readers. We have been too shaped by Walt Whitman's "Leaves of Grass." This exuberant display of American hubris abandoned rhyme and stanzaic form but kept a loose iambic meter at the center of the poetic experience.

> I believe a leaf of grass is no less than the journeywork of the stars
> And the pismire is equally perfect, and a grain of sand, and the egg of
>   a wen
> And the tree-toad is a chef-d'oeuvre for the highest,
> And the running blackberry would adorn the parlors of heaven,
> And the narrowest hinge in my hand puts to scorn all machinery,
> And the cow crunching with depressed head surpasses any statue,
> And a mouse is miracle enough to stagger sextillions of infidels,
> And I could come every afternoon of my life to look at the farmer's
>   girl boiling her iron tea kettle and baking shortcake.[7]

Everyone writes now in the shadow of Whitman. In terms of beat, Whitman keeps Shakespeare alive in the corners of our creative selves. Robert Frost once said that all modern poetry is either loose or strict iambic.

Rhythmic patterns in poetry have important psychological correlates. Like anything basic to experience, they begin in the self and have corporeal, physical, sensual, even sexual dimensions. We live in a world that starts (and ends) with the beat of the heart, an absolutely rhythmic and cadenced sound that is the ground of all being. But the significance of beat hardly ends with the heart. Life abounds in rhythmic experiences, from breathing, to walking, to love making, and includes in a larger sense the sequence of the seasons, the cycle of human life from birth to death, and the pattern making we find in all kinds of experiences that might otherwise seem confused and contradictory. Meter is so inborn that if it is not there, we impose it. The clock in fact goes tick tick tick tick when we are out of the room. But as soon as we walk back in with our coffee, we hear tick tock, tick tock, accenting the tock and creating feet of pure iambic. We have a kind of lust for rhythm.

Our attachment to such forms, in other words, is deeply imbedded in self patterns that can be thought of as central, orienting images. The organized rhythms in poetry reflect the cadence of the self as imbedded in the body and in culture. It is unlikely that the human heart beats in iambic rhythm, even though Americans (and English) may hear it that way, as with the clock. Other principles must be at work, because other languages vary so widely in the way they accent different syllables and therefore construct both poetry and reality. There may well be a synergistic interaction of culture with potentials in the self of newborn babies who make what is at first a wild assortment of sounds—surely itself an inborn process—as they feel their way into the world. In that matrix of the self and world, beat and language emerge as a unified whole that blends an entire cultural tradition with the rhythms of the tiny body. The two cannot be separated—except in trauma.

Trauma, which means a set of fairly defined responses to a direct or symbolic encounter with death, profoundly disrupts the continuity of self and experience. Trauma leaves us empty, confused, disoriented. In it we lose those ties to those we trust, to family, community, and in a real sense to ourselves and our identity. Nothing and no one feels safe. The body is disrupted and often collapses into a psychosomatic muddle. The mind struggles for grounding. Flashbacks haunt the imagination, we startle, and in general we display the myriad of symptoms so neatly, and now almost tritely, described as "post-traumatic stress disorder." Language also suffers in trauma. In the scientific literature, writers tend either to ignore the relationship between trauma and language, except those physical and neurological ways in which language mediates memory, or to include it simply as one obvious way in which one's story gets confused and disjointed in acute or chronic trauma. I would suggest, however, that the connection between trauma and language is much more complicated and contradictory, and touches transformative sources of healing.

Consider Paul Celan (1920–1970), a Holocaust survivor from Austrian Poland who knew many languages, especially French, yet insisted on writing only in German. Nazism, as John Felstiner, Celan's biographer, has noted, "organized its genocide of European Jews by means of language slogans, slurs, pseudo-scientific dogma, propaganda, euphemism, and the jargon that brought about every devastating 'action,' from the earliest racial 'laws' through 'special treatment' in the camps to the last 'resettlement' of Jewish orphans."[8] Celan sought to undo that violence and to heal himself and his grossly violated mother tongue together. His poetry is a counterpoint to propaganda and cliché. His most famous poem, "Deathfugue," is about the "passage of the language through the violence and the passage of the violence through language." The subject of the poem is the concentration camp commandant ordering an inmate orchestra to accompany their own grave-digging with an ecstatic fugue. The first stanza of John Felstiner's translation captures in English some of the anapest of the original German:

Black milk of daybreak we drink it at evening
we drink it at midday and morning we drink it at night
we drink and we drink
we shovel a grave in the air where you won't lie too cramped
A man lives in the house he plays with his vipers he writes
he writes when it grows dark to Deutschland your golden hair Margareta
he writes it and steps out of doors and the stars are all sparkling
he whistles his hounds to stay close
he whistles his Jews into rows has them shovel a grave in the ground
he commands us play up for the dance[9]

Among my respondents there was not of course such finished poetry, constructed in a metrical scheme that can be scanned and set in lines and stanzas, shaped by the hands of a master craftsman. From a formal, linguistic point of view, what my respondents said was much more naïve, halting, and incomplete. I did return to the sections in the taped interviews that I thought from reading the transcripts showed a move into a different poetic voice and noted as precisely as I could the cadences, natural stops, and breaths that distinguished "lines" in what they were saying. In listening again to the tapes, there was no question that something very profound happened as the respondent moved from a prosaic account in the narrative to describing a scene of death and trauma. What these poetic moments expressed was some process deep in the self that reflects a profound relationship between trauma and the healing potential of language.

Deirdre, for example, was describing to me in some detail her descent from the forty-ninth floor of WTC 7 (across the street from the north tower). The mood on the stairs was calm because no one had any sense of what was happening outside. She noted the point at which she heard a loud rumble that in retrospect she realized was cause by the second plane striking the south tower. She could feel the building move but lacked a context in which to explain it (or feel terrified by it). Deirdre was with her friend Leticia. Even after the loud rumble the mood on the stairs was one of increased anxiety and confusion but not of mass panic. When she reached the lobby of the building, however, suddenly it was a scene of fear. The large glass windows were broken and a security officer was directing people to leave the building by a safer exit. Deirdre followed the crowd and suddenly burst out onto the street, directly facing the north tower in the full flush of the disaster.

At that point Deirdre's language in the interview changed. She said, "And I look up at the building, and I saw this man on the side of the building, holding on, and then just pushed back and let go, and then I closed my eyes. And I looked down and I grabbed Letitia's hand, and she had turned around to do something else. And I said, 'Letitia, people are jumping from the building.' And then I went to grab my bag and I looked again. And there was another man just did a swan dive out of the building. And people were crying and screaming."

It does not seem too much of a stretch to cast this remarkable passage, which moves mostly between anapest (two short and one long beat to each foot, a beat that evokes action and drama) and iambic metrical feet, into lines of poetry that follow her natural cadences and insistent use of "and" to connect the frightening images in her mind that she was conjuring up in the course of telling her story, and further to note that there are two clear parts to the account that have some logic as two stanzas. Deirdre's "poem" is thus:

And I look up at the building,
And I saw this man on the side of the building,
Holding on,
And then just pushed back and let go.
And then I closed my eyes.
And I looked down and I grabbed Letitia's hand,
And she had turned around to do something else.
And I said, "Letitia, people are jumping from the building."
And then I went to grab my bag
And I looked again,
And there was another man just did a swan dive out of the building.
And people were crying and screaming.

Another example that I will analyze in greater detail is that of Renee, who was a "participant" in zone 3 (and thus did not directly encounter death on 9/11) but had a rich imagination, some early sources of trauma that were never entirely clear to me, and a powerful ability to use language in evocative ways. Renee was relating to me in the interview in a prosaic narrative in which she was in midtown as she learned about the unfolding disaster when suddenly her use of language changed. She said, "I think just a million things are going through my—at that point I was kind of trying not to—it was like every second something worse kept happening. And between what was actually happening and, you know, what they were saying was happening, it was like every time you—as soon as you thought it couldn't get any worse, a building fell down. Or as soon as you thought it couldn't get worse than that, the second building came down. The planes are—you know, they're saying that planes crashed into Camp David or there are fires burning on the Washington Mall. I—it was like as soon as you thought it was all over, something else kept happening."

To cast this passage into lines of poetry, it would look as follows:

1 I think just a million things are going through my—
2 at that point I was kind of trying not to—
3 it was like every second something worse kept happening.
4 And between what was actually happening
5 and, you know, what they were saying was happening,
6 it was like every time you—
7 as soon as you thought it couldn't get any worse,
8 a building fell down.
9 Or as soon as you thought it couldn't get worse than that,
10 the second building came down.
11 The planes are—
12 you know, they're saying that planes crashed into Camp David
13 or there are fires burning on the Washington Mall.
14 I—it was like as soon as you thought it was all over,
15 something else kept happening.

Renee's "poem" falls mostly into an iambic beat with a good deal of anapest. The very first line is illustrative. It is in iambic beat with one falling syllable at the end: "I think / just a mil / lion things / are go / ing through / my –." The incomplete last word, "mind," in the last iambic foot is more powerful by its absence. "Mind" cannot be said; it is in too much disarray. Line 2 introduces anapest in its first two feet ("at that point / I was kind"), as does line 9 ("Or as soon / as you thought"), or the beginning of the very powerful last line 15 ("something else"). The familiar, comforting iambic alternates with anapest that intensifies the underlying dread.

In some lines an even greater degree of order is imposed, as the iambic becomes iambic pentameter, or five feet, the basic meter of Shakespeare and the King James Bible. Such is true of line 1 (with the exception of the dangling last word) and of line 12 ("you know / they're say / ing that / planes crashed / into Camp / David" (though the "David" could be heard as an additional foot). It is less remarkable that some lines are not pure iambic pentameter than that each approaches Shakespearean and biblical forms. Renee, after all, is not a poet herself and certainly is under no internal pressure to conform to literary conventions as she talks. She—and all my respondents—are naïve in that sense, though also authentic.

One characteristic of Renee's poem is her frequent dropping of a word at the end of a line, as in line 1 (already discussed), or 2 ("at that point I was kind of trying not to –"), or 6 ("it was like very time you –"), or 11 ("The planes are –"). The "mind" that goes missing in line 1 is evocatively repeated in line 2, where one assumes "think" is what she cannot say. Line 11 then returns to the absence, in this case of planes that are crashing into buildings and Camp David, and one can only imagine what else. In each case the missing word that we unconsciously substitute pulls us into the drama of the unfolding poem. The lines end with falling feet, as people from those windows who desperately gulped air and then fell or jumped to their death.

Renee also imposes an elegant set of connections between the stanzas. The first and last lines of each stanza are conceptually linked. The poem opens with the image of a million things going through Renee's mind that then finds its logical extension in the beginning of the second stanza, line 7 ("as soon as you thought it couldn't get any worse"). That line sets up the naming of just how much worse it could get, which becomes the story of the second stanza. Renee further makes the last line of the first stanza, line 6 ("it was like every time you—"), serve as the first half of the sentence that ends in the final line of the poem, line 15 ("something else kept happening"). The two stanzas reflect in content as well these connections in language, so that the first stanza creates a mood of dread and malevolence, whereas the second tells the story more fully of what Renee is thinking about.

Finally, there is a narrative sequence to the poem that gives it coherence and meaning appropriate to the unfolding drama Renee is describing. The first stanza sets up the scene (as well as the mood) in her mind, the images of confusion but also of contradiction ("at that point I was kind of trying to –"), but "it was like every second something worse kept happening" and the disorienting experience of having commentators telling you things, as in line 5 ("and, you know, what they were saying was happening") between what you could see going on, line 4 ("And between what was actually happening"). Furthermore, the first stanza from lines 3 to 6 intensifies the dread that Renee evokes at the outset, those "million things" going through her mind. It is not yet clear in the poem what is happening every second, but the fear mounts in the way she juxtaposes the impact of all the voices of commentators with what she seems to know, or thinks she knows.

Lines 7 to 10, the beginning of the second stanza, then recount the central horror of the towers falling in parallel couplets. First, line 7, "as soon as you thought it couldn't get any worse," leads to line 8, which simply and dramatically states the fact of the first tower collapsing ("a building fell down"). Line 9 returns to the motif of the poem of knowing and not knowing, of thinking and not thinking, with the idea that "Or as soon as you thought it couldn't get worse than that," culminating in line 10, which again states the bald information that the "second building came down." From lines 11 to 15 the fear spreads. Renee evokes the many rumors that proliferated that day, those dangers that were on everyone's lips. In her case she must have heard something about bombing Camp David and fires on the Washington Mall (lines 12 and 13). It is the ending, however, those last two lines, that makes the poem profound and terrifying. "I—it was like as soon as you thought it was over," Renee says in language that returns her meditation on the violence to her own inner imagination, "something else kept happening." That last image of never-ending destruction is powerfully apocalyptic. The death will never stop. The escalating process of violence can only continue, though part of the subtlety of the poem lies in the way it leaves exactly where the process leads open to our imagination.

Other survivors talked to me in a similar vein and with equal beauty, though to carry the analysis much further would take me well beyond my purposes in this book. Much more remains to be learned about the nature of these poetical forays as they relate to trauma. It was a great surprise for me to stumble on the idea of "traumasong" as I carried out the research for this book, but I suspect further research will extend the idea, deepen its meanings, and open up avenues of interdisciplinary cooperation and exchange between clinicians studying trauma and poets attuned to nuanced linguistic expressions. But even based on my limited sample, I take from the "poems" of my respondents a measure of hope in the healing power of language.

8

TELEVISION: NUMBING AND RAGE

MOST AMERICANS came to know of 9/11 via television. The disaster entered our lives on screens that by then were not all that small. In retrospect, given the rise of the Internet, of iPhones and iPads, and of elaborate video games played on all kinds of screens, we can now recognize that 9/11 marked the end of television's hegemony that began sometime after World War II, perhaps with Richard Nixon's Checkers speech in 1952 or with Kennedy's assassination in 1963.[1] We learned, in that era of television's hegemony, about great events through television. It was, of course, not only television that made the experience of 9/11 unique. Among other things, it was extraordinary the way the disaster unfolded at a time of day when many could watch (including those in Europe, the Middle East, and Asia). Unscripted, the disaster felt for many like a movie made for television, something many survivors I interviewed mentioned. Henry, for example, said he felt as though he was in a horror movie as he was fleeing from this great white blob of dust and debris that was chasing him down the canyons of the city. The knowledge of 9/11 through television brought countless millions into the story. There is something potentially positive in that. Certainly the reach of television made the disaster a human drama that universalized its meanings. But learning of the disaster via television may also have had serious psychological and political consequences.

There is much that is positive and even hopeful about television as the focal medium among the many media that make up modern mass communications. It has vastly enriched the cultural experience of many hundreds of millions of people. One can never ignore this democratic aspect of the medium in bringing entertainment and awareness of the world to people whose lives before the modern era were significantly narrower and more constrained. Television educates those with low or moderate literacy. A viewer can travel on journeys to faraway lands and into imaginary realms, gaining understanding of history, culture, and life that was previously possible only for those with resources and educational opportunities. In crises such as war and disaster, such knowledge can serve as an important buffer against trauma. It gives context and a sense of history that can insulate and prepare one for brutal encounters with death.

In relation to 9/11 specifically, television also had the potential for expanding the empathy of the viewer by facilitating participation in the suffering of others. To see the disaster unfold was potentially to touch the deepest sources of empathy among all Americans. In fact, as the disaster unfolded it was difficult not to imagine the suffering of those escaping the burning towers, even without the images on the screen of people falling or jumping to their death. Once the towers collapsed, the immediate scenes of terrified people running imposed themselves on viewers. Their hurt became our pain.

Television (like good writing since the beginning of narrative art in the West with Homer) knows the art of humanizing larger events such as war and genocide by focusing on individual stories. In that tale viewers can imagine themselves into the experience of those caught up in events that might otherwise seem remote. Sometimes, as with images of famines or tragedies like the tsunami, the result is to inspire people to act, give money or even travel to the scene to help. Television wires our global village. Without it we often would not see beyond the road that leads over the horizon. Television, in this sense, creates the potential for witnessing.

To witness is to participate in someone else's suffering, whether in the religious context (as in the death of Jesus), the therapeutic (empathizing with someone else's trauma), or the social (as with those who suffered on 9/11). The immediacy of witness by the mere fact of empathic presence ennobles victims and brings them into a context of understanding and meaning. The tale of suffering that is then told in a conversation between witness and survivor becomes a mutual experience of deepening empathy, as the witness transmutes into a survivor. Each reenactment of that process of suffering and telling expands the horizons of empathy. The stories move away from the event, whether the crucifixion, personal trauma, or the disaster, but the possibility always exists of finding empathic energy from a witness connecting with a new source of suffering on the part of a survivor in ways that energize.

But the witness, as Avishai Margalit has stressed, must be a "moral witness."[2] The chronicler of a disaster—for example, the uninvolved journalist—merely records what happened but cannot tell us what it felt like to be in one. For that we need a moral witness, who must experience the disaster, be at risk within it, and provide testimony for others that brings them a measure of hope. There is no reason such hope cannot be secular, and in the modern world our need to locate hope in disaster has special resonance for those who feel separated from specific forms of religious and even spiritual traditions. Nevertheless, for many the varieties of hope Margalit is describing is religiously charged. Not only is it a theological virtue—along with love, faith, and charity—but the etymology of hope lies in an "eschatological expectation of future salvation." In the Christian tradition, God is described as "God of Hope" (Romans 15:13), whereas the original meaning of *sahid* in both the Greek and Arabic is "witness," though of course it has come to mean martyr. But Margalit stresses the redemptive meanings of witnessing: "the religious witness, through his suffering and ultimate sacrifice, expresses in times of trial his confidence in a world that against all appearances is still governed by a moral authority and a supreme and just judge, that is, by God."[3]

A moral witness is nothing if not authentic and as such describes but most of all uncovers evil. He or she is a "species of eyewitness." The canon of judging the reliability of both is similar. One must trust the truthfulness of the moral witness's story; otherwise it is meaningless. At the same time, it would be pointless to "put Primo Levi under oath." Or is it? We must have absolute conviction that we can trust the survivor's tale, and it is only within that trust that one experiences the horror and meanings of the disaster.[4]

Television, however, as it functioned in covering 9/11, may have not only interrupted witnessing at its source but offered up a false alternative. It is important to keep in mind, of course, in this regard the dynamism of the World Trade Center disaster as it unfolded in real time on TV. Its very spontaneity heightened the contradictions. A fully impermeable screen filtered the pain, the loss, and the death of what we saw on television. Many felt something profound, but for the most part none of what was evoked could be communicated to those who seemed to enter our living rooms as desiccated images. Television, in this way, objectified the human suffering on 9/11. The images we saw were concrete, detailed, and evocative. We saw many details, the fright, the contorted faces, and heard the screams and cries. Other senses, however, were cut off, especially smell and touch, which are crucial for the full experience of witness. The very concreteness of what we saw on television during 9/11 in fact confused our sense of the actual, making it seem as though we were there as witnesses while cutting off the possibility of such experience. Nothing could become real, and just as something was within our grasp it immediately disappeared, only to return in seemingly endless and deeply confusing repetition. We were left without context. Only the objectified image remained, whether of a falling building or of a contorted face or the unblinking eyes of most commentators, and that not usually for very long as we slipped back, numbed again, into our lethargy. True witnessing breaks through numbing and expands empathy. Television on 9/11 fostered numbing and false witness with its realistic image that hung in the air, outside the self.

Marshall McLuhan, the great philosopher of media, made us aware of what he distinguished as hot and cold media.[5] In his terms, the coldest of all media is print. The printed page embodies the potential for great imaginative leaps but requires on the part of the reader full engagement to bring to life the sights and sounds that lie within the text in the form of metaphors and the simple beauty of the right word. McLuhan's basic theoretical construct is that a medium extends our senses, and in the process alters the form of our experience in such fundamental ways that the medium itself can become more important than the content that is conveyed by it. This idea is what McLuhan intends by his famous, if admittedly somewhat obscure, idea that "the medium is the message." The telephone, for example, is warmer than conversation, because it extends the capacity of our ears to take in communication and our speech to convey our ideas. Radio, in this sequence, is significantly warmer than the telephone because of the range and diversity of the way it expands speech and hearing through music of all forms, conversation, chat, dialogue, commentary, and so on. The hottest of all media in this sequence is the movies, which envelope viewers and vastly extend all their senses in a way that exhilarates and completely absorbs. Television, on the other hand, is much cooler as a medium (at least as McLuhan saw it in what was then, in the 1950's and 1960's, the early days of television). Television was technically inferior: It operated on very small screens, was restricted to three major networks and thus offered little real choice, and mostly involved live people talking in political or news formats or performing in shows such as those produced by Walt Disney. McLuhan was struck by the difference between television and the movies in terms of his distinction between hot and cold media.

Since the 1960's we have witnessed a huge increase in the sophistication of all media and the blurring of lines between its different forms. Television has gotten enormously hotter in McLuhan's terms and has merged as a form of communication and entertainment with other media. It may be that the relatively easy distinction between media that McLuhan identified in the early days of mass communications is much too simplistic at the beginning of the twenty-first century. What matters now is not so much the difference between television and the movies and even radio as the remarkable degree to which mass communications flood us with images. We read the newspaper online and engage in interactive dialogue with columnists. We watch movies on television, and the evening news is so highly produced and choreographed as to amount to an entertainment show itself. The average evening drama may well contain action scenes of technical if not artistic sophistication far exceeding anything seen in the movies up to the 1980's. And so on. The psychological question is therefore how we are changed as human beings within this world of flooding images; and nothing flooded viewers more intensely than the World Trade Center disaster.

Four principles are relevant for understanding in new ways the psychology of television in relation to the disaster. The first is what might be called a *multiplier effect*. One of the more remarkable aspects of contemporary media is the way they feed off each other. A significant story in a major newspaper like the *New York Times*, for example, will prompt discussion on talk radio throughout the day and separate television news coverage in the early evening. The networks might well then spin off more extended coverage of the story on their cable networks, which in turn prompts further commentary on talk radio and perhaps some ironic commentary on late-night television talk shows. If the story is at all significant, further reverberations along these lines will occur in the following days, often moving in many directions at the same time. For example, a major story in the *Times* that spawns TV network coverage in its news outlets might well bring on camera some of the major participants in the story itself, which often creates additional news and feeds the story in intriguing ways that turn back on themselves and reverberate in other media. It is an incredibly complicated process that, at its best, can deepen the experience of the ordinary citizen in what otherwise might have been a one-dimensional story. The other side of the vast synergies of mass communications, however, especially in relation to something as large as the World Trade Center disaster, is that one never escapes the story, which is presented in so many forms and with such intensity that one can easily feel haunted and overwhelmed by its proliferation in the various media.

The second relevant principle is what I call the *overstimulation effect*. Television was able to capture in exquisite and realistic detail the experience of violence, fear, and chaos on 9/11. The endlessly repeated images of violence from 9/11 had the effect in its graphic detail of overstimulating the viewer and stirring, perhaps inevitably, desires for increasing levels of additional excitement. Onlookers in innumerable anecdotal reports exhibited increasing signs of dependency on, if not addiction to, television, after the disaster. We got a rush from the drug but needed constantly to increase the dosage to maintain satisfactory levels of contentment. It could only be endlessly repeated, adding commentary and maps and the inevitable expert that called forth more commentary and maps and experts and more replay.

The third principle is what could be called the *anticipatory effect*. The intensity and ferocity of media images of violence are especially significant in an apocalyptic age, one with nuclear weapons that were so much part of the subtext of 9/11. Perhaps we need stories to prepare us psychologically for such a future. The foretelling of the end is widely celebrated throughout the media: Sometimes it seems that half of the movies coming out of Hollywood, which after an appropriate time are replayed on television, deal with apocalyptic themes that in turn serve to evoke such yearnings in the self. In this anticipatory dimension we live in our imagination with future public tragedies. In this sense we are all survivors of a future nuclear holocaust. It was remarkable the extent to which 9/11 evoked these apocalyptic fears.

The fourth dimension is the *numbing effect*. Numbing, described in psychological terms first by Robert Jay Lifton in relation to the survivors of Hiroshima, is an active psychological process of closing off feeling because impressions and experience become too overwhelming. Different people have widely varying levels of tolerance for when they will reach the point at which such a closing down of feeling, or numbing, becomes absolutely necessary for survival. The deeply traumatized will respond much sooner to images of horror by shutting down than the relatively better adjusted. But large events like 9/11, and especially in the way they are brought to us through television and other media, tend to flatten out such diversity and overwhelm most people. As a principle, it is fair to say that the larger and more tragic the event, along with the more extensive the coverage—and of course both criteria were met on and after 9/11—the more likely widespread numbing will be.

These principles worked on 9/11 to diminish profoundly the sense of agency for most viewers. Agency is the key issue in coherent self-functioning. Nothing is more striking in trauma than the sense that survivors have of not owning the decisions of their lives. Such paralysis can reach extreme forms in paranoia but is evident in less virulent ways for all survivors. Other people are experienced as shaping, if not determining, what will happen in the self in feelings and actions. Survivors are besieged and helpless, left with a keen sense that events are beyond their control. It leaves them adrift. Lacking agency exacerbates an already aggrieved sense of victimization. The trauma lingers. The New York experience of the World Trade Center disaster was such that, in time, agency returned to survivors. They suffered, to be sure, and many, like Miranda, will probably never fully heal, but most New Yorkers eventually recovered more or less in the actuality of their textured and nuanced experiences of death immersion. In zone 4, where it all played out in virtual reality, however, few experiences allowed for what in psychoanalysis is called "working through," or finding ways to integrate and heal traumatic experiences. The confusion in agency left the country adrift and open to manipulation and control by an administration with a set and mostly secret agenda.

The endless repetition of the disaster and its scenes of destruction that kept Americans tied to their televisions for days and sometimes weeks simultaneously intensified the experience and the fears the images aroused. Watching television became obsessive. The more viewers watched, the more they were scared and confused, and the more they watched. The psychological result was an empathic overload that in turn generated a sense of rage and a pervasive paranoia, affects that were channeled into action by an authoritarian regime led by a Christian fundamentalist leader. America after 9/11 was a perfect storm of a determined and overly certain leader meeting the fertile soil of collective trauma.

POLITICAL EFFECTS

After 9/11 the United States turned in radically new political and geopolitical directions. A mass psychology of fear that emerged from 9/11 provided the underpinnings for this transformation. There were real reasons after 9/11 to fear continued threats to our existence from abroad. Jihadis were in fact plotting our demise. The dangers were not a figment of George Bush's imagination, conjured up for purposes of political calculation, but the extreme reaction of Americans to these threats resulted in paroxysms of xenophobia that played into Bush's hands. And this culture of fear after 9/11 had much to do with the way most Americans encountered the disaster through television. Watching it all rendered the viewer helpless. The experience was inauthentic and left the viewer full of rage and frustration, feelings that were well suited to meet the needs of those seeking to accomplish their geopolitical objectives in the Middle East long before 9/11.

The contrast with New York in this regard is striking. Many people in the city, of course, watched the event on television, both that morning and in the blur of days that followed. But in the city it was also outside one's door. In office buildings everywhere people fled. It was hard to escape the sadness of knowing people, or knowing of people, who died. In New York City we lived with the enduring echoes of the disaster, none of which was more significant than the smell of death that we all breathed or the real fears of further attacks. Henry, as a "news junkie," derived some important meanings through his little radio as the disaster unfolded. When he finally made it home, he spent days watching TV to find out all he could about what had happened. The fears he felt took a long time to dissipate. He kept waiting for something else to happen. In that period of waiting like Estragon for Godot, Henry often reflected on how different it must be for those outside of New York. "If you were completely removed from it," he says, "like living in Arizona somewhere watching the whole thing on TV, you probably don't have the fear that there's going to be some kind of attack where you're at." Standing there in the subway entrance covered in dust made him feel, as no one could outside of the city, "What's going to happen next?" In New York, in other words, there was no escape into the false security of one's living room with one's television. The disaster was in our lives in very palpable ways.

Now it is true that it is risky to distinguish the politics of the city from that of the nation based on something as tenuous as the television experience of the World Trade Center disaster. Many other factors were at work *and* the political differences between New York and the country must not be exaggerated. There were many in the city who, in the nature of their response to the disaster, might as well have been in Kansas, whereas in many pockets of the country wise and good-hearted people resisted the pull to war and violence as the primary response to 9/11. Furthermore, New York City has long been much more liberal politically than the rest of the country, so that any difference between its politics and those of the country after 9/11 may be purely illusory. But from the outset it was striking how citizens in New York for the most part refused to participate in the project of war-making as the primary response to 9/11. Union Square became the epicenter of that dissent in the weeks after 9/11, though it soon encompassed the rest of the city in large demonstrations as one war led to another, outrages like Abu Ghraib became known, and the consequences of domestic surveillance altered much of the fabric of our democracy. New Yorkers were less likely than many others in the country to buy into the Bush project. Many of those who saw it on television called for killing people in response. Those who experienced it simply cried and survived. However confused or traumatic or full of despair the experience of 9/11 was for those living in New York, it was at least a psychologically authentic experience.

Deirdre put it well. She struggled at first to describe what she found so disconcerting about her conversations with her family members in California and with other friends and more distant relatives she talked with after the disaster. As she put it in terms that she herself found confusing, "Now as time went on, other people who came into the picture I wasn't as comfortable with because they didn't know how I had been three days before, and one day I'm happy and one day I'm sad and one day I'm upset, and they were perhaps feeling the same feelings." She continued with her self-analysis in trying to explain what she felt. As she put it, more clearly: "I mean I do get a sense that it's not as intense for other people. I mean I've talked to a lot of people from California, a lot of people from the West Coast and down south and they're getting involved very politically you know . . . but they don't have the same sensitivity—they're not as sensitive to the effects it has on other people around them or losing people or seeing—you know, there's something that's a little bit different. They're angry. Some of them are angry and pissed off and upset or it's so horrible, but they just seem removed generally."

Removed, indeed. Everything from within the virtual reality of the disaster had a cartoonish quality to it. For one thing, it was oddly derivative. The 9/11 plotters would never have gotten the idea of flying hijacked planes into the

World Trade Center without Hollywood doing it first, from *Independence Day*, to *Die Hard*, *Armageddon*, and *Executive Decision* (a 1996 movie of Middle Eastern terrorists who hijack a plane and attempt to fly it into the Washington area in order to release a powerful biological agent that would kill 40 million people). Some of these images drew in turn on literary antecedents, such as Tom Clancy's *Debt of Honor*, which has people flying planes into tall buildings, and William Pierce's 1978 *The Turner Diaries*, which ends in a wild flourish with the protagonist, Earl Turner, on a suicide mission flying a Cessna loaded with a nuclear weapon into the Pentagon. Such images were stamped on the template of our unconscious as a kind of wrap-around screen long before 9/11. The disaster as seen on television in this sense was mere replay.

The events of 9/11, a disaster that had the form and length of a movie, occasioned Norman Mailer's quip, "Our movies came off the screen and chased us down the canyons of the city."[6] It was just another script, and in Hollywood the world is always saved, the survivors noble, and evil punished. Our post-9/11 wars are just final acts in the already revealed future of the narrative. The unconscious expectations of appropriate revenge in which virtue will triumph fended off the dread. But events kept breaking out of the mold and stirring the fear and malevolence. The numbing had trouble holding. There was a constant contradiction between a contemptuous familiarity and dreaded, irrational fear.

The very protections television offered—the screen, the context given by commentators, the ability to leave it easily—came with the costs of potentially numbing the watcher. The television experience of 9/11—whether or not in real time—was vicarious and removed. Such numbed encounters with death can have many meanings. In this case, in part because of the general political climate into which 9/11 got inserted, many television viewers throughout the vast expanses of America became vulnerable to rage at their helplessness. That rage was to be channeled into forms of action—most of all in the wars we were to fight in the next few years that in turn fostered a radical set of new laws curtailing our civil liberties.

9

HIDDEN CHILDREN: TELEVISION'S EXCEPTION

DURING WORLD WAR II many thousands of Jewish children were spared death at the hands of the Nazis by altruistic Christian families and some institutions, such as monasteries and convents. Jewish children in Europe faced death on a cataclysmic scale. At the outset of the war approximately 1.6 million Jewish children were living in the territories that the German armies or their allies would occupy. By war's end, more than 1 million of them, and perhaps as many as 1.5 million, had been killed by the Nazis' program of genocide. Those who survived lived with disguised identities, often physically concealed from the outside world, and faced constant fear and danger. Some could pass as non-Jews and live openly. Those who could not had to live clandestinely, often in attics or cellars. Children posing as Christians had to carefully conceal their Jewish identity from inquisitive neighbors, classmates, informers, blackmailers, and the police. Even a momentary lapse in language or behavior could expose the child, and the rescuer, to discovery and death. The child *and* all those providing protection would be executed or deported to a concentration camp.

For decades the Jewish children who survived the war never realized the extent to which they were part of a larger community. Their direct experience had been one of isolation and miraculous survival. Through the concerted work of people like Myriam Abramowicz and eventually with the help of Abraham H. Foxman and the Anti-Defamation League, some 1,600 former hidden children from twenty-eight countries met for the first time in May 1991 in New York City at the First International Gathering of Children Hidden During World War II. The purpose of the gathering—which I attended—was to share memories, help those who were too young to remember, and speak as witnesses of the atrocities committed against Jews. The gathering inevitably led to the formation of an organization, the search for other hidden children, a major exhibit at the Holocaust Museum in Washington, and other such activities.

That conference spawned a number of local chapters of what became a movement all over the country of this special group of survivors. I became intrigued with one such group of hidden children in Chicago as I considered the question of television and 9/11. I interviewed this group in Chicago on April 24, 2004. I wanted to explore my idea that there was a qualitative difference in experience between those who more directly encountered 9/11 in New York and most Americans, who came to it from the very different vantage of television. I felt, to paraphrase T. S. Eliot, that the television encounter of 9/11 made it possible for Americans to experience the disaster but it robbed them of its meaning. I suspected that this unusual group of adults, given their extraordinary childhoods of survival, might articulate profound meanings about 9/11 that were mostly unavailable to Americans outside of New York. In searching out the hidden children, I hoped to find the kind of exception that would prove the rule. I was not to be disappointed.

I sat in a circle with my new friends and put the tape recorder on a chair in the middle of the group. They began by wanting to know more about my study before opening up about themselves. They did not want to be exploited. I therefore began by explaining my work, the interviews I had conducted, and some of my ideas about the apocalyptic. I defined the term in a very brief way as "world-ending" and noted that we have such images of extinction in our imagination from historical events such as Auschwitz and Hiroshima and that part of my theory about 9/11 is that it evoked the apocalyptic, even though as an actual event the disaster in no way should be defined as world-ending or equated with the attempted genocidal elimination of the Jews during the Holocaust. In such an interview situation I would not normally talk so much at the outset and certainly not about my general ideas on the subject of the interview itself, but these hidden children insisted that I talk first so that they could understand what my study was all about and why I had been so eager to interview them (which was not exactly self-evident). I therefore answered their general questions as best I could and in sufficient depth to explain my purposes.

My opening comments sparked immediate discussion. A couple of people in the group were confused by what I meant, which was probably too abstract. Jill[1] spoke out with feeling: "It doesn't sit well with the survivor to think about universal extinction. We don't accept it. I don't accept it." Cindy disagreed strongly. She said to her friend Jill, "You don't accept it. I do." She then told a vignette of flying in a plane over a part of Africa where there had been a terrible disaster (Rwanda after the genocide in 1994). She looked down at what she first thought were thousands of logs on the ground, only to realize with a start that the logs were dead human beings. That, she said, was an "image of extinction." It was also one that was part of her imagination from her childhood during the war, and such images came back to her on 9/11. Jill added, "It's on again. War. The end," to which Cindy replied with more hope, "We will not be annihilated. There will always be humans." Saul added that millions of people are dying just as millions more are being born. "That's the way it is. I don't think humanity is going to disappear." But in the same breath he contradicted that hopeful note: "I don't think that humans will stop doing things to each other. And when they finish, nature will start doing it to humans."

It should be noted that the variety of wartime experiences represented in this group was remarkable. One woman stayed mostly in the barn of a peasant during the war as a mute relative to hide her accent. She never opened her mouth between the ages of ten and fifteen. Now she never stops talking. A man hid in the cellar of a monastery. Another woman was always on the run with her mother and younger sister. As soon as there was the slightest hint of danger, the mother scooped up the children and ran into the woods and another destination. Such were some of the amazing stories of just this small group of Chicagoans.

I asked them how they found out about 9/11. Several replied at once that they saw it reported on TV. They didn't believe it at first. Jill was playing tennis that morning and someone came running with the news. She said it made her think there would be World War III, thus immediately connecting the violence of 9/11 with the World War II in ways that evoked the possibility of future apocalyptic violence. Jill said she was nearly crazy that morning until she was able to track down her daughter, who lives in Manhattan, and make sure she was okay. She then brought home her fears: "This [9/11] made me feel like I had totally lost control. Like the war in Europe. I couldn't believe it was happening again."

Jill said, "I was horrified. But I was fascinated by what happened. It's mind-boggling. I was not in a camp, but I was hidden. I cried because it brought back memories. We lived through bombings, those of us who were not in camps, and all that. I thought I was safe in America. And now I find out I am not safe. Six million of us died, and for what? The strife continues." And then: "It's very sad. If there is a God, if you follow what the Bible says in creating humanity, he made a big mistake on his part." Pauses. "A big mistake on his part. No good has come from it. We kill everything." Elsa took exception to such pessimism. "We will never agree as long as we have people on this Earth. This is a simplified statement I am making. I don't think we will be annihilated."

Cindy associated to the people who "jumped out of the windows" of the towers on 9/11. "What did they feel?" she asked rhetorically. "It's like what I have always wondered about the people in Auschwitz. What did they feel?" That thought led several others to discuss how 9/11 made them feel unsafe. Before that there were things that scared them, but most, as Cindy put it, were things "you could control." "But this [9/11] I couldn't control, like the war." That comment prompted Jill to recover specific memories of the war from her childhood connected to planes: "I remember when we went into the forest and the planes came down really low." That memory was connected to how low the planes flew that went into the towers. How could this happen? This is the United States of America. David said, "I cried because it [9/11] brought back memories. I thought I was safe in America. It brought back memories."

Cindy wondered about the experience of the people in the planes. "And this goes for the people in the [death] camps [during the war] as well." "How can a human being do this, knowing what the results will be? That you are instrumental in killing thousands of people." "It happens all over the world," she added. In Africa, "they hack each other to death. If I catch an insect, I don't like to [kill it], I put it on a piece of paper and [put] it outside." "How can they do what they did to other people?" she asked of the terrorists in the planes as they hurtled toward the towers.

Saul at that point wondered why I was meeting with them at all. "Do you really feel our reaction [to 9/11] is going to be that much different from that of the general public?" I explained why I thought their reactions were unique and worth exploring. He accepted my explanation and went on to say that at first when he turned on his TV and saw the north tower burning, he thought it was a movie. "Suddenly, as the second plane fell into the second tower . . . it's been said before . . . fortress America came to mind. This is not fortress America anymore. America has been attacked *in* America. That has never happened before. We have never fought a war in the United States." What he thought about was the pain of the people dying. That is what has preoccupied his thoughts since childhood. He wonders about the pain one feels at the moment of death. He asked of those who jumped to their death: "What kind of pain did they go through? Did they die in a hurry? Did some suffer? What happens to you when you jump out of a building 100 stories high?" he asked himself. And he continued: "I have always been preoccupied with the pain of death." All of that flooded him as he watched the disaster unfold. "But then I started to think, 'This is New York, not Chicago. And I thought of the Sears Tower, and how far away am I from the Sears Tower? Is this going to affect me?'"

Jill recounted the five wars she has lived through. I asked how she felt about the piercing of "fortress America." For her it was like 1967 in Israel, when she had to take her child and hide in a cellar. "Security," she said in a thick accent with phrasing that was as poetic as it was obscure, "is as long as I am."

Saul said everything changed with 9/11. There were kamikaze fighters in World War II but they were a relatively minor part of the story. Now it is different. How do you fight people who are willing to die, convinced they are going to heaven. And not just "one, two, it is happening by the hundreds. Their life must be so miserable or they are so convinced by their teachings that this is the right thing to do. . . ." Cindy said 9/11 could have been prevented. Why weren't they more suspicious at those flight schools about people only wanting to learn how to fly planes but not land or take off?

Elsa said her reactions and those of the group were largely based on their war experiences. "We didn't understand then why someone was arrested, why the Gestapo came in, or whatever. Some of us reacted [to 9/11] as we did as children. Maybe it wasn't this sort of cool, objective assessment of another act of terrorism." It seemed it was an "initial fear, of what can happen to me now" that arose in us. "That is what seems to be so unique about our group. How can it happen again? It is like 1941, 1942, 1943. America just fell apart." I asked if it was difficult to distinguish her memories of her childhood experience from her reaction to 9/11. "I do remember having the same fear. What is going to happen next? What's going to happen to us?" Saul said he had a different feeling. "In 1942 or 1941 they were looking to kill me because I was a Jew. This [9/11] happened to all kinds of people. My reaction was relief." "You mean you felt safer?" I asked. "Absolutely," he replied. "It was a horrendous happening but it wasn't against me as a Jew."

Jill noted, on the other hand, that she never feels completely safe now. She has her "antennas out." Ruth said that somewhat ironically she feels completely safe only in Israel but not in America. Here things feel dangerous after 9/11. But Jill reiterated her more general feeling that nowhere is really safe now. "That they can do what they did, that life doesn't matter . . . They have no conscience, nothing." Ruth expressed surprise that people in this group feel less safe now, presumably after what they all went through in the war. But then she answered her own implicit question, namely, that America for the first time was attacked. "Well, America, welcome to the human race." Furthermore, Ruth went on, with the Patriot Act and other such things happening in America "it looks more and more like Nazi Germany." Some neighbor can call you a terrorist and all of a sudden the FBI is beating down your house. "We're not free anymore."

Cindy commented that though all the hidden children had similar experiences during the war, they reacted to 9/11 more in terms of their personalities and characters. "I remember as a child always being fearful. I don't know if our reactions were based on our group experiences but rather on how we are." I asked if Jill (but also everyone) thought that if I had come to Chicago and assembled a random group of Chicagoans to talk about 9/11 their discussion would have been like what we were having. They all said in unison, "No, it would be very different." Eleanor asked me what would be the reaction of that imagined group of random Chicagoans. I said I could not say for sure but I would have thought such a group would not be as likely to be in touch with their fears and able to express how their feelings connected to their childhood experiences.

Cathy said, "No one came to help us. From 1938 to 1945 my mother, my sister, and I were on the run. We were always one step ahead of the Germans. The minute she got some kind of sense that things were dangerous, we were off. And that's how we survived the whole war. So I know that activity is my immediate reaction [to danger]. Other people, as well, who are not Jewish must tune into their own childhoods."

The new themes in the conversations at this point seemed to stir specific memories that led to a flood. Jill said, "We were still afraid even after the war because we traded the Nazis for the Communists." Cindy added, "I was raised to believe it was never bad being a Jew. I was raised Orthodox and taught that even if you were in a monastery it was okay to be a Jew." And she continued, "I was never a child. I had responsibilities. We were hidden. I took care of my younger brother, a three-year-old. I was eight years old."

Jill said, "I was taught by the other schoolchildren, by the Christian children, that I had killed Jesus. I was ashamed. And when I first came here [to America] I didn't want anyone to know I was Jewish. On the first day of Yom Kippur I had to take off and said I was ill. I was embarrassed to say I was a Jew."

Jennifer told a story of a little boy she had in treatment after 9/11 [she is a psychotherapist]. "He came from South America. He had been traumatized as a little boy. He had been in an orphanage. I knew the family was on hard times and actually going hungry. He had a sister whom I had seen before. The mother wasn't around. The father was scheduled to bring in the child [for her appointment]. I called and told him, 'You come and we will meet in such and such a restaurant. All of you come and we will all have dinner together.' So they came and the father went to the bathroom and I talked with the children." She asked herself as she was telling the story, "Why am I telling this story?" She continued, "Because somewhere along the line I decided this happened to me. I am going to change things. No one is going to persecute children. I was so surprised at my reaction that I decided to feed this entire family. And it was absolutely the right thing to do. It was just absolutely wonderful. It had lots of good repercussions [including on me]. Denial in me runs so deep."

Cindy said, "As a child [during the war] I was always afraid of being abandoned. Later, when my new husband died, I felt abandoned. This time [9/11] when I saw what was happening in New York I could almost visualize myself being part of it, or my family being part of it, and then what happened is that everything would be gone." She then interpreted herself and said that her reaction to 9/11 of feeling abandoned has all these antecedents. It is always there. "We don't change as we grow older."

Saul disagreed. He said he was a youngster when he came to this country. "I was struck by the power of this country. Nobody could defeat this country. And that gave me a certain feeling of security. Even when I went into the army [he fought in the Korean war in 1952] I felt I was with the best and the strongest. And now you can get a guy with a suitcase to come and blow up Chicago. One suitcase. So warfare has changed." He added, "This whole country is different. And to me that is frightening." I asked how new those ideas are. "Before 9/11 I would never imagine suicide bombers. Suicide bombers? Never. Nobody could defeat this country. [That was my attitude before 9/11.] But now you can have a dozen people with suitcases and they can destroy millions of people."

Elsa added, "You are not safe on the train. You are not safe on the airplane. You're not safe in the car." I asked, "Is 9/11 over?" A number in the group answered together, "No," and repeated it several times. "No, never," someone added. Saul noted the idea in Israel is that it is not whether it is going to happen but when. And now we live with the same kind of thought. "It is going to happen again," he added with certainty. "They are figuring out a way to do terrible damage. And it's going to happen." Another woman said with anger, "We have all these codes now, code 11, code yellow, purple, everybody, like the government, is waiting for it to happen." I said, "This is a very pessimistic group." Elsa reacted against that idea. "No. The worst thing we can do is give into fear. This is getting at our minds. And for me that is one of the two things I was happy [about] at the end of the Nazi era: that my mother survived and my brain survived. Nothing else survived. They didn't get at my brain. I didn't hate. I feared. But when fear was over I do not hate. To this very day I am proud of that." And: "We need to be inoculated against fear. Not to give in." Cindy added, "It takes a lot of courage to live without fear."

Jennifer said that if she lived in New York now and had children she would be very careful. "My life would be planned." When she is in New York and on the train, "I think about it. I think about it constantly. I know it is irrational. But I feel it." She went to Paris and London recently. "I wasn't so sure we would make it back." Elsa interrupted to say, "But you went. You went outside. You went." I said that I have talked with people in New York who basically never go outside and live with the covers over their head [I was thinking here of Miranda]. Several people noted in unison, "That is very sad." "A real tragedy." Saul said, however, "I think that woman had a problem well before 9/11." Elsa softened that a bit: "We never know how we will react for the first time."

THE CONTRADICTORY EXPERIENCE OF AMERICANS

The reaction of most Americans who only watched the disaster on television contributed to the rage, xenophobia, and fear that became a staple after 9/11. The intense experience of the disaster on television in its endless repetition contributed to the numbing, for it deepened the fears of most Americans. It would be foolish to overstate the role of television in shaping our culture and politics in the years after 9/11. Many factors contributed to the making of our lives in the last decade. But I would say that the world we have created for ourselves in this period is unimaginable except in the context of 9/11 and that the disaster was a felt event only because of television. The peculiar psychological workings of the medium made it, in McLuhan's terms, the message.

It was refreshing therefore to encounter my small but remarkable group of hidden children who grasped deeper truths of the disaster despite, rather than because of, their encountering it on television. Jill and Saul and Jennifer and the others brought their survivor wisdom with them as a sharp arrow in their psychological quiver when they turned on the television that day. The disaster was startling, unsettling, and sad for them, as it was for millions of Americans, but despite the important differences among those I talked with, the hidden children related their feelings of what they were watching to their wartime experiences, to their struggles to survive, to what they knew of death and clawing their way back to life. As Jill said, "I think the things that happened to us as [hidden] children made us stronger and better able to deal with things later on in life. I think it made me stronger. I think it gave me strength to deal with things later on." Among this group there was no glib nationalism or self-righteous calls for crusade or numbed calls to kill and avenge in fury and rage. There was sadness, even despair, about the world and its capacity for violence, feelings that were entirely appropriate after 9/11. But there was also hope, without which there cannot be life.

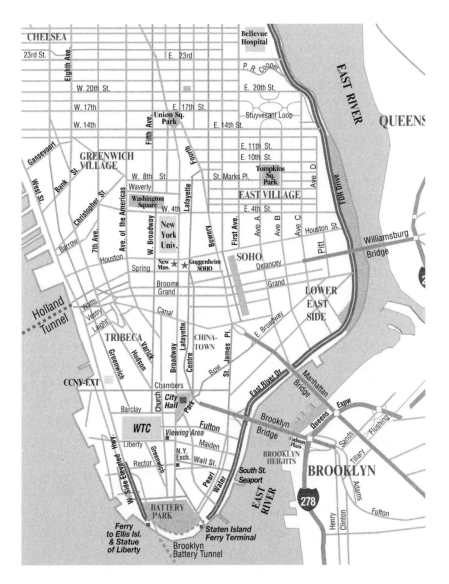

FIGURE 1 The World Trade Center complex was located in the far southwest corner of Manhattan and spilled over beyond the streets of what would come to be called Ground Zero. Once the disaster struck and the tunnels were closed, the only avenues of escape were north along the West Side Highway or on city streets through Tribeca and Greenwich Village, south to Battery Park and the ferries to Staten Island, or most of all, east, across the Brooklyn Bridge. (*Courtesy City Maps, Inc.*)

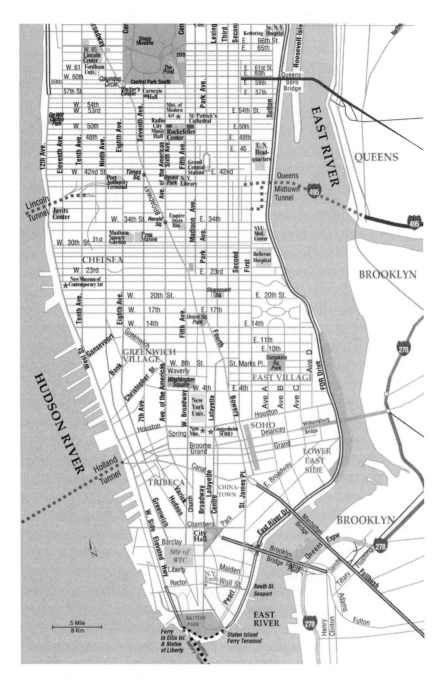

FIGURE 2 This map of Manhattan shows how the zones of sadness radiated out from the violence at Ground Zero. Parts of Brooklyn, especially along the waterfront and the neighborhoods closer in, as well as Hoboken, New Jersey, and the northern shore of Staten Island, were intimately caught up in the disaster because of the location of the World Trade Center near the southern tip of Manhattan. (*Courtesy City Maps, Inc.*)

FIGURE 3 The north tower was already on fire when millions of television viewers around the world saw Marwan al-Shehhi fly United Flight 175 into the south tower of the World Trade Center between the 77th and 85th floors. The plane, flying at 545 mph, nearly missed the building altogether, exploding its 10,000 gallons of fuel in a gigantic fireball. (*Courtesy Lyle Owerko.*)

FIGURE 4 American Airlines Flight 11 struck the north tower squarely in the center of the north face of the building between the 93rd and 99th floors, destroying all the elevators and stairways at and above the point of impact. United Flight 175, however, hit the south tower on its eastern side, thus allowing egress from upper floors until it collapsed at 9:50 A.M. (*Here Is New York, photograph of the events of September 11, 2001, in NYC, photo #112 by James Wentzy; Here Is New York Collection, PR 258.*)

FIGURE 5 This improbable image of a woman standing in the gash of the north tower shows how hopeless it was for anyone caught in the upper floors to escape. The woman unfortunately fell or jumped to her death shortly after this picture was taken. (*Courtesy Roberto Rabanne.*)

FIGURE 6 (*left*) Each collapsed tower produced a terrifying blob of dust and debris that enveloped Lower Manhattan and New Yorkers in the area like a monster in a Hollywood movie. (*Here Is New York, photograph of the events of September 11, 2001, in NYC, photo #1367 by Jacqueline Gourevitch; Here Is New York Collection, PR 258.*)

FIGURE 7 (*top*) Nothing matched the horror of the fires burning at Ground Zero. The stench was an awful blend of toxic chemicals and death, and left many workers with disabling lung diseases. The fires burned for 100 days (*Here Is New York, photograph of the events of September 11, 2001, in NYC, photo #2515 by Steven Hirsch; Here Is New York Collection, PR 258.*)

FIGURE 8 (*top*) A deadly silence soon fell on Ground Zero. (*Here Is New York, photograph of the events of September 11, 2001, in NYC, photo #7607 by Patrick McCafferty; Here Is New York Collection, PR 258.*)

FIGURE 9 (*right*) It became quickly apparent that the massive pile of debris from the collapse of both World Trade Center towers would require heavy equipment to clear. The cranes and their operators, however, had to work in the middle of the fires and amid the thousands of volunteers on the bucket brigade. (*Here Is New York, photograph of the events of September 11, 2001, in NYC, photo #5101 by Samuel Hollenshead; Here Is New York Collection, PR 258.*)

FIGURE 10 (*bottom*) Volunteer firemen from around the country officially and unofficially flocked to the pile to help save any of their surviving comrades after 343 members of the NYFD died in the disaster. This image is of Roman Kopinski from Company 2 of Niles, Illinois. (*Here Is New York, photograph of the events of September 11, 2001, in NYC, photo #6960 by Daniel P. Ryan, Sr.; Here Is New York Collection, PR 258.*)

FIGURE 11 On 9/11 some were hit with debris and suffered grievous injuries, requiring medical attention, as did those who got dust and debris in their eyes and lungs, but for the most part on September 11 New Yorkers either died or survived the disaster relatively unscathed *physically*. Local hospitals, however, especially St. Vincent's on 12th Street and Seventh Avenue, geared up once the disaster was under way for what they assumed would be a flood of victims. Most never arrived. The empty gurneys and doctors and nurses with nothing to do filled the sidewalk and street outside the hospital's emergency room in the hours after the disaster. (*Courtesy Roberto Rabanne.*)

FIGURE 12 (three images) Private and very personal memorials to loved ones sprang up throughout New York City, but they were especially numerous for several weeks in Union Square just north of 14th Street. Many of these spontaneous memorials showed the contradictory way in which we place death in middle knowledge, combining a picture asking for information about the loved one (hoping for life) with burning candles (signifying death). (*Here Is New York, photograph of the events of September 11, 2001, in NYC, photo #513 by Sally Davies; Here Is New York Collection, PR 258. Credit line for other two images: Courtesy Roberto Rabanne.*)

FIGURE 13 Two images of the 9/11 Memorial (based on models), located in the footprints of the two towers, show an elegant and moving testimony to those who died and continue to suffer from the effects of the disaster. (*Arial View of Memorial Quadrant and Memorial Pool Names Parapet, Courtesy National 9/11 Memorial and Museum.*)

PART 2
100 DAYS OF SUFFERING

10
ORGANIC PROCESS

THE WORLD TRADE CENTER disaster was not a static event that happened one day in September of 2001. It was instead an organic process that changed and unfolded week by week, day by day, even hour by hour throughout that fall and to some degree through the winter. It was millions of moments and episodes that evoked responses in all of us who were at the same time participants and observers, actors and audience in the making of a collective trauma.

The pile at Ground Zero embodied the disaster itself. It was a concentrated site of evil. It took some time for the full rescue operation to fall into place, but thousands of volunteers descended on Ground Zero the afternoon of September 11 to search for survivors. It was a "frantic, bloody business," as *The Guardian* reporters put it. "Firefighters, police officers and eventually the National Guard were scavenging under the rubble for the panting, blood-splattered injured and the lifeless, rubbery limbs of the dead. One man, barely alive, was humped into the back of an ambulance with his foot hanging loose by a couple of tendons."[1] The scene was incredible. The force of the collapse of the towers pulverized 425,000 cubic yards of concrete, and the collapse and fire twisted 200,000 tons of steel beams entwined with the cables of the 198 elevators (99 in each tower) and miles of rebar from the concrete. The resulting pile of debris that sunk 70 feet to bedrock and reached some ten stories into the heavens was life-threatening for anyone on or near it. The pile also had open fires, smoke, jet fuel, and extreme heat.

The magnitude of the burning, belching debris at the pile created great difficulties for rescue workers. Much of the infrastructure of Lower Manhattan had been destroyed or damaged, and it was difficult to get the right kind of equipment to the site. Shoes and boots melted from working on the hot surfaces. Zac Ungar, a firefighter from California, arrived at Ground Zero two weeks after 9/11. He was most surprised at how much metal was stacked over acres of ground, reaching into the sky. There were no visible remains of furniture, or wooden or plastic parts, or computer shards. All of that kind of material— and much else—had been pulverized in the collapse of the towers. Only the iron and steel remained, though the force that it underwent was awesome. Huge beams were ripped down the middle "like pages from a notebook."[2]

The burning fires defined the landscape of Ground Zero. They were not entirely put out until December 20, 2001. The reason the fires burned so long had to do with a peculiar fact of the design of the World Trade Center towers and the way they collapsed. Architecturally, the load-carrying beams were all in the middle, where the elevators were also clustered. Each floor, which allowed for about an acre of open office space, hung between those beams and the many redundant outside columns placed 22 inches apart. That façade provided reinforcement but did not carry the same amount of load for what was more like an elaborate deck of cards suspended in air than a solid and secure skyscraper. The raging fires on the inside of each tower, created because the planes plowed into the center of the buildings and released an enormous quantity of burning jet fuel, softened the steel supports for the floors, which caused the pancaking and collapse. The fires and the force of the impact also weakened the inside beams much more than those on the outside that held each tower rigid. As the buildings collapsed, those outside columns moved from side to side before breaking apart, helping to dig the hole that later contained the mass of the cascading building. The result was to bury vast quantities of still-burning material beneath the mountain of steel as well as create air pockets that fed the fires with oxygen. One other factor is relevant: It was many weeks before those working at the pile turned their attention to extinguishing the fires, as their first concern was rescuing anyone who might be alive.

The rescue process, which is the first phase in the immediate wake of any disaster, began with buckets and shovels. Vast numbers of firemen, police, and other volunteers moved cautiously as they searched for survivors. It was quickly apparent that heavy equipment was needed to move some of the steel pieces in order to search in pockets where there might be survivors. In the end, some 108,342 trucks and barges transported material to Fresh Kills on Staten Island, where it was all sifted a second time to be sure there were no human remains. Iron workers joined the crews early on, as did engineers. The stability of the pile was always variable and required daily, even hourly, engineering assessments before proceeding. Once the flames were extinguished, a huge clean-up job remained, which lasted another half year. On May 28, 2002, the final steel column was ceremoniously removed and taken away.

The behavior of the thousands of firemen and other rescue workers at Ground Zero in the months after 9/11 was enormously complicated and at times highly contradictory. There emerged early on a "jealous sense of ownership," as William Langewiesche puts it in his book *American Ground*, based on his months of reporting from Ground Zero. A pride in ownership of the disaster existed for those who worked it most closely. Langewiesche makes the interesting point that this feeling of ownership of the disaster extended throughout the United States but became progressively more acute with proximity to the site, reaching its ultimate sense of peculiar ownership within the boundaries of those working the pile. Three main groups made up the rescue workers: fire, police, and construction workers. Their task was unified, but sometimes their separate loyalties divided them against each other, as was particularly the case when the police and firemen got into a fight on November 2nd. The greatest sense of ownership at the pile undoubtedly came from the firemen because they had lost 343 of their peers out of a force of 14,000. Certainly, as well, they responded to the national idealization of firemen as epitomizing the heroic martyrdom in response to the disaster. There was at times, however, a good deal of grandstanding, and the striking of tragic poses for newsmen and the signing of autographs outside the perimeter gates. Most, however, stuck to the task at hand. The police, who had themselves lost many of their own people, felt resentment, and the construction crews, who assumed the responsibility for honoring the civilian deaths, doubled over in anger at many points. No more dramatic example of the differing reactions of rescue workers existed than the responses of the different groups to the recovery of body parts. Whenever the remains of a fireman were uncovered, there was always an elaborate flag-draped ceremonial. The other dead merely got a "bag 'em and tag 'em" approach. Langewiesche comments, "It was a surprisingly gang-like view, and encouraged a gang mentality among the others on the pile."[3]

Despite all the posturing, most of the men felt a continuing and acute sense of sadness. The depth of pain that people felt was not always obvious. Certainly the determination of all workers to toil at extraordinary lengths is evidence of the pain they felt. Many barely left the site, leaving to sleep on cots in St. Paul's Chapel or to sleep on the pews in Trinity Church, before returning to their work.[4] But they also took a lot of risks for no good reason. Sometimes they would jump into newly opened debris holes or stand for hours on unstable cliffs. Many workers, especially firemen, "seemed to have surrendered to an attitude of reckless self-abandonment." Langewiesche argues that such behavior was the expression of a "creative and courageous impulse, linked to the need for action and improvisation," that spoke to important depths of personal freedom. The outrageousness of the risk-taking, in this sense, was a response to and part of the sheer magnitude of the disaster.

And then, of course, there was the pile. It had been the focus of ferocious energy during the collapse, and now was the focus during the unbuilding. The pile was an extreme in itself. It was not just the ruins of seven big buildings, but a terrain of tangled steel on an unimaginable scale, with mountainous slopes breathing smoke and flame, roamed by diesel dinosaurs and filled with the human dead. It heaved and groaned and constantly changed, and was capable at any moment of killing again. People did not merely work to clear it out, but went there day and night to fling themselves against it. The pile was the enemy, the objective, the obsession, the hard-won ground.[5]

A number of other factors contributed to the scene of chaos at Ground Zero in the extended period after 9/11. For a variety of political reasons, the formal declaration of the end of the rescue phase and the start of the recovery phase was delayed for nearly three weeks, something that should have happened at least within a week after 9/11. In all, twenty-one people were found alive following the attacks, including sixteen in a stairwell and at various other places within the rubble. One woman was rescued near where a West Side

Highway pedestrian bridge had been, and two Port Authority police officers, John McLoughlin and Will Jimeno, were found miraculously alive in a void between where the towers had been. (Their story was later made into a movie by Oliver Stone.) All were found, however, in the first twenty-six hours after the attacks.[6] During rescue operations, all effort is focused on finding survivors. The focus on recovering survivors influences the allocation of resources and determines the kinds of decisions made about allowing volunteers to participate in the process. Those on the pile knew the truth. John Norman, for example, the Battalion Chief heading the rescue and recovery operation, knew a few days after September 11 that it was hopeless to expect to find anyone else alive.[7] The extreme losses suffered by the FDNY contributed significantly to the enormous pressures to delay the declaration of a formal end to the rescue phase of the operation. Once into recovery from the beginning of October, the search was relentless and much delayed in the hopes of finding body parts. Feelings ran very high at the level of the rank and file, and the firemen were determined to leave no stone unturned in first rescuing their fallen colleagues and then finding their remains.

The work of finding the remains of victims in time became regularized. The various contingents represented at the site worked out their complicated relationships, often with tension and sometimes with outright rivalry, but eventually with a degree of regularity. The work was divided into twelve-hour shifts, and many groups of fireman came in and out of the work. New workers were constantly arriving and needed to be initiated into the grim, tedious work. For the most part, crews of rescuers stood by the side of diesel excavators as they pried loose the steel and other debris from the pile. After each movement of something, the workers would probe at what lay beneath with their pikes and shovels. Then the debris would be carefully transferred out and inspected for any kind of remains. This elaborate and detailed searching for body parts was then repeated when everything was taken to the landfill at Fresh Kills, a landfill that was specifically reopened to accommodate the vast amount of debris from the disaster.

Body parts constantly appeared in the pile as the rescue operation proceeded. Many of these body parts led to the identification of victims through DNA analysis, but most were either too partial or degraded. Sometimes the scattered body parts looked merely like "lumpy cakes," mixed in with the other debris. At other times, one could see a piece of clothing or the striation of flesh and know that there was something to uncover. It was also possible to spot body parts just below the surface because of the smell, though this could be deceptive. It turned out that there was a good deal of leftover chicken and meat and hot dogs strewn about the pile from the remains of meals tossed on the ground by all the workers.

Astonishingly enough, it took a full forty-eight days, that is, until October 29th, before any kind of viable health and safety plan was worked out at Ground Zero to protect the workers. Only after this plan was issued could it be implemented. This meant that formal training on-site to protect health and safety did not even begin until November 29th. And it was only by January 29th that there were a little fewer than 1,500 recovery workers who had attended a mandatory three-hour safety and health awareness program. By then it hardly mattered.

Yet another complication in the chaos of the recovery is that 85 percent of the members of the Special Operations Command of the FDNY died at the site during the disaster period. Included in those who died were a number of hazmat experts for the city. Those, in other words, most needed to guide this kind of complex response to a disaster had perished. Besides some of these experts, more than 400 emergency responders (other than the 343 firemen) died at the site.

Another health hazard at Ground Zero resulted from the refusal of many workers to wear respirators. The site was incredibly loud, and with a respirator on it was impossible to talk to anyone. Workers were constantly tugging at respirators to talk to someone. As a result, many stopped wearing them. Data from a two-week period in October, when respirator use by operators of heavy equipment was studied, show that the daily range was as wide as 20 to 50 percent, and for the most part only about a third of such operators used respirators regularly. The dire consequences for workers at the pile are now becoming apparent in the increase among them of lung and other ailments, heart problems, and cancers.

As if all these complications were not enough, Ground Zero quickly became a site that many celebrities visited. It became *de rigueur* to have yourself photographed on or near the pile, perhaps talking to a fireman, as George W. Bush did on Friday, September 14, his arm wrapped around the shoulders of a worker and speaking to the multitudes with a bullhorn. A steady stream of celebrities, including politicians, professional wrestlers, race car drivers, movie stars—even Miss America—visited the site. None, of course, wore hard hats, which further contributed to the pervasive sense of informality and desperate urgency but disregard for personal safety.

TOXIC AIR AND THE HEALTH CRISIS

Disregard for personal safety proved decisive in light of the toxins in the air at Ground Zero and the failures of officials at all levels, but especially the EPA, to report the potential public health crisis after 9/11. By far the best account of this crisis is that of Juan Gonzalez in *Fallout*. Gonzales is particularly hard on EPA director Christine Whitman, but he notes there was pressure by all city, state, and federal officials to get the stock market open and the city functioning so that the American economy would not go into freefall. There even seems to have been pressure put on Gonzalez's editors and publishers to suppress his courageous reporting. Their compromise was to publish his pieces but far in the back of the paper. Consequently, few at the time understood the real dangers of the air in the city, the toxic wastes that were everywhere in and near Ground Zero, and the huge potential long-term consequences to workers at the site and indeed for all New Yorkers.[8]

The extent of the obfuscation was considerable. For the two months after 9/11 three crucial institutions repeatedly reassured citizens that the air around Ground Zero was safe: the New York City Department of Health, the federal EPA, and the Occupational Safety and Health Administration (OSHA). Alternately promising there were no indications of long-term health risks, that the health effects resulting from the disaster were negligible, and that, as EPA director Christine Whitman put it, "There's no need for the general public to be concerned," the official voices of those responsible for public health spoke in unison to try and reassure the citizens of New York. One official, however, spoke out in outrage—Congressman Jerrold Nadler, whose district included the World Trade Center. Nadler was particularly incensed that the EPA refused to implement the Superfund Act (the National Contingency Plan of the Comprehensive Environmental Response, Compensation, and Liability Act), which would have empowered the EPA to deal with the clean-up indoors as well as outdoors and forced it to inspect and decontaminate homes in the area. Instead, the EPA deferred on the issue of clean-up in the apartments to the NYC Department of Health. The department in turn left the issue up to individual apartment dwellers themselves, who were advised to use a damp cloth to clean up.[9]

There were also emotional issues of concern, because it was clear from the outset that many New Yorkers were traumatized from their experiences on 9/11. The Department of Mental Health had its LIFENET referral phone line up and running within twenty-four hours in English, Spanish, and Asian languages. Staff from DMH were dispatched to the Family Assistance Center on Pier 94 and to the morgue. Throughout the city a host of local agencies established grief and counseling centers. More troubling for officials was the small army of some 9,000 psychotherapists who flooded Lower Manhattan, offering their services, sometimes desperate to help. There was no real way to handle all this volunteer labor, and most were turned away, to their consternation. The DMH meanwhile within two weeks after 9/11 had established its own network of services at Pier 94, Ground Zero, Emergency Operations Center at Pier 92, various hotlines, and through 230 community-based agencies in the city. All the major hospitals in the city also launched a variety of outpatient mental health services that reached thousands of people in Lower Manhattan and in the greater New York area.

It quickly became apparent to professionals involved in this massive effort, especially someone like Neal Cohen, a psychiatrist and the city's commissioner of health at the time, that long-term planning was necessary for the care of the workers at Ground Zero. The city sought to unite the efforts of the myriad of therapy programs then ongoing, but the efforts came up against the radical decentralization of the delivery systems and of course the general chaos after 9/11. Within about a year, however, the locus of effort (and money) came together with the September 11 Fund that developed policies for long-term financing of mental health services for all those affected by 9/11. It is a remarkable statement of the wisdom of this approach that this fund continues to support psychotherapy for traumatized survivors of the disaster.[10]

Located just north of the Trade Center complex, Stuyvesant High School, one of the city's most famous elite and selective schools, came to symbolize the debate over air quality near Ground Zero. On 9/11 the school had been evacuated, with most students walking north up the West Side Highway to safety. In the next few weeks repeated tests, both local and by the EPA, were held to determine the safety of the air. It seemed safe by October 9, when the school was reopened. But the site was too close to the disaster for the comfort of many. Barges loaded with debris floated in the Hudson on the way to the Fresh Kills landfill on Staten Island. Dump trucks continuously roared by the school on the West Side Highway. Dust that many feared was toxic filled the air and debris was everywhere. Students began to develop coughs, asthma, bronchitis. Parents were furious and some demonstrated regularly outside the school. The Board of Education, relying on reports of officials with the city and EPA, tried to reassure the school community. At the end of 2001 some extremely high readings for asbestos were found in the school auditorium, further inflaming passions. By May of 2002 a CDC report documented that more than half of the employees at Stuyvesant had contracted respiratory illness after 9/11.[11]

THE DNA STORY

For many years before the 1990's the Office of the Chief Medical Examiner for New York City was mired in inefficiencies and corruption.[12] It struggled with the huge rise in crime in the 1980's, often coming to wrong forensic conclusions because of the sloppiness of its methods. In 1989, however, Charles S. Hirsch, a distinguished forensic pathologist, became the city's Chief Medical Examiner and was charged with reforming the office. He went to work and within a few years had recruited an outstanding staff, improved methods, and both expanded and streamlined the local offices, each of which was in one of the boroughs (the large central office is in Manhattan). By 9/11 the Office of Chief Medical Examiner (OCME) was a respected and efficient entity in the bureaucracy of city government. It was readily able to handle the determination of death for about 25,000 New Yorkers each year and gather and analyze the forensic evidence for some 700 homicides and anywhere from eighty-seven reported rapes in 2007 to 115 in 2008 (keeping in mind that many more rapes go unreported in a city the size of New York).

Hirsch and his team also had in place practiced protocols for handling bodies during a disaster. When Charles Hirsch first heard about the attack on the World Trade Center, he therefore rushed to the site with members of his office to set up a temporary morgue, according to plan. This disaster, however, was not to fit the mold. Things were hardly in place at what would soon be called Ground Zero when the most immediate victims became the members of the Office of the Chief Medical Examiner itself. When the first tower fell, one member of the staff had her leg broken so severely that the bone was showing. Another was struck by a piece of metal, which hit him on the back of the head with such force that he required months for recovery. A slight young woman was thrown head first into a wall. And Charles Hirsch himself, covered in dust, was thrown to the ground, cutting his hand badly and bruising his body. He remained a pitiful sight for the rest of that busy day.

Some destruction of the medical infrastructure is one of the characteristic first effects of a major disaster. It was nowhere more radical than after the bomb fell on Hiroshima. The majority of the doctors and surgeons, along with their nurses and other support personnel, were killed or injured, and their offices, hospitals, equipment, and medicines destroyed or scattered. Before August 6, 1945, there were 150 doctors in the city. When the bomb fell, sixty-five died instantly and most of the others were injured. Of the 1,780 nurses in the city of Hiroshima, 1,654 were dead or too injured to work. The Red Cross hospital was the only one working and in it only six of thirty doctors were able to work. Dr. Sasaki, whose story John Hersey follows in depth, was the only uninjured doctor on the staff.[13]

New York City never faced this level of destruction. In fact, with the exception of the injuries to Hirsch's staff, the opposite occurred. The disaster in New York was highly localized. The city itself was the home of major medical centers with some of the best doctors in the world. Medical personnel throughout the city mobilized their facilities to help, and all major medical centers were on high alert to prepare for what was assumed would be an onslaught of injured victims. Once the towers collapsed, doctors joined emergency workers in places like the skating rink at Chelsea Piers (one of the first temporary morgues). St. Vincent's Hospital, the closest to Ground Zero, was especially prepared to take in the injured. All doctors were on call, space was made ready, medicines were checked, and so on. Gurneys were brought to the emergency room, some borrowed from other hospitals. In fact, so many gurneys were on hand that they were taken outside to give more room for medical personnel to navigate the emergency room. With some exceptions, the injured never came. In this disaster, most people either died or survived. One of the most jarring images from that day is the scores of empty gurneys lining the sidewalk outside St. Vincent's Hospital.

It took a number of weeks to figure out a process for storing bodies and body parts, for establishing procedures for identification, and most of all for dealing with the huge task of DNA collection. After Hirsch and his colleagues were sent reeling from Ground Zero, there was not even a temporary morgue. Temporary makeshift morgues slowly surfaced in places such as Brooks Brothers, where clothing bags were used as temporary body bags to house the remains.[14] Ellis Island was utilized as a temporary morgue as well as a triage center, and hundreds of patients were ferried over to New Jersey to the Jersey City Medical Center as well as Liberty State Park (NJ State Police handled this area) due to the overflow of patients in other nearby New York City hospitals.[15] Bellevue Hospital, one of New York's premier medical centers, treated those who survived and identified those who didn't in a temporary morgue located within the hospital.[16] Ground Zero itself was the home of many temporary morgues set up by recovery and construction workers in the immediate aftermath of 9/11 and continued on for the next three months after the attack.[17] The temporary morgues were located on piers along the West Side, including Chelsea Piers, as well as on barges between the west side of Manhattan and Fresh Kills landfill.[18] The skating rink at Chelsea Piers was commandeered until something more permanent could be worked out.

It took until late in the fall before Charles Hirsch and the OCME regularized the process for handling the human remains from the disaster. There were two sources of the remains: those found directly at the site and those missed in the first pass but later recovered in the debris from Ground Zero that was all hauled off to the landfill on Staten Island, where it was carefully sifted. But whether from Ground Zero or the landfill, all human remains were taken by an escort, usually a police officer, to an open-air bay on the East 30th Street side of the OCME facility at First Avenue. Dan Barry of the *New York Times* described the scene: "In close and hectic surroundings, they [the remains] were examined by a succession of experts—the pathologist, the forensic dentist, the fingerprint analyst, the DNA specialist—all in search of something distinguishable, from an inscribed wedding ring to a set of genetic markers." Once examined, the remains were carried across the street by the escort to the refrigerated trailers in a white tent for storage, either to be relinquished later to the appropriate family or to be kept for future analysis, when the science of analysis might improve.[19]

In this process, some mistakes inevitably were made. Two firefighters from the same firehouse had the same anomaly in the same neck vertebra, which led to a false identification. Once a forensic dentist gave the wrong folder to someone in the conference room, confusing the identity of a victim, after which Hirsch required two dentists to sign off on the identification of a victim if done solely through teeth and dental remains. Hirsch himself was at times remote and seemingly cold. He could be blunt. In November 2001, in a meeting with family members, Hirsch said with scientific accuracy but in cold tones that many victims had been "vaporized." Some in the audience heckled him for being insensitive. Another time he said, "If reinforced concrete was rendered into dust, then it wasn't much of a mystery what would happen to people." Hirsch was not consciously or intentionally making the comparison, but the World Trade Center disaster in this respect was a bit like Hiroshima. In Hiroshima, within half a mile of Ground Zero temperatures reached 10,000 degrees Fahrenheit. Not only were nearly 100,000 people vaporized in a fraction of a second, but some left eerie silhouettes on the pavement. John Hersey, who reported from Hiroshima in 1946, described the story of a painter on a ladder who was "monumentalized in a kind of bas-relief on the stone façade of a bank building on which he was at work, in the act of dipping his brush into his paint can."[20]

Most observers in New York after 9/11, however, gave high marks to the professionalism of the OCME. The same family members who had heckled him in November of 2001 eventually gained great respect for his devotion and Herculean efforts to do everything humanly possible to identify victims who left precious little of themselves with which to work.

Mayor Rudy Giuliani was greatly impressed with the work of Hirsch and his staff at the OCME. On the evening of 9/11, he said later, "None of us thought you would have been able to identify a third of the people [who died in the disaster]." Hirsch himself aimed in those first 100 days after the disaster to identify 70 percent of the victims, or about 2,000 people. "That's been our whisper number around here," he said. Unfortunately, many of the remains were too degraded for identification (at least at this stage of science). The whisper number was about 25 percent too high.

At the heart of the identification process within the OCME was the work done on DNA. Hirsch called this forensic process a "dialogue with the dead." "Who are you?," he said of the scientific efforts to identify someone from burnt fragments. The key figure in Hirsch's office in charge of the DNA analysis was Robert Shaler, who was more voluble with the press than Hirsch but, like his boss, a genius at responding on an ad hoc basis to the enormous challenges of the moment after 9/11. In Shaler's account, he emphasizes the chaos and pressures he and his staff were under in the early days of the disaster. As early as Wednesday, September 12, in the midst of bomb threats and general disarray, Shaler began receiving many calls from the FBI and city officials to set up some kind of DNA laboratory to identify remains. No protocols existed for establishing a Family Assistance Center, where samples would be collected, or for creating a temporary morgue in the event of such a disaster, because nothing on this scale had been imagined.

On Thursday, September 13, Shaler began to set up some facilities, order supplies, establish shifts for workers. His labs were located downtown, not far from Ground Zero. The Family Assistance Center was established at Pier 94, though it was at first moved from one place to another between Wednesday and Thursday. Shaler was under great pressure to deal with the sudden influx of work and new samples to analyze, keeping in mind that the forensics for other crimes still needed to be kept in place. Interestingly, the one relief he got in this area was that there were no rapes in Manhattan for all of the next two weeks, an extraordinary and baffling byproduct of the disaster.

On Friday, September 14, Shaler was able to work out a helpful division of labor with the New York State Police laboratories, which agreed to take on the responsibility for handling all the collection of the family samples, while he and his labs would assume responsibilities for all the WTC site samples. Another bomb threat forced an evacuation of the entire medical examiner's office that Friday (which was the day President Bush visited Ground Zero), creating fear that existing samples would be destroyed. Part of what complicated the planning, ordering of supplies, arranging for staff, and such things, is that Shaler—and everyone else—assumed some 20,000 people had died in the disaster and that he would end up with something in the neighborhood of 35,000 samples. Instead, fewer than 3,000 people died and he ended up with some 20,000 samples of human remains.

All these organizational problems in dealing with the DNA gathering and testing resulted because there was no comprehensive plan for such a problem in case of disaster. New York City had a disaster plan, but dealing with DNA was not part of that plan (and a systematic disaster plan detailing how to collect and handle DNA samples only came about four years later). It was left to Shaler to improvise. Given the significance of dealing with proper storage of organic, human remains, decisions had to be made quickly. Shaler recognized he would need help and therefore enlisted outside agencies to assist the work of the city. He enlisted several different groups around the country and worked closely with the FBI, which set up a sample identification network in the city similar to one they maintain for the country as a whole. Shaler worried as well about the stress on his staff and did all he could to ease their work. He acknowledged how often he had to make wild estimates because of the relentless questioning. He tried, of course, to do his best, but in the early days there was no way of knowing, for example, whether 20,000 or 500,000 body parts would be recovered from the disaster.

The work at the Family Assistance Center, which was located at Pier 94 at 54th Street and Twelfth Avenue, was particularly chaotic. It is customary to follow some standard kinship protocols in gathering DNA samples from family members. None of the workers gathering the samples knew anything about such kinship analysis, and there was no time or opportunity to train them. As a result, many of the samples gathered from families were useless for the purposes of confirming identification. It was only after January 2002, that the process of collecting viable samples was regularized, a hot line established, and 3,500 appointments made and 10,000 consultations with family members carried out.

"Immediately after the collapse of the World Trade Center, the New York Police Department (NYPD) set up collection points in the city to take missing persons reports and collect materials that could be used for DNA testing. Police departments outside the city established reception points in their communities and forwarded their collections to the NYPD. Within a week, the city of New York established a Family Assistance Center (FAC) on the west side of Manhattan at Pier 94, where they consolidated the missing persons intake process. Thus, the collection of reference samples and victim information is often referred to as 'Pier 94,' even though some of these activities took place elsewhere."[21] The Family Assistance Center at Pier 94 was the location of an elaborate process for establishing a match between DNA samples from family members and the human remains found at Ground Zero (and in time at the resifted debris at the landfill on Staten Island).

"Family members, friends and co-workers went to Pier 94 to provide information about a person they thought was at WTC when it collapsed. If possible, they brought in the victim's personal effects for direct DNA matches and gave cheek swabs for indirect DNA matches. At this point each missing person was assigned a P number and each collection of DNA reference material was given a DNA Case number."[22] A large number of volunteers worked with OCME staff professionals taking the samples and carefully storing them. More than 5,000 cheek swabs were taken from blood relatives, and more than 15,000 personal articles were collected. Some items yielded no information, but many, from the 1,400 toothbrushes, 140 razors, and 126 hairbrushes, proved valuable sources of DNA samples.

Much else went on at the Family Assistance Center in the vast space of Pier 94, from assistance with displaced residents, to free counseling, to financial assistance, to help with life insurance policies, to assistance in obtaining death certificates, to applications for benefits from the New York Crime Victims Board, to assistance from the Human Resources Administration, to emergency food stamps, and to welfare applications. The Red Cross was basically in charge, though much that developed was spontaneous and of the moment, as with the creation of the "Kids Corner" by Desmond Heath in collaboration with the Disaster Psychiatry Outreach.

Pier 94, however, was not the only Family Assistance Center. New Jersey, home to many families that had lost loved ones, on September 19th set up the

New Jersey Family Assistance Center at Liberty State Park. A visitor was first greeted by a volunteer from the National Organization for Victim Assistance (NOVA) who stayed with him or her for the entire day, helping to negotiate the myriad of services available in the trailers pulled into the park to create the complex. These services included counseling, financial advice, help with obtaining a death certificate, and the taking of DNA samples. If a body was unrecovered and deemed lost, there was a simple ceremony in a waiting room that became a kind of impromptu chapel. Dust from Ground Zero was used to fill an urn that, with a tricornered military flag, was presented to the family in a respectful ceremony overseen by a rabbi, priest, minister, or imam, according to the wishes of the family. If they chose, the family could make a specially arranged trip to Ground Zero.

One of the most interesting witnesses to the New York Family Assistance Center was Robert N. Munson, an articulate social worker sent by the Red Cross for three weeks in late September 2001 to help with grieving foreign nationals. He got this assignment because of his position on the International Family Linking On-call Team, a specialty group of the American Red Cross International Disaster Response Team. Nearly every evening during his stay in New York, Munson wrote long and detailed emails to his family and the Minneapolis Red Cross as "debriefing therapy" for himself. Later, he donated his letters to the 9/11 Digital Archives. These notes are an unusually valuable contemporary source.

Munson wrote on September 25:

I work on Pier 94 which is the building in NYC where all families who have a missing relative need to come to access any and all services. To say that we have been busy since my arrival at the center on Monday AM is an understatement. Currently Red Cross Family Service in this building has a waiting list of 5 hours for families. We are in a giant pier warehouse building—set up like a trade show with full carpet, poles with drapes, and some 75 agencies with all their staff and stuff, service agencies, government, immigration, FBI, child care, etc. It is a comfortable building in order to be welcoming and calming as can be to the families. The City of New York has done a good job. It is a full city of people in this building—with free meals for families and separate 3 meals a day for workers. The dining areas are nice (as they can be)—donated fresh flowers daily, tablecloths, and an ambiance of peace and calm different from the noisy, bustling activity everywhere else. There are clients and workers everywhere. Lots of noise.

People come here to access a broad array of services. Security is the tightest I have ever experienced anywhere. You can't get near the place without going through several barricades, body and bag checks—and once in, all workers need to be separately badged daily even though we have permanent clearance badges.

"Tomorrow," Munson said, that is, September 26, "promised to be unusually busy, because the city has said they are going to begin issuing death certificates." The issue here was that normally the city refuses to issue a death certificate without the body, or some semblance of a body that is clearly identifiable, but there was tremendous pressure on city officials to soften the requirements for death certificates in this disaster.

On September 27, Munson wrote:

The most macho of men, the smallest of children, people of all ages are warmly clutching teddy bears of various breeds. None are casually carried. They are everywhere. . . . Another kind of bear sits against the back wall. It is a wall, which, according to my pacing, is 200 feet long. The wall is covered with pictures of missing family members—all with hand-written notations: "wearing green dress," "tattoo of eagle on shoulder," "last seen on floor 96 Tower One." . . . (This wall is different than the one you see on TV—that one is on the street in front of the building where the media gathers. This wall is inside—protected from all but family members and people involved in the response.) On the floor like guardians of these precious "wanted posters" sit rows and rows of multi-breed teddy bears. All these bears were sent by the children and friends from Oklahoma City to their new brothers and sisters in NYC. I remember that I visited the Oklahoma Memorial only some 16 months ago at the Fifth Anniversary of that bombing, and how moving that was. The still hurting are comforting the newly hurting. Amongst the bears, there are lighted candles in glass holders and fresh flowers. The sight is amazingly peaceful given the bustle around. All is roped off—family members are allowed to be at touching distance to the photos—a rope keeps workers who are going about their business separated so the families can weep in peace.

No activity was more appropriate at the Family Assistance Center than weeping in peace.

AD HOC MOURNING RITUALS AND THE TERROR OF NUMBERS

The peculiar form of the dying on 9/11 forced survivors to create a number of ad hoc mourning rituals. The absence of the body, for example, or clearly identified remains, made it difficult to obtain a death certificate. The old and time-honored procedure was that families of a deceased had to petition the Surrogate's Court to have a person declared dead. Usually, the Medical Examiner's Office required physical evidence of a body before issuing a death certificate. But after 9/11 bodies were not available to prove death, and families could not proceed with insurance claims and other benefits without the death certificate. Mayor Giuliani got directly involved and assured families he would change the procedures. Soon there were hundreds of additional workers from the state department of health to assist city workers. The National Center for Health Statistics, which did not have a category of death from terrorism, also set up emergency procedures and soon developed a category called "Death and Injury Resulting from Terrorism." All these efforts made it possible by early October for the city to start issuing death certificates to families of victims.

A more psychologically troubling issue in the weeks following September 11th was the way the figure for the numbers of those who died that day kept changing. During the disaster, commentators on television frequently noted that some 50,000 people normally worked each day in the twin towers, suggesting without actually saying that the number of those who died could have reached such proportions.[23] There was no reason not to believe in the immediate wake of the disaster that somewhere near that number might have died when the towers collapsed. I know I thought as I watched the disaster from the street and on television that at least 25,000 must have died. Figures in that range also appeared in the press. On September 12th, for example, *The Guardian* journalists on the scene reported that there were said to be 20,000 people inside when the planes hit. On September 15th Diane Cardwell of the *New York Times* reported that thousands of people who were in the towers at the time were assumed to be dead, even though the official body count stood at 124 and the medical examiner had identified only a few dozen victims. Cardwell wrote that it could be months before many of those killed could be officially confirmed dead.[24]

On September 21st city officials told Eric Lipton of the *Times* that the number of people listed as missing and feared lost in the World Trade Center disaster, a number that was then at 6,333, could fall significantly. Part of the problem lay in the reports of missing people from foreign countries. Mayor Rudolph W. Giuliani said the reports of missing foreign citizens, which had contributed to the high number of those listed as missing and perhaps dead by about 1,000 over the previous three days, probably involved many people who had been counted twice or who were neither working at nor visiting the twin towers. Lipton reported, however, that it was also unclear what kind of database of names the city had created. He suggested it was all very sloppy in the chaos of the moment. There was probably much redundancy. Police Commissioner Bernard B. Kerik said that the city had compiled its list of the missing from the Red Cross, companies that had offices at the Trade Center, and a number of police departments across the region. He said the multiple sources of reporting could have led to some duplication even beyond that involving foreign citizens.[25]

And so the numbers kept dropping in the following weeks, most of all because names were compared on different lists but also because foreign visitors to the city reported to their families that they were in fact safe, and so on. It was a relentless process. Down, down, down the numbers went, from 25,000, to 6,333, to 5,000, and to 3,300 by December 2nd, which made it less than the bloodiest day in American history, the battle of Antietam during the Civil War on September 17, 1862, when at least 3,650 died and thousands of others were wounded, many of whom died later. Mere numbers, of course, did not diminish the nation's sense of horror. Nothing, for example, could change the deep sadness of more than 3,000 children losing a parent.[26] Yet as the number of victims fell, people reacted in a variety of ways, and not all of them simple relief: One sister of a victim watched the number shrink and felt all the lonelier, briefly fearful that people might think the wholesale devastation that took her brother was somehow less epic; the mayor of New York excoriated reporters for chronicling the declining totals, describing it as a macabre exercise; and military and political leaders have said the total does not for a second change their sense of outrage. The loud protests betrayed the underlying anxiety that the significance of the disaster would fade too soon.

PUBLIC AND PRIVATE MOURNING RITUALS

The major collective mourning ritual in New York City was the event at Yankee Stadium on September 23rd. As conceived by Mayor Giuliani, the event was called "A Prayer for America." The afternoon event, which was broadcast worldwide on television, lasted two and a half hours and included a wide range of political and religious leaders, as well as celebrities like Oprah Winfrey, and many guest singers, including Marc Anthony, Bette Midler, Placido Domingo, the Boys and Girls Choir of Harlem, and Lee Greenwood, among others. David Benke has called "A Prayer for America" a "lesson in the civic ritual of healing" that was as important as any in our recent history. The afternoon event was an almost interminable display of public grief. Scores of thousands of people wept openly. There were prayers, songs, speeches, and much wringing of hands. Giuliani spoke briefly but sat near second base looking into the sea of grieving faces of survivors who filled the infield sobbing and clutching photographs of their lost loved ones. The event, which Giuliani had decided on two days after 9/11, was an ad hoc affair but intentionally designed by his appointed committee to constitute something of a public funeral. It was "a collective expression of a multiplex spirituality in which a variety of religious traditions of mourning were played out." The event transformed a baseball field into a kind of temple or "outdoor cathedral" where the dead had the power to raise a new kind of consciousness in its participants. The variety of the religious figures who participated and the variety of traditions they represented was remarkable and expressed a "kind of universalistic civil religion."[27]

The Yankee Stadium event was part of a universal tendency of those trying to memorialize death to light candles as a way of sanctifying space and time. Another important example of this deep human impulse was the array of mini-altars throughout Union Square; near some churches, especially Trinity Church on Wall Street near Ground Zero; and hospitals, especially Bellevue and St. Vincent's. In almost all cases, the form of the altars evolved spontaneously. Beneath the display of a picture of a loved one who was being sought or who by that point was half-recognized as being lost, sat one or more lit candles. These remarkable mini-memorials thus captured the contradictions of the mourning process, that "middle knowledge" of the space where death and death equivalents live in our consciousness. On one hand, the picture, often with some phrase indicating that the person shown was being sought, represented the hope for life in the search process. At the same time, however, the memorial included a burning candle, which symbolized and honored the death of the loved one. Within each memorial, in other words, hope and despair were joined equally, if in contradictory ways.[28]

11

DISRUPTED LIVES

DISRUPTION DEFINED THE lives of New Yorkers after 9/11, though it took many and varied forms. For Renee, the fear she felt after 9/11 was palpable and imminent. It hung in the air as she waited, and waited. There were frequent bomb scares in the many buildings that made up Rockefeller Center, near where she worked. Thursday, September 13th, was particularly bad in this regard, though it was hardly the only time that buildings near where Renee worked were evacuated. Fear about continuing attacks in general and about bombs in places like Grand Central Station was widespread. These fears left Renee with a constant sense of dread about going into Midtown and returning to work. They haunted her constantly the entire week after 9/11. This made her experience of the disaster much keener and heightened her sense of insecurity and dread.

For others the dread came in fits and starts, opening up awareness slowly, and sometimes in contradictory ways. It came unbidden, unexpectedly, and erratically over time. Kyle, for example, completely ignored the event when he first heard about it on the radio as he was getting dressed. He then went down to the street and absentmindedly watched the burning towers without seriously considering what was happening. Only later in his office did he realize fully what had happened and begin a long process of trying to understand it. Even then he felt not fear but a general numbness. Between that Tuesday and the following Saturday, when he returned to his apartment, he was reluctant to take the subway. He says it was not because he thought it would be bombed but because he assumed service would be erratic. Nevertheless something was happening inside him to keep him with friends on the Upper West Side for the rest of that first week. On Wednesday in the afternoon he was with a friend on 86th Street when the smell from the burning pile drifted to the Upper West Side with a change in the wind. "Then it really sort of hit." Kyle was very aware of that smell. "I sort of assumed it was the sort of steel and the rubble and all that, but people had begun talking about the fact that as you're digging through it and uncovering people, you know, that you're actually smelling some of the human decay." That same day, Wednesday, September 12th, Kyle had worked some phones at the New School on a volunteer basis in a missing person's bank. As he notes, after some of those calls, "I sort of fell apart." It was then that he cried for the first time, though even then he is not sure a week later whether it was precisely on Wednesday or the next day that he cried for the first time. The confusion is important, as it reflects Kyle's deeper struggles with opening up to the full extent of his feelings while numbing himself at the same time to the terror and pain that those feelings raised in him.

Death could be quite visibly present for some New Yorkers. Serena and her family lived on the Lower East Side, less than half a mile from Ground Zero. Serena comments, "I didn't sleep for about two weeks, nightmares like crazy, and they were all associated with my daughter Karrie and buildings falling and my not being there." Karrie, for her part, lived with her own extensive fears. As she walked around outside she would constantly ask Serena, "Mommy, is this building going to fall? Mommy, are we going to blow up? Mommy, are we going to die?" In the evening Karrie was only able to go to sleep if she was being held tightly by her mother. Since Serena herself was not sleeping she would simply lie in the bed with her husband holding Karrie and try to make it through the night. She felt so confused. "You know I can't explain it, but it was just a deep sadness, a deep sadness that I can't explain except for the devastation so many lives that were lost, but also the different world that we have now." One day Serena and her family came home to find a huge number of boxes lined up against the wall of their building. On the sides of the boxes was written "body bags." There they were, "right outside, right outside in big bold letters Body Bag, Body Bag, Body Bag. Oh my God, this is just too close for comfort."

Eric's fears and traumatic reactions to 9/11 prompted him to search out in a quite serious way the possibility of self-defense in the event of social chaos following another attack. He pondered purchasing a gun (even though he had grown up as a Quaker). The reason for considering such a purchase had to do not with defending himself against a potential terrorist, something he recognized was a relatively foolish idea, but with protecting his family from mobs that might emerge following the social chaos after another attack. He was particularly concerned about this chaos occurring in the country, where he and his wife owned a home. His idea was that everything would "go to hell in a handbasket," that he and his family would have to "flee the city," and while out there things would "get really ugly and people start fleeing the city," and that he would need a gun to protect himself against such mobs.

For some, like Felicia, the posttraumatic symptoms were completely debilitating. She jumped at the sound of trucks passing over her on interlocking highways, and her skin crawled when a train ran overhead as she walked under a trestle. She could never relax, hating to be on the street, hating any loud sound, hating the city itself. She grew scared of heights and of planes and felt constantly claustrophobic. No matter where she was, whether at home, in a movie theater, in a car, or in a restaurant, Felicia planned her escape. Everything startled her. She jumped if someone dropped a book in another room and could not stand to see someone running. She felt out of control of her body. Her dreamscape was tormenting, with a recurring nightmare of being stuck in the towers. But the absolute worst part of it all was that she "hated having the fear" itself. She felt inadequate and crazy, which in turn filled her with shame. "I just feel very stupid for being so scared about everything."

And, finally, the disaster served for many to reawaken earlier trauma. Angelica, a patient who had been sexually abused by her four older brothers, found ways to develop her significant talents in school, where she studied to become an occupational therapist. She married early and had two children, then divorced, but by the fall of 2001, Angelica was nearing thirty and feeling better about her life. She was almost at the end of her training program, which when completed would allow her to obtain a job with a salary reaching six figures. She was in a relationship with an older and quite rich man who seemed to be taking advantage of her but did bring real excitement and fun into her life. She was in class that morning at the community college just north of the World Trade Center. She and the other students poured out onto the street and watched the people falling and jumping for nearly an hour, transfixed by the horror, unable to leave. When the first tower fell, she ran north in terror to escape and was overcome with fear as the cloud descended on her. After she got home later that day, she crawled into her bed and hardly got out for most of the next week. She lost weight. She never got dressed or even bathed. All the confused feelings from her years of abuse came flooding back. Her childhood asthma returned and often left her unable to breathe adequately. After a few days she finally called me and we talked on the phone because she was unable to come in for a therapy session. Even months later, after she was out of bed and back in school, Angelica talked about 9/11 in hushed tones. It only gradually faded.

COUNTERFEIT NURTURANCE AND THE SPECIAL CHARACTER OF NEW YORK

Kyle commented in his interview, "We were in the play. They saw the movie." Nothing more dramatically captures the unique experience that New Yorkers had of the disaster. Kyle sensed early on the nature of this difference in shared suffering between those in and out of the city. His complicated and nuanced understanding of the difficulty in communicating his experience of the disaster to those outside of the immediate community of sufferers and witnesses was part of what he interestingly analyzes as the geography of the disaster. Quoting from an article in the *New Yorker*, Kyle noted how the rest of the world was saying, "Isn't this awful that this happened in America"; everyone in America was saying, "It's awful that it happened in New York"; while in New York they were saying, "Isn't this awful that this happened downtown?" No one could fully own an event of such gigantic proportions. Kyle attempted as well as anyone could, however, to locate himself within this moral geography.

Those outside New York had no way of comprehending the enormity of the brush with death experienced by everyone in the city, even though the psychological contours of that experience varied greatly. A survivor in a disaster such as 9/11, as Robert Jay Lifton has made clear, experiences any attempt at empathy and nurturance from outsiders as illegitimate and counterfeit. The survivor distrusts even effusive displays of empathy, because it feels like an attempt to interfere with and even rob the survivor of the experience of suffering. No one outside the event is able to comprehend what it meant in that moment to come so close to death. That leaves the survivor alone and only able to communicate with those in the immediate community of other survivors.

Eric felt the falseness of those outside voices so keenly that after some initial conversations he was unable to take calls from anyone in the first few weeks. "I didn't want to talk about it, but the excuse I had in my mind and maybe part of the reason I didn't want to talk about it, too, was I was talking to people in many cases who lived outside of New York." Renee, for her part, felt keenly that people outside of New York were simply not as "scared as I am." "I don't know if it's that safe that they're out there flying planes around. You know, the military could be surrounding the city and I don't feel that safe." She did not even feel safe on the streets. "I feel like I can't walk around." "The more psyched out I get, the more I just have to be out there and I have to do it."

FAILED ENACTMENT

Failed enactment describes the sense survivors have that in the moment of their trauma they failed to act in a way that might have warded off or even prevented their experience of victimization. Some sense of failed enactment is almost universal among survivors, leaving them with a sense of shame and humiliation, often mixed with despair. Eric blamed himself for getting off the local at 14th Street as he headed north because it removed him from the reassuring community of people on the train who understood exactly what he had just been through. Deirdre felt terrible for weeks for failing to dissuade the three women with babies and strollers from continuing their odyssey toward the disaster. Miranda harshly blamed herself for being stupid in returning to work in the Trade Center after the bombing in 1993. Sometimes during my two interviews with her she unconsciously slipped into talking about 1993 when I thought she was still talking about 9/11, forcing me to ask her for clarification. For example, in one sequence toward the end of her first long interview, she was talking about returning to work and how she was "just stupid, just stupid, like how did I ever go back?" At that point I asked her whether she meant after 1993. She replied, "Yeah, and if I was stupid enough to go back then, I don't want to do it again, 'cause now … I mean if we're nuked and the rest of my family goes, I'm fine. You know, if we all go together, you know, or we all drink the water, it is what it is. But I don't want to run, I don't want to get stuck under cement, I don't want to be there the next time." This extraordinary passage suggests how close to the surface Miranda's nuclear fears are, and in this case how they had been mobilized and made salient by her sense of failing to learn from her experiences in 1993.

Tina developed a keen sense of failed enactment in the months after 9/11. She said, "Part of me thinks that I never should have gone out there. I mean it was obviously a dangerous situation. Why did I walk into it? Why didn't I walk away? There were other people who walked away … but I needed to see it. I needed to be part of like what was going on and I had no fear, none at all, watching it." Later in the interview, Tina added that her tendency to rush into things has been a part of her character since she was a child. It's like if there was a "fire down the block when I was a kid" she would automatically run to go see it. The same was true as a child going to watch a car accident. Tina harshly condemned herself for rushing toward the disaster and ending up as a witness to an event that brought such a high degree of trauma into her life.

PERSONAL REFLECTIONS

Although I am finishing this book ten years after the event, I have been amazed to recover in detail (through my journals, research notes to myself, copies of emails, etc.) how deeply the disaster affected me personally. No one in my family died, nor was anyone close to me in danger at any point. Yet from my notes in the early weeks after 9/11 I realize the disaster cast a shadow over all aspects of my life and those I love. For myself, from the outset I felt a certain destiny to study the disaster, as though, given my training and long-standing interests, fate had dropped me into it. That sense of mission only deepened with my involvement with patients and their 9/11 stories, my students and teaching about terrorism and 9/11, and the early talks I gave about my work to scholarly audiences.

But the disaster has also touched the lives of every member of my family. My wife Cathryn, who suffered many losses as a child, cried continuously for the first week, and for some time after that seemed unable to stop watching television about the details of the event. As late as December 2, 2001, she wrote:

Today, I still jump and startle easily when someone surprises me unexpectedly. I absolutely loathe the sounds of airplanes and shudder every time I hear an airplane overhead in the sky. I track it and follow its direction. When I'm in subway stations, I plan the best ways to get out should the walls come crashing down on my head. I tearfully read the "Portraits of Grief" in the *New York Times*. It's so unfair that their young lives were cut short. I often think of Lars Qualben, whose son Kai was in my daughter's class for ten years. Lars happened to be on the looth floor of WTC and he was never found. At his memorial, there was just one large poster of him. I grieve for a young student in the school where I teach who lost his mother and will never know her nor she her son. I am constantly reminded of 9/11 when my young 3- and 4-year-old students build towers in the block corner or paint those magnificent buildings on the art easel. A heavy sadness fills my heart and those around me and I realize that it is not over.

The story with my twelve-year-old daughter Alison was more contradictory. I think at first she felt some guilt about not being able to express her sorrow. As late as September 23rd, I finally realized that part of the problem she was dealing with was her initial nonchalance because some teacher reported to the students that while the towers had collapsed only six people had died. This preposterous story meant that Alison was psychologically unprepared when her mother showed up an hour or so later, crying and hysterical. Alison and her friends never did figure it all out and were then pleased to have the day off from school and played happily on that Tuesday afternoon. But as with all New Yorkers, the disaster was to strike home. She learned in a few days that a boy in her small class had lost his father.

My son Christopher, then twenty-five, left New York in August of 2001 to find a job as a chef in Las Vegas. He had had a troubled adolescence with too many drugs but eventually found his niche in cooking. That is something I always harbored as my own secret ambition, and my experience of his involvement with cooking was that he seemed to realize that part of my own unacknowledged ambitions. It was with genuine pleasure that I therefore watched him get his first job as a sous-chef in a French restaurant in New York City and then study with Paul Bocuse in France in an eight-week program. He returned to New York and held a number of jobs, some in good restaurants, as he moved into his twenties. He reached a glass ceiling, however, as a sous-chef, unable in that world to make the leap into actually running a kitchen. He felt Las Vegas, where his older brother Michael lived after getting out of the

Air Force, might offer new opportunities. There were lots of restaurants with high turnover and 25 million visitors who kept the economy thriving.

Two weeks after he arrived 9/11 happened. Las Vegas came to a standstill, because a good number of those 25 million visitors arrived by plane. The Las Vegas economy stalled more than anywhere else in the country. Christopher could not even get work flipping burgers, let alone making foie gras with a fine burgundy wine. He was also by then not getting along very well with his brother, who had his own personal problems. By the end of September my wife and I told Christopher we would pay to bring him back to New York and that he could stay with us until he got his feet back on the ground. He jumped at the offer, returning three weeks after 9/11. It was good to have him back home safe and sound. He sprawled on the couch and drank too much beer, depressed at his prospects but secure in his family setting.

My oldest son Michael had just been discharged from the Air Force in the month before 9/11. He had served two tours but was ready to leave after eight years. In the first few weeks after 9/11, I was convinced he would be recalled in what was clearly going to be a war in the Middle East. I was distraught because he went through something similar during the Gulf War. Michael had then been in the army, where he went after high school, and was in the fall of 1990, at the end of an eight-year enlistment. From the beginning of the crisis in August, all enlistments were extended indefinitely. He was sent to Saudi Arabia, served in battle as part of the invading force (VII Corps), and remained in southern Iraq until the spring of 1991. It seemed a cruel fate that he would serve in both Middle Eastern wars. As it turned out, he was not recalled to the Air Force, saving his family that measure of anxiety, though four years later Christopher joined the army himself and ended up fighting in Iraq. That brought the consequences of 9/11 exceedingly close to home.

12

DEATH AND FUTURE

THE DEATH-DRENCHED World Trade Center disaster called into question the comfortable assumptions about God and the future for many survivors. Such existential questions extended their apocalyptic confusions. Helen Whitney, who produced a very good documentary for the first anniversary, "Faith and Doubt at Ground Zero," explored such meanings with the families of firemen as well as some ordinary New Yorkers commenting on the spiritual meanings of their losses. One grieving man said, "I'm losing respect for Him. I know there's a Trinity. I believe in the Son, but the Father I'm having a rough time dealing with . . . I can't accept this, unless I can have an answer as to why all this occurred . . . I look at Him as a barbarian. I think I'm a good Christian, but I have a different view of Him now." And another: "How could God be in the horror of what I saw?" That was a common complaint: "There is no answer. Only anger. A lot of anger," another said. A fireman's widow (Marian Fantana) commented, "And now I can't bring myself to speak to Him anymore, because I feel so abandoned." "God seemed absent," an Episcopal priest said. "If there is a God, He's a very indifferent God." Perhaps the most interesting comment in the documentary is that of an anonymous observer commenting on the image of a couple who jumped to their death holding hands: "A couple leaped from the south tower, hand in hand. They reached for each other and their hands met and they jumped. I try to whisper prayers for the families of the dead, for the screaming souls of the murderers, but I keep coming to his hand in her hand, nestled in each other with extraordinary, ordinary naked love. It's the most powerful prayer I can imagine, the most eloquent, the most graceful."[1]

The firsthand immersion in the death that surrounded many of my respondents evoked a continuing search for spiritual meanings and often grew out of a profound sense of existential threats to the future. The ultimate issues of personal and collective death so central to the survivor experience of the disaster called into question whether the future could be trusted (something that has also bothered many philosophers in the last half century[2]). Deirdre, for example, in her despair commented, "Some days are not so bad, [but most of the time] I feel pretty depressed. I can't sleep. I feel kind of sad." Deirdre felt unsure about her future, "unsure about what I should do, what I'm supposed to be doing, what's important, what's not important, what the best decisions are to make right now." She was under some pressure from her family to go home to California but could not make up her mind whether to abandon all her projects and previous plans for the future in New York.

Deirdre was "not sure what's going to happen." She continued to be haunted by fears. When her subway crossed the Manhattan Bridge, she had trouble stopping herself from imagining that the bridge would collapse and everyone in the train sink into the icy waters. That prompted her to wonder why there were no exit doors in subway cars as there are on airplanes. "Things like that are on my mind all the time." Sometimes she managed to get excited about various job opportunities, but found that such enthusiasm "only lasts for a few minutes." Then she asked herself, "Well, is that really what's necessary right now?" Her existential questioning of things continued in all directions. She was unable to return to her movie project. "I don't feel real positive about anything like that right now." In the past, she noted, "I was very focused. We were going to make these movies, I was going to continue with my photography career, this is what was going to happen, this is how it was going to happen, these were my goals and next summer I'm going to go to Maine and go to the Rockport school for cinematography and this is going to happen and then I'm going to do this." All of that was radically transformed for Deirdre. She could hardly get beyond wondering, "Am I going to have cereal this morning or am I going to have grapefruit?" She tried to imagine where she would be in the next few minutes, the next day, the next year. In general, however, "I'm not so much projecting into my future. I feel very unsure."

SURVIVOR GUILT

Survivors of a disaster such as 9/11 often struggle with guilt for having lived when so many others died, asking themselves such questions as "Why have I lived?" "Do I deserve to live?" "Was there a divine force that delayed me for just a few minutes so I missed that train and lived when so many of my colleagues perished?" There are many ways to take such questions, and one can simply accept an explanation of good fortune and move on. But for those with a more existential bent, including most of my respondents, it can be tormenting to explore why one lived when so many others died. Felicia, for example, knew that she was very lucky not to be further into the World Trade Center mall when the first plane hit, to have been led to safety by the unknown man when she froze in fear, and not to have been killed by falling debris as she ran across the West Side Highway. She asks herself, "How come nothing happened to me?" "Why was I running late that day?" "What if I had been on time?" The idea that God was watching over her gave her no satisfaction as an explanation for her luck. She felt such an explanation for her survival was facile and troubling. How can it be, she asked rhetorically, that, "I was really blessed and somebody was watching out for me?" It is the logic of that thought that most bothers Felicia. Did all those who died reach "their time" all at once? And, she asks, pushing herself philosophically, whether she was worthy of surviving. "I almost wish," she says hesitantly, "like maybe I should have gotten hurt 'cause if I was hurt, all those other people . . ." as her voice trails off.

These musings had a personal dimension for Felicia. She grieved especially for all those children of the men who died (over 3,000 children were left without a father). Her experience of having lost her own father suddenly at sixteen years of age alerted her to that dimension of the disaster. After his death she had come to feel he watched over her. It was almost like he was a kind of ghost whose immanence she could feel, though she never took this feeling literally or trivialized it. She had moved well beyond such beliefs as she matured, but a feeling of God's presence in her life was evoked by her searing experiences on 9/11 and the amazing way she escaped harm. "[I was] thinking about all these kids whose fathers went to work and never came home. And it's so sad to hear of one case that, but, oh, the thousands of children whose parents left for work and never came home. And I just think it's so sad. . . . It's almost like too much. It's just too much sadness."

RELIGIOUS DOUBT AND COMFORT

Renee, who was raised Catholic, found that 9/11 forced her to confront some of the more hoary aspects of her religion while at the same time finding ways of drawing spiritual strength from her faith. Her immediate response to the disaster was to turn to familiar religious rituals and prayers in the days and weeks after 911. She often walked over to St. Patrick's Cathedral to pray in one of the chapels in the back, attended the large memorial service there at the end of the first week, and began attending her local Catholic church on the Upper West Side. She also was in constant touch with her family, who lived outside the city. The difficulty this interaction posed for Renee, however, was that her family, especially her mother, insisted on sending her unsolicited prayers and religious advice. One particularly annoying time for Renee came when her mother called and said about the Virgin Mary, "Our Mother said something like this would happen." Renee found that incredibly offensive and intrusive. She refused to believe that the Mother of God would have willed 9/11 on anyone but also seemed to feel that her mother's obtuse religious advice came from a place of complete ignorance about her feelings and those of anyone caught up in the maelstrom of the trauma after the attack. The comments of Renee's mother reflected not only a highly limited notion of divine interaction with human affairs but was, as Renee experienced it, part of the general lack of understanding that people outside of New York brought to bear in their interaction with those inside the city.[3]

Curiously, Renee's struggles with her mother over her musings about the Virgin Mary were part of a complex of interactions that she had with both her parents that led to new insights about their personalities. She had always thought, growing up, that her father was the strong one in the family and her mother the weak, retiring partner who needed the support of her strong husband. "I've come to realize that my mother was never the fragile one, that she was really the strong one, and it was my father who was a lot more, you know, who doesn't ever deal really with anything, doesn't really ever talk about anything." This insight was very much a product of her experiences after 911. Her father was much more "visibly freaked out" and kept wanting to fly to New York to take care of his daughter. Renee's mother, on the other hand, kept trying to reassure her, in part through her annoying comments about the Virgin Mary, but more generally with concern and calming comments.

The mother's attempts to calm her, however, brought Renee into a new and troubling place in relation to her mother, who had a remoteness about her that left Renee confused about her mother's capacity for authentic engagement with Renee's experience. The mother worked as a special education teacher and generally dealt with that difficult group of teenage children well, though largely because of her ability to cut herself off from her students' huge emotional needs. Renee tells of when she was eight and had hit her head against the door and needed ten stitches. Her mother's first response was to put a Band-Aid on it and tell her to lie on the couch. As Renee comments, "She's never been kind of a—I mean she doesn't act overly concerned. She's calm, but I think she's more, I think she ignores it a little bit more—like she's a little bit cut off." Renee's point in telling this story about her mother is that she felt that her mother's numbed calm failed to provide her with much support in the wake of Renee's own trauma during 9/11. As she comments, "I mean I needed somebody to say that it wasn't necessarily all okay. Okay, I understand where she was coming from, but, you know, it wasn't all okay, and it isn't, and that's what scares me to death."

As Renee explored her feelings about her mother more deeply in the course of the interview and recovered memories like the scene after she hit her head when she was eight, she became visibly more upset and even mildly dissociated. She talked about how she had been harassed in an elevator at work by a weird man. She talked to one friend, who encouraged her to seek counseling, but Renee felt that would not be helpful in her moment of crisis. The only person she shared the story with was the director of security for the museum in which she worked, a man with whom she felt safe. After 9/11, she reported, she found herself once again thinking that she needed to find a therapist. One close friend suggested that she definitely should find a therapist for herself, but in the meantime she might find being interviewed by me for my study helpful. As her friend told her, "You need to tell your story over and over again." Renee talked about that advice but was also aware of how confusing it was for her to recover her feelings about the disaster and especially those relating to her mother. She says, "I'm like really dizzy." That comment prompted Renee to remember how on Wednesday, September 12th, she had gone into Central Park and lay down on the grass to rest. "It was like I laid down, I closed my eyes, and was like dead for half an hour," after which she felt "resurrected."

THE PREMONITORY AND THE EXOTIC

An event as large as 9/11 tends to evoke responses in some that are equal to it in spiritual significance. They feel part of a larger plan (not always for the better), or caught on the wheel of fate that some higher power moves. Many found, for example, as they recalled things after the fact, that there were warnings they tended not to heed. Rosemary pondered, sometimes with a sense of survivor guilt, why she had been moved by her company from her office on the ninety-first floor of WTC 1, the north tower, to the midtown offices just five days before 9/11. Polly Weiss, a respondent in the Columbia Oral History Project, had a haunting, but touching, experience with her husband on the morning of 9/11. They had had an argument early that morning. Weiss felt bad about it and wanted to make amends. When she made her husband a lunch she cut the sandwich into the shape of a heart. She took the lunch to give him, but he was distracted because he was busy feeding the cat. He failed to respond to her. Perhaps he was still angry and feigning unawareness of her presence. But she refused to let him ignore her. She told him, "You know, I could die today, and you would feel so bad for not taking the time to kiss me and say goodbye." That broke the ice. He stood up and hugged her and they parted with love. Later, he sat on the roof of his midtown office building watching the disaster unfold, knowing that his wife worked in the area and that he could not reach her. He kept looking at his little heart-shaped sandwich.[4]

Other stories of such premonitions are more esoteric, even though all their tales are inevitably ex post facto. The most dramatic case in my personal experience came from one of my patients, Roxanne. A sensitive woman prone to such experiences, Roxanne began to feel a sense of darkness and despair on the Monday afternoon before the attacks. She struggles with depression and felt her mood was simply part of a familiar experience in which she cannot distinguish between sadness and the uncanny. She spent much of the first part of the night crying. She asked an ex-boyfriend to come over and stay with her for a while. He did, talked with her for several hours, but then had to leave. She called another ex-lover who remained a good friend and asked him to stay with her. They talked for hours into the night and when they were finally exhausted he went to sleep on the couch and she went to bed. Even then she felt no relief from her misery and cried herself to sleep, not having any idea what was happening in her uncanny awareness (as she understood it in retrospect). The next morning she woke up feeling exhausted but actually somewhat refreshed. At 8:46, while she was sipping tea with her friend, the first plane to attack the World Trade Center came roaring over her apartment and made such a thunderous noise that the plates rattled on the table and in the kitchen. She ran to the window and looked out to see American Flight 11 turn and then ram into the north tower.

Another esoteric story came from my patient William, who was walking his dogs at the dog run on the West Side near 23rd Street at around 8:30 in the morning on September 11th. Usually, he said, people remain in the dog run with their dogs until well past 9 o'clock. That morning most had already left by the time he got there at 8:30. He was surprised to see that both his dogs were riled up in ways that they never had been. The larger one ran around apparently in great distress and the smaller one followed, seeming not to know what was happening. When he left, both were reluctant to walk and flattened themselves on the sidewalk, which was extremely unusual behavior them. At that moment he looked up as the first plane flew over and hit the north tower.[5]

Such retrospectively rendered premonitions cannot be called predictions, however powerful they were for those who experienced them. For many, however, though not for me, a more convincing variant of this same theme was the keen interest after 9/11 in Nostradamus, who has a way of popping up in the wake of great events. Nostradamus, who was born in France in 1503 (died 1566), was a mystic and seer who was drawn to the occult and wrote an estimated 6,338 predictions in his annual *Almanac*. He also did psychic readings for many French nobles and others who came to know of his fame in this area. Nostradamus, however, is best known for his book *Prophecies*, published in 1555. It consists of highly symbolic and often obscure quatrains (942 of them), which many feel have accurately predicted wars, natural disasters, and the rise and fall of empires. There is no question that Nostradamus intended his quatrains to be read in this way. Within hours after the towers fell, email boxes around the world were filled with references to a quatrain Nostradamus wrote in 1554:

In the City of God there will be a great thunder.
Two brothers torn apart by Chaos, while the fortress endures,
The great leader will succumb.
The third big war will begin when the big city is burning.

The "City of God" is taken to be New York; the "two brothers torn apart" are the World Trade Center towers; "Chaos," Osama bin Laden and Al-Qaeda; the "fortress," the Pentagon; the "great leader who will succumb," the United States itself; and "the third big war" that will begin, World War III (though thankfully not yet under way, the war in Afghanistan did begin while the pile still burned, which is where the quatrain ends).

At a different level, I encountered in my patients and among the respondents in my study a number of examples of mystical experiences of 9/11. Jenna, a strict Catholic to which she joins her own forms of spirituality, said decisively, "We are not alone. I always sense that He is there, that He is listening, God, the angels." It is the angels that particularly intrigue her. "I love angels, and my whole house has angels everywhere . . . I have all kinds of little statues of angels." She quickly called herself silly for having such beliefs, as she has probably been cautioned against being too literal about angels by her priest and perhaps by her family. In our interaction, she eventually told me that she was worried I would think she was crazy for such beliefs. As she came to trust me more, however, she elaborated on her beliefs. The presence of God in her life was matched by the equally powerful immanence of the devil. "Hell was deeply ingrained in me," she says, "anything you do, there's a big eye looking at you." These beliefs frame her unique interpretations of 9/11: "Sometimes I feel that those souls are still lingering down there, 'cause they still don't know what happened, you know, like it caught them."

On October 4, 2001, my patient Betsy referred to disturbed souls. I noted it and explored her meanings, though she was reluctant to elaborate. When she could tell I was not only accepting of her use of such a dramatic spiritual image, she said she had had a conversation with her cousin from Seattle, who is a witch, as well as another mystical relative from Chicago, about the idea of the deaths of 7,000 people (her figure then) as a sacrifice for the world to move to a higher level of meaning. All these disturbed souls, she said, were still in the air and troubled and searching for a home. Betsy then talked about twice visiting Ground Zero when she had to go to her former office to retrieve some files. She talked at length with various workers and felt incredibly moved at the destruction. She felt the death, experiencing Ground Zero as a vast graveyard. I encouraged her to write down her thoughts, as that might give greater coherence to ideas that were otherwise mostly troubling for her. She was distressed at having to work for a company that hoped to profit monetarily from the crisis by raising consumer debt, and at having to relate to her boss, whom she called Mr. Rational Man. I pointed out that she was not entirely passive in her environment. She was a witness to an awful event. She was spared the actual violence but could now bring something important to her understanding of the disaster. It would also strengthen her. "Pay attention to the spiritual," I said, "it is the other dimension of the psychological." She replied with warmth that I obviously believed in all this as well, by which she meant the disturbed souls in the air. It was an odd moment for me. I cannot say I believed anything she was telling me. At the same time, I realized I had extended my empathy in ways I often do in therapy and enveloped her world that in the moment became true for me. This experience with Betsy reminded me of when my daughter Alison at the age of four asked me if I believed in angels. I said, "Yes, of course," because at that moment with her I did believe in angels.

REINCARNATION AND KARMA

On 9/11 Ellen, a sensitive psychotherapist, sought to grasp the spiritual meaning of the disaster in ways that connected with her experience raising her daughter Samantha, who was born with Williams syndrome, which is not unlike Downs but makes a child mystically musical. Ellen's experience with Samantha led her to ask, "What is the spiritual meaning? What is the karma of those [who died that day]?" Ellen takes it as a given that "we're all spiritual human beings and we all have a soul." All those people who died on 9/11, she assumed, were reincarnated, but her other concern was to try and understand the "deeper meaning for those people's destiny, that they were like sacrificial beings for our, the rest of the world's, sins." Ellen's ruminations move in two directions. On the one hand, she feels that those who died inevitably move to a higher karmic realm through the experience of reincarnation. In her beliefs, some kind of process occurs after the body dies. "Over a period of three days or so, there's a release, and back to the spiritual world." In this way the suffering and death of those on 9/11 served to elevate their spirits to a higher level. Ellen came at this idea from many different directions in the course of the interview, but it is an idea she tenaciously holds to. She is equally clear in her mind that the death of all those people on 9/11 had a sacrificial quality to it and that their deaths serve to elevate the rest of us spiritually. Nor was the disaster an accident. Nothing, in fact, is accidental for her. It had to have a purpose from some kind of divine being, and that purpose inevitably was to change the world spiritually and elevate us.

DEATH IMAGERY

"I have a very acute fear of death," Henry said. That fear drew him to his research on serial killers for his doctorate and informed his response to the disaster. He took in the more profound meanings of the death that unfolded before his eyes. In the immediate wake of 9/11, for example, he worried about another attack. It made daily life almost unbearable for a time. "I'm not paranoid about it," he said, while acknowledging his deep concerns. This whole tragedy did not "make me like obsessive about it." But it did cause him to reflect on the transitory nature of life. One minute, "you can be working in your office and two minutes later like something happened and two minutes later if you don't make the right decision, you know, you're dead." Life can end "just like that, absurdly." Henry continued about what he called his "mathematical brain." He did some counting. He was thirty-two and could expect to live to eighty-five, so he was about 40 percent done with his life. That prompted him to reflect: "40 percent of my life is—like what have I done?" Time was "running out." That thought led him to associate to his grandmother's death. She got cancer and took a long, slow year to die. "She had lung cancer and one of her lungs had collapsed and I mean she knew she was dying." Toward the end, it was almost unbearable for Henry to see her, though, he notes ironically, she was always "much more at ease with it" than he was. She was a simple, grounded person and took death in stride. Henry contrasted that with the character in Tolstoy's "Death of Ivan Ilyich," who screams for three days at the knowledge of his imminent death.

How does one deal with that knowledge? And how can one deal with the absurdity of 6,000 people dying (the figure at the time of the interview)? All those people went to work for an ordinary day. They had no reason to fear anything. No one took a particular risk that day when leaving for work. "What could be more innocuous?" Such reflection led Henry to think about his work on serial killers. The connection between 9/11 and such killers is that awareness, ever so fleeting, that "you know you are being murdered." It is like a "death camp." You wait to die. "I mean I can't imagine how like horrible that is." Henry thought of all those final cell phone calls. People trapped in the raging fires, desperately afraid, knowing that death was not far off, talking for one last time with someone they love. It was an almost unbearable thought. In the same vein, he imagined his way into the experience of the flight attendant on American Flight 11 who was on the phone reporting the hijacking and trying to report where the plane was flying. She described some buildings and some water without really knowing what was happening until suddenly "she started screaming like she figured out what was happening." That kind of horror was difficult for Henry to imagine fully.

For her part, Rosemary felt like psychologically she was treading water after 9/11, an image that brought back to her an experience she had swimming in some water off Long Island. She got a cramp in a leg and began to panic when she swallowed a little water. She realized, however, that she was in saltwater and could tread water easily. Treading water thus became an image of survival for Rosemary that day.

Rosemary reflected on her deep sense of spirituality and connection with nature. She felt strongly that a "sense of connectedness ... somehow hits the fringes of our consciousness and possibly binds people to one another as a sort of bond of human nature." She was convinced that there are "mysteries about human consciousness that we don't understand" but that she felt part of in an important, spiritual way. It is also interesting that Rosemary on a vacation to St. Lucia took with her to read on the beach Melville's *Moby Dick*. She had tried two other times in her life to read *Moby Dick* but had always found it too long, complicated, and difficult. On this trip, however, she recognized for the first time what an extraordinarily good writer Melville is, especially in his discussions of evil. Something in her led her to take this particular novel with her on her vacation as a way of reflecting on the deeper meanings of evil as she herself moved toward overcoming her depression and numbing. That recovery process even left Rosemary with a feeling that her 9/11 experiences had deepened her in profound ways by breaking through her own emotional wall. She noted that it is perhaps a common experience to erect such walls. "We all have reasons and I had good reasons." She also understands the psychological cost of numbing oneself to feelings. "But I've had an emotional wall against what was happening to human beings in the world and it [her 911 experiences in general] broke that wall. So what was vague horror has become tangible." Rosemary's point here is extremely subtle and important. As she elaborated: "Instead of some vague, terrible threat out in the distance that happened to other people," she understood that "it almost happened to me." Her point was that this incredibly close brush with very large-scale death that evoked apocalyptic destruction broke down some of her emotional walls. That left her very confused and full of pain and depression for a long time but at the same time deepened her own experience by cutting through much of her numbing.

Rosemary called herself "kind of an Earth nut in my soul." She described the small town in which she grew up in West Virginia as having some of the worst industrial and human pollution in the nation, second only to Birmingham, Alabama, and even worse than Pittsburgh. In the river that ran through her town "you could literally see fecal material floating on the surface because it was just open sewers into the river." She says that as a child she used to "dream about a fresh river" where she would be able to swim and play with her friends. She once went to Scout camp in the mountains and encountered a "real river" that she could swim and play in. It was a startlingly wonderful experience for her. Her river, however, literally caught fire when the coal engines drove by and sparks dropped on top of the water. There were also many forest fires in her area, sparked by the generally devastating destruction to the environment caused by the coal mines. It seemed to her that that was simply how it all had to be. She noted with great enthusiasm that in the last few decades the whole environment of her town and West Virginia in general has been cleaned up. She found that really remarkable. "You can clean it up. It was so hopeful."

She was less certain about the future after 9/11. "I mean I don't know. I don't know. For myself, I feel like I've walked into such a new reality. Not that it wasn't there before, but just nothing ever made me look at it and I'm standing here looking at it. And it's really hard to look at. And I don't know what to do about it. And right now I don't feel like I have a whole lot of strength to do anything. But I'm hoping that it doesn't last too long 'cause I really have to do something. I have three grandchildren and a lot of kids that I care about, a lot of kids."

13

PREGNANT WOMEN

IN THE FALL of 2003 I was well past the period I had
allotted for formal interviews in connection with my
study of New York City and 9/11. Those were conducted at a furious pace in the immediate wake of
the disaster and were completed for the most part by
early 2002. By 2003 I had already begun to process my
enormous amount of data, had given some talks, and
had written one article. But I was dimly aware that I
was missing a full understanding of what 9/11 meant
for the way people imagined hope. Despite disaster,
war, genocide, suffering, life goes on, and the question
I was pondering was how ordinary people dealt with
hope in a compromised world. I was therefore alert to
new possibilities when, after one of my presentations
in October of 2003 to Lifton's Wellfleet psychohistory
meetings, Shareen Brysac, having listened closely,
suggested that I interview women who got pregnant

right after 9/11. It would tell you, she said, much about the meanings of hope in a world of danger and malevolence.

I immediately knew that the idea of such interviews was exactly right. Finding the appropriate women was another matter. I thought of hanging out in playgrounds and trying to approach women with children between the ages of two and three, or putting a formal request in various newspapers, or just asking women on the street with children the right age until I found some respondents who could help me find others. Any such method, however, seemed both difficult and haphazard, not to mention ethically questionable to approach women on playgrounds without an introduction. It risked making them feel accosted. But my wife came to my rescue. She had then been teaching many years in a preschool in Park Slope, Brooklyn, named Huggs Preschool. She talked with the director there, Randy Bader, to see if she would help me recruit a cohort of women for my study whose children were then in the two's class and thus would have been born in the summer of 2002. Ms. Bader agreed and proved an invaluable ally. She talked with all the mothers and weeded out those who were ambivalent, so that when I called the others they knew who I was, had a trustworthy connection in my wife who was a teacher in the school, and had basically already agreed to be interviewed. This cohort was perfectly suited to provide insight into the questions I wanted answered. All were educated, middle- and upper-middle-class New Yorkers; all lived in one neighborhood in Brooklyn; and all shared the common experience of having their 9/11 babies attend the same class in the same school.

There had been some errant nonsense in the press after 9/11 that the hospitals would be filled with babies in the summer of 2002. Such an urban myth grew out of the notion that people must have been making a lot of love cooped up in their homes after the disaster. Such a myth is implausible on the face of it and, perhaps even more important, fails to take into account the presence of birth control in the contemporary era. Even if people were making more love—which is highly unlikely, given the widespread panic—they were not making more babies. A simple look at demographic data confirms that nothing changed in the way of live births in the summer of 2002, either in the nation or, more important, for my purposes, in New York City.

It is a very different matter when, in the wake of 9/11, a woman, with her partner (in the case of my sample, all husbands), chooses to get pregnant and bring a baby into the world.[1] I discovered that the motivations for these women to get pregnant were enormously complex, but their pregnancies had nothing to do with sitting around in their homes cooped up for too long without work. These were decisions that were shaped profoundly by the new world after 9/11 and their personal hopes to create life despite all the dangers.

JENNIFER

Jennifer is a calm, appealing woman who was thirty-seven in 2001. She and her husband, along with their daughter who had just turned two, lived in a small apartment between Greenwich and 13th streets in Greenwich Village. They had bought a country home in Pennsylvania, where they spent many weekends that they extended as long as possible. On that Tuesday, they were driving into the city so that they both could get to work. At the approach to the tunnel they saw the smoke and turned on the radio, learning that a small plane had crashed into the north tower. It seemed innocuous enough, so they continued their drive.

It was their anniversary, a symbolically important day that made the subsequent events auspicious in memory. As they got closer to the entrance to the tunnel the amount of smoke increased and they learned of the crash of the second plane. Just as they were about to enter the tunnel it was closed and all cars were turned back. It was 9:14. Jennifer's precision about that moment is telling. After being turned back from the tunnel, they decided to return to their Pennsylvania home. Jennifer feared that "nobody knew the end of it. I felt the precariousness of the infrastructure of this country. What if someone tampered with the money machines?" She feared that all the planes might be downed and the trucks and trains somehow immobilized and that there would be no food in Pennsylvania. They therefore stopped at a deli for water and supplies, at which point they saw the first tower fall down. "We cried when we saw it. I thought of the people in the street [around the WTC] and I thought how could that debris fit on the street. How was that going to work?"

They returned to Pennsylvania in a state of shock. Jennifer proceeded to call everyone she and her husband knew in Manhattan. She was especially worried about a cousin who worked at American Express, across from the World Financial Center, who, it turned out, had gone to a dentist appointment that morning. Another cousin, who lived on Grand Street, was harder to reach. Because the phones were out, it took until the next day before Jennifer could track her down and find out whether she was okay. She was mesmerized by watching the television coverage. "It was constant. It was riveting. It [the disaster] was in my backyard." She was on edge and felt paranoid. Her response was visceral. She felt vulnerable to an "imminent attack . . . I definitely did not feel safe."

In this heightened state Jennifer got pregnant at the end of September. She had been trying to get pregnant since the middle of the summer and "never thought of not trying" to continue after 9/11. "It never entered our minds that we should not, because this horrible thing had happened and what would it be like to be pregnant, which we probably should have frankly, but we didn't at all." Her mild self-condemnation about getting pregnant just after the disaster is clearly a retrospective idea and even then came up against all her human impulses to proceed with her life in the way that was most important and creative. "I was thirty-seven," she said, "so I thought, 'This is when I should be doing this. I am not going to not do it now.' Perhaps if I had been twenty-eight I would have said, 'Well, we should stop [trying to get pregnant].' Isn't that funny?" The wording in this passage suggests that the question of getting pregnant was perhaps in her mind, even if at unconscious levels. "Totally weird when I think back on it."

Jennifer was also influenced by her mother's insistence that it would be best to have two and a half years between her daughter and the next child. That was not Jennifer's childhood experience with her sibling, nor was that particular gap what existed between her niece and nephew. But for some reason Jennifer had been convinced by her mother and started to try and get pregnant in August of 2001 so that her second child would be two and a half years younger than her daughter. Her mother's shadow hung over Jennifer's continued commitment to getting pregnant.

The fact of pregnancy at the end of September, which was confirmed in mid-October, changed everything for Jennifer. Both she and her husband (and her doctor) were worried about the quality of the air in the city, not to mention the chaos, especially in the area below 14th Street, where they lived. "I also didn't feel I could make that decision [to move back to the city] for my daughter (who was then three)," she said. "I thought that I really didn't want her to be where, the scene at the time, we were all in danger, so that's when we decided we would commute." So Jennifer decided to live in Pennsylvania with her daughter while she was pregnant and have her husband commute to work each day. She stayed in the country for the next six months. She did return occasionally to her Village apartment for doctors' appointments and such things, for she mentions in her interview how badly it smelled in the area. "It was so sad." She could see the empty sky where the towers had stood from their window. "I thought that I just knew everybody in those towers, even though I didn't know anyone. I absolutely felt that I knew who all those people were." Jennifer was a woman of great empathy.

As it turned out, Jennifer's fears about the city after 9/11 were not entirely a result of the disaster. Rather, the disaster evoked an earlier dread about being trapped in the city. She had been in New York since she was twenty-four but always feared being caught. "All the doors would be closed," she said, "and all the bridges and all the tunnels. I had always felt it was a precarious place to live in the city. So I had these dreams of being locked in and things like that." New York seemed to her something of a "tin can." It was "very compressed and seemed clear to me that if you were in any kind of emergency, you know, [in the] subways, there'd be no cabs. It's clear to me that all the people in the high-rises coming down [would be stuck] . . . so I always sensed that it would be more than awful."

In the country Jennifer kept herself busy during her pregnancy taking care of her daughter, who began to attend a Waldorf school that required mothers to be with their two-year-olds while in the program. "I had a lot of fears," Jennifer says of what the air quality might do to her growing child. "I knew they were lying. I knew it because they said it was fine after about three weeks and I thought that was bullshit." Jennifer's fears were aggravated by living in Pennsylvania among many poor people who had an unusually large number of babies with birth defects. She began to feel the very ground she walked on was contaminated. Though at the same time she labeled such fears as irrational, they made her feel somewhat crazy. In that confused state she condemned herself for being pregnant. It was a "pretty stupid time to be pregnant," she said, even though she was basically pleased and excited about having a second child.

Then Jennifer had a paradigmatic experience that she felt was an omen and filled her with dread. She had taken her daughter to a "godawful mall" in Philipsburg for some pizza. Suddenly, a group of caretakers wheeled a large number of severely disabled children from a nearby institution. Jennifer was horrified (and felt guilty at her reaction). "It was heartbreaking and sad and they [the children] couldn't talk and they were sort of drooling." She asked herself, "Where do they go? And where do they live? Do they live forever in these hospitals like that?" She immediately connected the dread she felt with 9/11 and her "extreme sensitivity towards people with defects." Pennsylvania itself seemed tainted, a state built over ancient toxic coal mines, poor people with sick children, all profoundly unhealthy. "I felt that Pennsylvania was poisonous, that there was stuff there that was not good." She recognized in the interview, though somewhat vaguely, how her 9/11 fears got expressed in the reality of the disabled children and her basically irrational fear that Pennsylvania was the real threat to her unborn child's health, not New York City. "It's interesting. I used to blame Pennsylvania, but isn't that funny? Of course it was the experience of the towers [that made me feel that way]."

The scene in the pizza parlor mobilized Jennifer to decide to leave Pennsylvania immediately, sell the house, and never return. She was seven months pregnant that April of 2002 when she moved back into their small apartment on Greenwich Street. She was elated to be back home. "I was happy, so happy, to be home . . . I felt so much safer. I was so happy to be near [her husband]. It was a beautiful spring and she suddenly was full of hope. Jennifer was keenly aware of the contradiction in her feelings. "I was ten times more miserable in the country than when I moved back to the city, even with the danger." Her return brought her back into the world she best knew and loved. "I felt I knew everyone and that I was far away from people who were hurting, and that I was part of it in many ways." She wanted to be part of the hurt, to connect again with her natural community, to feel New York in its time of greatest danger and recovery. It is extraordinary that the main reason for leaving in the first place—the potentially toxic air—vanished after the pizza parlor scene in Pennsylvania. Now she felt only relief and safety in the city, even relatively close to Ground Zero, where she lived. "I was worried," she says, "but I wanted to be back."

All went well until a final checkup just before she gave birth revealed that her fetus had only one kidney. Her dread returned. Was it because of 9/11? Was it the ground in Pennsylvania? Had she made a terrible mistake by getting pregnant so soon after 9/11? Jennifer was tormented. All her worst fears seemed realized.

> I didn't know. I thought water [was the cause]. I thought the air. I thought because I spent most of this pregnancy, seven months in the country, I don't think that I thought it was the air quality. Although, who knows? Maybe it could have affected me after seven months. I don't know. I thought there was something in Pennsylvania. My initial thought [was] that the ground quality was poisonous there. Pennsylvania had been a huge industrial state with coal and metal. We were right near those very famous ironworks that are now defunct, sad, and depressing. Now it's one of the biggest agricultural states in the country, so they are growing on top of what was a coal state, a metal state. You see so many deformations there. It's just a very odd place, where we were and I felt that that was affecting. I did not connect

ultimately September 11. Although, again, that was my fear. The reasons for not being here. Perhaps I worried too that it was those last three months in the city that did make this happen.

Everyone in the hospital clinic where she got the test, knowing of her 9/11 background, was fearful as well. Several pediatricians were called in, and there was general unrest and distress. Finally, the head of the sonogram unit, a blunt Israeli, was called in to evaluate the test. Jennifer asked, "Oh, my God, what does this mean?" He turned to her and said matter-of-factly: "People live fine lives, no problem [with one kidney]. He isn't being born in the desert." Jennifer had to laugh at this reassurance by the Israeli doctor that her son would not be born in the West Bank. The doctor also told her that the amniotic fluid was fine, which meant the one kidney in the fetus had enlarged and was performing the work of two. Everything was normal, and in fact Jennifer gave birth a few days later to a perfectly healthy boy. But at the birth there were three pediatric specialists on call.[2]

SANDY

Sandy is a very friendly, outgoing woman with short dark hair; big, wide expectant eyes; and a warm smile. Her new duplex apartment is spotless and has wide windows with sun streaming in and immaculate shiny wooden floors. I sat at her clean wooden dining room table for the interview. After greeting me, she served water and soda, which she placed on the table along with a tray of cheese, crackers, and grapes that she had prepared in advance. Before she had her two children, she had been a professional stage manager, so her hospitality seemed a natural extension of that previous experience.

Sandy was married in 2000 at thirty-five years of age. She and her husband knew when they got married that they wanted children and had begun to try to get pregnant in June of 2001. After two months of failing, her doctor recommended she consult a high-risk fertility specialist. There was nothing especially to be worried about, but she was then thirty-six, and because it took four months to get an appointment with the specialist, her doctor recommended that she begin the process. Her appointment was set for the day before Thanksgiving. In August, as in July, she had not become pregnant.

Then came 9/11. On that day Sandy was working on the production of a new Broadway play with Sarah Jessica Parker. The first rehearsal was to begin that day. When the director heard of the disaster, he instructed Sandy to call everyone and cancel the rehearsal. She therefore spent the morning on the phone, first reaching her husband, who was okay, and then all the actors to notify them of the cancellation. Occasionally, she had the chance to watch television for a few minutes, but in general she feels she "sort of missed the 9/11 experience because I was so concentrated on what I had to do."

Sandy, however, was deeply affected by the disaster. She seemed not to have thought much about her feelings about 9/11 until the interview four years after the event, so that the more she talked, the more she remembered about her anxieties. These were intense and included isolated memories that became retrospectively activated. For example, Sandy recalled overhearing a conversation of a couple on the train the morning of September 11th on the way to work. She overheard the woman, a recent mother with a four-month-old, talking of her feelings about going back to work. She was telling her husband that she did not have a moment to herself. "It's so hard," she had said. "I can't even dress right, I can't even shower, I don't know how this is going to work, honey." The husband was being patronizing and trying to reassure her that it would all work out, but Sandy felt he was not hearing his wife's plea for help. Sandy regularly took the F train to Jay Street, where she switched to the A. The couple remained on the F train and in retrospect Sandy worried that they died in the disaster and left that baby all alone.

Such newly revived and interpreted memories were part of Sandy's dread about herself and the world after 9/11. She felt "our country is going to be taken over, that our whole way of life was going to change, and we would be put in concentration camps." She suggested to her husband that they get some cyanide pills so that when "they come for us, we can kill ourselves so that [we will not] suffer." She actively entertained fears of bombs in the subway. After the anthrax scares she refused to open her mail for a few weeks, and it was clear in the context of the interview that there were a host of other fears that she never elaborated. "Anything could happen," she said. Sandy seemed to feel some shame about her fears, especially in retrospect. Twice she contrasted her own "hysterical" fears with the more "realistic" attitude of her husband, which was that there was a definite "long-term danger but that you could put [it] in perspective." In this contrast she was self-critical about the extremity of her fears. At the same time, there was a hint of her resentment about this contrast in her telling the story of the couple on the F train on the morning of 9/11. Sandy seemed to be equating her own rational husband with the man who treated his wife's postpartum struggles with condescension. Perhaps she felt he was not really listening to her pleas that the world was not safe.

Yet Sandy never stopped trying to get pregnant. Nothing happened in September, but she did get pregnant in October. She knew from her sudden sensitivity to smell. Coming out of the subway once she could almost taste the smell of burnt almond. Another time she was exceedingly revolted sitting next to someone who smelled of cigarette smoke. She said to herself: "Oh my God, I am pregnant." He pregnancy was confirmed at her prearranged appointment with the specialist the day before Thanksgiving.

Sandy was overjoyed. In fact, she wondered what happened to all her fears. "I guess in a way it sounds like I recovered from my anxiety awfully quickly." Nothing, it seems, could intrude on her joy at being pregnant, not even fears of Nazis banging down the doors. Sandy does recall feeling sad to the point of tears for women who gave birth on 9/11 and how scary it must have been for them. She also felt deep empathy for all the women who were pregnant on 9/11 and lost their husbands to the disaster. That thought and her general anxieties stirred in her the fear that something might be wrong with her own baby. As a result, for fourteen weeks she told no one except her husband that she was pregnant, or until well into 2002.

LESLEY

Lesley was an exception in my sample but such an interesting one that I have included her. She gave birth in St. Vincent's Hospital on 9/11.

In the early morning of Tuesday, September 11th, at around 4:00 A.M., Lesley, then forty-two years old, went into labor. She called her pediatrician and they agreed it was time for her to get to the hospital. As the mother of two other children, Lesley was familiar with the labor process and knew it was time. But these things are often not what they seem, for at around 6:00 A.M. her contractions began to lessen. The doctor felt, however, that she was dilated enough to justify staying in the hospital. "And then I don't know how much time passed, but I was like in contractions, not in contractions, sort of like time just sort of vanishes in the middle of that." To urge things along a nurse suggested she walk around. Lesley wandered down the hall on the seventh floor and noticed a crowd standing by a large window looking south at the World Trade Center. They told her there was a fire in the building. As she stood there she began talking with another woman who had given birth to her baby ten hours before. Suddenly, the second plane hit the south tower and Lesley saw the giant explosion. All the nurses, mostly Caribbean American women, started screaming hysterically, "It's the terrorists, it's the terrorists." Lesley tuned it out. "I was kind of in that labor zone, like the world is falling apart but my job is to deliver this baby."

The next few hours are a blur in Lesley's mind. She remembers the announcement over the PA system insistently repeating, "Code 3, all personnel, Code 3." Her doctor was with her at that point and looked at his identification badge and read on the back that Code 3 meant disaster. He said, "Oh, this must be some kind of drill" and ignored it at first. But very quickly he realized it was not a drill and then kept leaving Lesley to join the other doctors in preparation for what they assumed would be the flood of victims into the hospital.[3] The doctor also became increasingly nervous as the morning progressed, which raised Lesley's anxiety. "You know, the person of a doctor is not supposed to crack," she said. Lesley's husband was with her as well, but he also kept leaving to watch the little TV in the father's room so that he could figure out what was happening in the world. When the towers fell, he came back into the room, "just shaking his head." Both were exceedingly anxious about their two children back in Brooklyn. Lesley, meanwhile, when her contractions stopped, would walk down the hall to watch the burning and then collapsing towers. She said, "It was the spookiest thing."

Sometime after 11:00 A.M. the doctor advised Lesley that he felt he should expedite delivery by putting her on Pitocin. His concern was not her or the baby's health but the urgent need in the hospital to free up beds for what they still believed would be all the injured survivors. With Pitocin Lesley began virtually continuous contractions that dilated her more and brought her near giving birth. She said she felt close and asked to have her epidural. At first, the nurse said okay but came back twenty seconds later and said that, unfortunately, she could not get an epidural because all the anesthesiologists were in the emergency room and could not be called away. The best they could do was give her some Demerol. Now Lesley got very nervous. The doctors were not there for her in the hospital. What if something went wrong during delivery? What if she needed blood? What if they had to do a Caesarian? She felt in an "existential [state], like you're born alone, you die alone."

The Demerol had a distancing effect on Lesley but did nothing to relieve her pain. It was as if she was "sitting there rocking in the middle of the bed ... writhing pain ... but like ha ha ha, I'm in so much pain, ha ha ha." But the baby finally did come and all was well. The nurses quickly took the baby to clean her up and moved Lesley into the recovery room so that they could take her hospital bed down to the emergency room. There was a TV in the recovery room, and in her drugged state of exhaustion she watched the images of 9/11 endlessly replayed, of the second plane flying into the south tower and of both towers collapsing, of the Pentagon, while she listened to the frantic and confused commentary. "And I'm like, I really am, what the fuck is going on?"

She was also alone. Not only was her doctor in the emergency room, but her husband, as soon as he knew all had gone well with the birth, left her to be with their other children. The best train for him was the F, which also happened to be the only line in service to Brooklyn. The F train has clusters of seats that means if the train is full, as it was that day, people sit facing each other. Everyone was in shock and asking what had happened and how and why. Lesley's husband listened for a while but then took out of his pocket two Polaroid pictures he had taken of his newborn baby and said, "Well, something good happened today. My daughter was born." He then passed around the pictures, and many cried. It was sweet and touching and tragically sad all at once to welcome life in the wake of death.

Lesley, meanwhile, was getting scared and increasingly lonely. She had figured out enough of what was happening to know that all of Lower Manhattan was being evacuated, that the tunnels were closed, and that no cars were allowed anywhere below 14th Street. She had a cell phone with her but it was not working. She could not reach her husband. She feared she would be trapped. "I'm not going to get out of here. I'm not going to get to the people I love, and they might die. I might die. And I did have that [idea] that like if we're going to die, I want all of us to be together."

Somehow Lesley made it through the night and learned the next day she could go home. Her husband at first found it difficult making it below 14th Street to fetch her. The police were not letting anyone but those part of the official rescue teams through the lines, as well as reporters and other family members of victims. But her husband luckily had with him the piece of paper with the baby's footprint on it and the St. Vincent's logo. He was able to show that to the police and convince them that he had to get to 12th Street and Seventh Avenue so he could bring his wife home. Lesley was overjoyed that her family was now united.

Lesley put her three-year-old in the stroller, the four-year-old walked, and her husband carried the baby in her carrier. They walked out of the hospital into a "sea of people and reporters and police." St. Vincent's, as the hospital closest to Ground Zero, quickly became a magnet for those searching for survivors. Just as hospital staff the day before had made massive preparations for the injured who never came, now family members frantically searching for their loved ones flocked to the hospital where they assumed survivors might be found. It was a chilling scene for Lesley and her husband.

Lesley also had to confront the terrible smell of smoke and death that hung in the air. It smelled to her like "tar, tar burning, that really like viscous dirty [smell]; it did not smell like a clean wood fire at all." Her first thought was that she did not want her new baby to breathe the awful air. But soon the need to get through the crowd and to the F train focused her thoughts on the moment. Once on the train, however, the dread returned. She was no longer drugged and had a good understanding of the scale of what had happened around her the previous day. "Now I'm thinking, 'Oh my God, now reality is starting . . . I'm on the F train with a one-day-old, and my universe is going to fall out on the train.'"

In the next few days Lesley found her fears spreading and becoming apocalyptic. On Thursday on her block someone speaking loudly into a megaphone suddenly ordered an evacuation of everyone from their homes. There was a suspicious package in the street. She began to fear there was going to be another attack and that "they're going to drop chemicals from airplanes." That was part of broader fears of "contamination stuff," such as poisoning the food supply. She also felt vulnerable in her neighborhood, Park Slope, because of all the Jews who live there, including her husband. The news of the twelve firemen in the local firehouse on Union Street (Squad 1) who died made the death immediate. Dave Fontana, one of the dead firemen, not long before 9/11 had come into the preteen classroom her four-year-old attended in full uniform, much to the delight of the children. And in time the anthrax scare further fed her fears. Lesley tried to pull into herself and "find that quiet place inside of me," but the world kept impinging on her sense of safety and hope. Everywhere danger lurked.

SHERRY

Sherry was a forty-one-year-old African-American woman with two children at the time of the interview on February 14, 2005. We sat in her living room overlooking Grand Army Plaza in Park Slope. Her oldest child, RJ, was seven years old and in second grade at St. Ann's School in Brooklyn Heights. Her 9/11 baby is named Ryan, conceived in December of 2001 and born the following October, in 2002. The great tragedy in the life of Sherry and her husband Rich was the death of RJ's twin, Brandon, in 1998, some fourteen months after his birth. The cause of his death was freakish. He choked on a piece of rice and Sherry and her husband were unable to dislodge it. That personal tragedy had a huge effect on Sherry and Rich, leaving them ambivalent about risking another birth but also wanting to create life again. Sherry said, "Rich and I still haven't gotten to a place where we've really both gotten over the loss of Brandon in a way that we can [make sense of]." Perhaps one never fully gets over the loss of a child.

But by the summer of 2001 Sherry and Rich had just gotten to a place where they could begin to think about getting pregnant again. By August for the first time they began to talk about it. "Do we do this again?" Sherry asked herself. "Can I even deal with this again, and should RJ have a sibling because he did have one?" Those intensely personal questions expanded after 9/11 to a profound doubt about the future in a dangerous world. "Babies are the hope," she said, "I will always believe that. [But] what am I doing? This country is crazy; we can't do this." The danger is too great. "What if New York gets attacked again?"

The situation in the city deeply contributed to Sherry's ambivalence about getting pregnant. Her office is near the World Trade Center. She had been in Park Slope on the morning of 9/11 (and thus saw the disaster on television) but that fall returned to work every day. Her train is the Seventh Avenue line that runs directly under Ground Zero. Nothing matched the horror of the Fulton Street stop on the 2 or 3 train. "The smell, my God, it was awful," she reports. Her problems that fall were compounded by the fact that she and her coworkers, whose business had been disrupted, did not have much to do. They would take long lunches and drink too much. "We could barely work because of, between the smell and the systems being screwed up, and we were close enough to the disaster that it affected our buildings and systems so much that we just kind of like, the smell bothered me the most and I really was focused on, well, is the air quality really good?"

On the other hand, Sherry found herself fascinated by pregnant women that fall of 2001. "I was obsessed," she says. She followed particularly closely newspaper articles about women who had gotten pregnant immediately after 9/11, holed up that week with their husbands. "I was kind of hopeful, and then I do remember thinking, 'Well, this tells you that the future is, you believe in some future, whatever that is [laughs].'" The laughter at that moment in the interview is not trivial, for it reflects Sherry's profound self-doubt in thinking about the experience of other women: "What do they [the pregnant women] know that I don't know." She was drawn to such women because she hoped that in understanding them she could begin to comprehend what was stopping her from getting pregnant. "I had to consider, 'Does this [getting pregnant] make sense?'"—and that not only in terms of 9/11 but also in terms of RJ.

The issue of RJ may have been the decisive factor overcoming Sherry's ambivalence about getting pregnant. She felt terrible at many levels about the death of Brandon, including remorse that RJ's twin had been taken from him. He was now potentially alone in the world. She worried a great deal that if she and Rich died, RJ would have no one. That haunted her. Besides, curiously, RJ himself got into the family drama and began pestering Sherry to have another child so he could have a sibling. At seven years of age, he would ask regularly: "Mommy, when are you going to get pregnant?" RJ seemed to want a new Brandon, a brother, a playmate, but perhaps he also responded to something working unconsciously in his mother and sought to bring it to the surface.

Sherry and Rich never did resolve that fall in any clear and conscious way whether it was time to get pregnant again. Instead, the possibility of getting pregnant simply opened up between them in new ways. Their ambivalence was revealed in the contradictory ways they used birth control. Sometimes they practiced it, but at other times they said to each other, "Why bother?" It was magical when she did discover she was pregnant just before Christmas. Her heart had led her into it despite all her misgivings. But there was a shadow. Had she done the right thing? Would this end in another personal tragedy? Was the world too awful to bring a baby into? The best she can figure now is that, "Probably biology just kind of took over." In retrospect, however, and in a more considered view, she feels that, "I would say, I wish we had waited a little longer because I think that, I felt that I wasn't really really ready in my mind in real time."

NANCY

Nancy, who works for Citigroup, is a tough, determined, competent, assertive, outdoorsy, athletic woman who is also tender and deeply devoted to her girl, conceived just after 9/11, and a boy born two years later. Her husband, Tony, who sat in on the interview and frequently joined the conversation, is a round-faced, gentle, teddy-bear type who must be very good with the children.

They are deeply devoted to each other and very good with the children, who were in the room and played a not-so-silent role in the interview itself.

Nancy and Tony had been married since 1995 but had not begun to try and get pregnant. "We were going to wait," Nancy says, "because we wanted to make sure everything was right." At some level they had to know that the right time was fast approaching, because both were thirty-three years old on 9/11. It is equally true, however, that it was the impact of the disaster on their lives that convinced them to have children.

The day itself was quite traumatic for both of them. Nancy worked in midtown and Tony's office was at the southernmost tip of Manhattan. They had some communication after the second plane hit, lost contact with each other, then he finally got a page to her, saying, "Just go home. We'll meet at home." Since home was in Brooklyn, Tony began walking up Water Street toward the Brooklyn Bridge and was near the Fulton Fish Market when the first tower collapsed. He was covered in dust and debris. He kept paging Nancy but was not at all sure his pages were getting through (they were not). Nancy, meanwhile, was terrified. After the one page that came through, she had no idea where he was. Because she was out of sight of the towers, when she heard they both fell, she could not imagine them imploding and had visions of them falling over into Manhattan, perhaps south of where Tony worked. "Where the hell is Tony," she thought, "Oh, my God, I have no idea where he is."

Nancy and a friend heard that the Brooklyn Bridge was closed to pedestrian traffic and so headed toward the Manhattan Bridge. They were walking down Second Avenue and got near the United Nations when someone said the UN had been hit. She continued south toward the Manhattan Bridge, even though people covered in dust were now streaming north. Nancy had no cell phone and only the earlier page about getting home as her lodestar. Tony, in the meanwhile, made it through the dust to the Brooklyn Bridge but was turned back by police.[4] He too decided to keep walking north to the Manhattan Bridge, as that seemed the only avenue of escape to Brooklyn. As it turned out, he made it to the bridge first, crossed, and made it home. Nancy was able to borrow a cell phone when she was on the bridge and reached Tony at their apartment in Park Slope. The worst of their anxiety was over. Nancy reports that she saw many people, when they finally reached Brooklyn, get down on their knees and "kiss the ground. It was like Brooklyn was this haven."

At home, however, Nancy found Tony in a traumatic state. He was "stomping around here like a military man," furious at what had happened, still traumatized at the people he had seen jumping from the towers, unable to be affectionate, able only briefly to hug her. She and her girlfriend had a gin and tonic, took a walk later and then slept twelve hours. They apparently did not watch television. Tony, meanwhile, remained in his state of heightened anxiety and lay awake all night, still traumatized. He kept waiting for something else to happen, that "something else would fall," or in what he knew is a familiar trick of terrorists to set off one bomb to draw people into the scene and then explode the big bomb. That big bomb, Tony assumed, would be nuclear.

Nancy said, "I drank and Tony paced." Nancy had to go to work both Wednesday and Thursday at Citigroup to be sure "the dollar was stable, so the dollar wouldn't collapse." That focus on work kept her somewhat insulated from her own fears and anxieties. But Thursday, when she came home, a scene on television punctured her calm. Watching with her good friend, the camera "zoned in on a black Nine West shoe," a model she herself wore, and it dawned on her that, "Somebody like us died in that mess that day." She burst out crying. Tony, she said, did not really cry until the Super Bowl, when they did a tribute to 9/11. That was considerably later. One wonders what kind of psychological state he was in during the intervening four months.

Nancy and Tony determined to move up their plan to get pregnant. In a determined way, they wanted to do something "affirming and human." Tony at this point added, "It felt like the right thing to do at that time. There was something emotional about it. It is hard to rationalize honestly, because it was probably not the best time, but it was like a statement of confidence that everything was going to be fine." Nancy added, "I felt we should bring some joy into the world and that would be such a nice thing. I thought it would be nice to have something else to focus on."

CONCLUSION

Sherry felt that "Babies are the hope," while Nancy and Tony got pregnant after 9/11 because they wanted to do something "affirming and human." All the women in my sample felt such hope at varying degrees of consciousness. One has to get pregnant. It is often a difficult process. Pregnancy itself lasts for what seems forever. There are risks, both for the baby and the mother, and there is lots of pain in childbirth. But a woman, with her partner, gets pregnant for only one reason—to bring new life into the world. That is its only purpose. And that new life represents the symbolic immortality of its parents and, in a real sense, the future for all humanity. We cannot endure without new life continuously replenishing the old. A new baby is the future incarnate.

In the course of my work I talked with other women than those from Huggs Preschool about bringing life into the post-9/11 world. With these other women the topic entered our conversation spontaneously and at their initiative. When they did turn to the issue it had a decidedly different meaning for them. They felt the world was too full of evil and malevolence ever to bring new life into it. Miranda, the insurance executive who escaped from the south tower, voiced this attitude with great vehemence, shuddering somewhat as she said it. In her case, because she was well past menopause, the question was abstract, however meaningful. But for the beautiful young Felicia to have the same determination never to get pregnant felt in the interview as though she carried on her shoulders the full sadness of the world. How could she feel so strongly that she would never, ever get pregnant? Nearly a decade later, of course, it is impossible to know if she changed her mind and is now living in Queens with three lovely, black-eyed children. But in the moment, several months after 9/11, displaying many of the symptoms of posttraumatic stress disorder, huddling on the floor of a car if a plane flew over, Felicia set her jaw in grim resolve never to bring life into this dangerous world.

The women discussed in this chapter struggled at times with ambivalence about the timing of their decision to get pregnant. Jennifer escaped the city for Pennsylvania but felt paranoid there and vulnerable to another attack. She had always felt claustrophobic in the city (it was a "tin can"), fears exacerbated by 9/11. After the experience in the pizza parlor she felt for a time that it had been a clear mistake to get pregnant in September of 2001. Sandy felt we were going to be taken over after the disaster and "we would be put in concentration camps." She insisted her husband buy some cyanide pills. Sherry had to work all that fall in Lower Manhattan close enough to Ground Zero to be continuously sickened by the smell, and this as she was trying to get pregnant. Nancy finally felt the death on Thursday, September 13, watching TV. The camera zoomed in on an empty black Nine West shoe. She realized someone had worn it, and she burst into tears.

These frightened, vulnerable women, however, never stopped trying to get pregnant after 9/11. That September they were not all in the same place in their lives or in their relationship to their plans to have a baby then, but they shared deep fears and doubts about themselves, their future, and the safety of this world that they somehow overcame, or suppressed, in their decisions to get pregnant. They were full of contradictions. Most said their pregnancy had nothing much to do with 9/11, which they then contradicted in the course of the interview. None had a particularly rosy view of the future. The decision to become pregnant was perhaps only partly conscious but still an act of will to overcome doubts and push on, bracket their fears, and make a future happen.

PART 3
TEN YEARS OF EFFECTS

NG BROTHER

UCHE

14

THE SURPRISE OF IT ALL

MOST OF MY CONCLUSIONS about 9/11 lie embedded in the way I tell the stories of survivors and witnesses, the structure of the book itself, and the conceptual formulations that organize the narrative. Most of the emphasis is on the concrete and the human. I am most interested in how ordinary New Yorkers encountered the World Trade Center disaster, how they suffered from it, what their differences and similarities were, and how our world has been shaped by that event. This final section differs from the rest of the book, as it moves from the individual to the collective, from the immediate and palpable to the conceptual. This section is historical and philosophical, intentionally interpretive. I keep the lens in focus but pull back to wide angle.

I have constantly struggled to find hope in this book, which is its own form of resistance to atrocity. I sought to heal as I learned, imparting something to my respondents as they gave so much to me. I dug in odd corners of the landscape, as with the hidden children or the pregnant women, in large part to find some measure of hope for a human future. There is, however, nothing simple about the hope that I take from a close study of New York City and the World Trade Center disaster. I am not at all sure we are stronger as individuals or as a people for having survived 9/11. I rather think something broke in our souls and we have yet to find a way of healing. But 9/11 was surely the kind of peak experience and brush with death—the defining characteristic of the survivor—that prompts existential reflection. We may have learned, or tried to learn, something important in surviving the disaster.

One thing is certain: We cannot begin to understand the deeper meaning of 9/11 without contextualizing it historically. A disaster of this scale would have caused great distress and had enormous political, social, and economic consequences no matter when it occurred. It was large enough, the deaths sufficiently extensive, and the targets so symbolically compelling as to have wreaked havoc in our lives at any time the attacks might have taken place. But the disaster came at a very unusual moment in our national history, and our extreme reactions to it need to be understood in that context.

It all seemed like such an incredible surprise to Americans, though in retrospect we failed to heed many warnings. We directed our gaze elsewhere, resulting in a distraction fed by supreme self-confidence about our unique place in the world. That sense of exceptionalism had reached unusually fervid levels by the 1990's. We had won the Cold War and were dominant economically, going through a technological revolution in communications that was creating vast new sources of wealth and leading to loose talk of endless accumulation and recessions never returning. At least one cautious observer (Robert J. Shiller) worried about what he called the "irrational exuberance" of the age, though his voice was mostly drowned out by the cheering multitude.[1] The sense of overweening confidence extended from economics to politics, culture, society in general. We reigned unchallenged in the world, a new Rome, a superpower without match. We exalted in a grandiose sense of invulnerability. History, for some, had reached an end, a Hegelian synthesis of utopian proportions.

To attack America, to crumble those towers, and even penetrate the Pentagon, was so profoundly humiliating as to demolish in a heartbeat all that security. It literally rocked the ground of our being. We could not have been less prepared psychologically. The most common phrase used to describe the attacks by nearly all my respondents—"unbelievable"—was in some ways profoundly wrong. Terrorism was everywhere in the world before 9/11. Weapons of mass destruction were in our lives for half a century. An apocalyptic cult in Japan just six years earlier actively tried to initiate Armageddon. There was a very serious bombing of those same towers in 1993, and Osama bin Laden oversaw assaults on our embassies in Africa and the battleship *Cole* off Yemen in the late 1990's. We had even lived with home-grown terrorism in 1995. What Timothy McVeigh let loose was on a vastly smaller scale, but what he aspired to in the way of beginning an apocalyptic process was much greater. We ignored all this information, these signals and signs, out of excessive confidence, indeed arrogance. It is fair to say that before 9/11 we lacked an appropriate level of fear of the apocalyptic dangers in the world. After it we lived in a state of panic and hysteria.

America has a long history of feeling unique in the world, protected from the sins of others, able to endure while others perish. From the outset American exceptionalism blessed, or cursed, us with a sense of entitlement. The early settlers from England faced great hurdles in surviving rough conditions in the New World but felt that a divine purpose guided their efforts. Much of what drove them from England was religious conviction, bordering on fanaticism, a sense that the Church of England had truly lost its way and that the New World offered a path toward righteousness specially created for the elect. The phrase that became iconic to describe this sense of Puritan zeal was John Winthrop's adaptation of Matthew 5:14: "You are the light of the world. A city that is set on a hill cannot be hidden." The early settlers were creating a city on a hill. Winthrop said,

> For we must consider that we shall be as a city upon a hill. The eyes of all people are upon us. So that if we shall deal falsely with our God in this work we have undertaken . . . we shall be made a story and a by-word throughout the world. We shall open the mouths of enemies to speak evil of the ways of God. . . . We shall shame the faces of many of God's worthy servants, and cause their prayers to be turned into curses upon us til we be consumed out of the good land whither we are a-going.[2]

This sacred mission merged with more secular intentions that embraced the rich and abundant land, plentiful food, new freedoms. Dangers existed, of course, from the displaced Native Americans and the harsh conditions. But once the fragile communities became secure settlements and then villages and towns, a robust confidence spread throughout the land. The population grew and prospered, creating institutions that moved sharply away from the controls of Parliament. By the latter part of the eighteenth century the colonies even felt confident enough to declare independence from the Old World. A nasty war followed that easily could have been lost but for the military genius of George Washington and a democratic republic was founded, the first in the modern world, and, one could well argue, the first since the Roman Republic.

Henry Adams, writing in 1889, captured well the "hyperbole of enthusiasm" that Americans around 1800 gushed at foreign visitors:

> Look at my wealth! . . . See these solid mountains of salt and iron, of lead, copper, silver, and gold! See these magnificent cities scattered broadcast to the Pacific! See my cornfields rustling and waving in the summer breeze from ocean to ocean, so far that the sun itself is not high enough to mark where the distant mountains bound my golden seas! Look at this continent of mine, fairest of created worlds, as she lies turning up to the sun's never-failing caress her broad and exuberant breasts, overflowing with milk for her hundred million children! See how she glows with youth, health, and love![3]

By the time Alexis de Tocqueville visited the United States in the 1830's, Americans were fully confident that they owned the future. He did not disagree, and in fact came up with the phrase "American Exceptionalism." He felt the new republic was qualitatively different from all other nations of the world (which for him meant the countries of Europe). Its experiment with democracy singled it out for special attention. De Tocqueville was most concerned with the contrast between the feudal and hierarchical institutions of most European states with the values of liberty, egalitarianism, individualism, populism, and laissez-faire that prevailed in America. Much of his concern with America, in fact, was an indirect criticism of his native France, though in the process his trenchant observations have shaped American consciousness in fundamental ways.

At the heart of American exceptionalism was a military might that evolved over the centuries from the fragile vulnerability of the Puritans in relation to the Native Americans, to complete control of the continent in the nineteenth century, through a precarious half-century of Cold War with the Soviet Union, to absolute global dominance after about 1990. Much of what helped create the new country's sense of security after the end of the eighteenth century was the absence of any fear of attack from abroad. Many reflected on the way territorial isolation enhanced American security but none more enthusiastically than Abraham Lincoln. In his 1838 Young Men's Lyceum speech, he argues that we face no threat of foreign invasion. "All the armies of Europe, Asia and Africa combined," he says, "with all the treasures of this earth (our own excepted) in their military chest; with a Bonaparte for a commander, could not by force, take a drink from the Ohio, or make a track on the Blue Ridge, in a trial of a thousand years." Lincoln instead feared domestic unrest (the "mobocratic spirit") that will loosen the people's attachment to our democratic institutions and cause the emergence of a dictator. It is an analysis that seems almost quaint after 9/11.[4]

American exceptionalism did have a dark side. Violence was rampant on the frontier, and elsewhere. Millions of Africans lived in North American slavery (some 10 to 12 million in all, 3.5 million actively enslaved in the United States by 1860) because they were deemed inferior, and it was both profitable and convenient. God, it was argued, sanctioned expansion (Manifest Destiny, first named in 1845 almost in passing), which led to the final destruction of Native Americans. And we clothed such violence in hypocritical and self-righteous rhetoric. Lincoln noted ironically that Americans were the "almost chosen" people, and G. K. Chesterton called America a "nation with a soul of a church." Sanctimonious self-righteousness provided cover for much brutality in the name of high-minded idealism.[5]

Some observers have argued recently that a new form of American exceptionalism took shape in the last half century or so. Michael Ignatieff, for example, pays particular attention to the contradictions, even the confusions, in the way American exceptionalism has worked in practice since World War II. For example, he notes the profound contradiction between the promotion by the United States around the world of religious freedom, gender equality, democratic rights, the abolition of slavery (with its support of rights-abusing regimes), attempts to scuttle the International Criminal Court, unilateral military action, failure to ratify crucial international treaties, and blithe disregard for United Nations bodies that criticize aspects of American law and practice. Ignatieff notes three insidious principles that have come to govern American exceptionalism. One is what he calls exemptionalism, or the insistence by America to have the right to withdraw from any international treaty or convention, even one it has initiated, if it feels that participation could in any way threaten U.S. interests. Second are the double standards the United States claims the right to impose. It routinely judges others more harshly than itself. Finally, American exceptionalism claims a right to legal isolationism. There can be no foreign law, international convention, or precedent that can in any way contravene the Constitution. One might also consider this last feature of American exceptionalism a form of constitutional fundamentalism.[6]

Ignatieff names four types of explanation for American exceptionalism that have been offered. First, realists stress our global power since 1945. The United States simply can, and perhaps should, dominate the world through its vast military might and democratic institutions that serve as a model for the world. Second, a strong messianic cultural tradition has long stirred an American sense of uniqueness in the world, and the resulting sense of destiny to impose that vision on others. Global moral leadership comes naturally to Americans. Third, a definite sense of exceptionalism is attached to American institutions. Judicial review, for example, is a striking aspect of American democracy that others envy and leads often to an American sense of superiority. There has also been remarkable political stability in the United States that contrasted sharply with European wars and internal divisions in the twentieth century. Finally, in the last half century America has defined itself morally as more conservative than much of the developed world. Many of those beliefs are also based in evangelical religious traditions that shape attitudes toward abortion, family values, women's rights, and gay marriage.

Stanley Hoffmann, in turn, argues that such contradictions left America with a "lofty feeling of democratic superiority and universal relevance" that went along with sometimes crass and violent pursuit of national interest. The expressions of American exceptionalism have also taken two forms. One is Wilsonian isolationism; the other is a crusading and militant project of exporting American ideals, of building democracy globally. In one case the emphasis was on protecting. The emphasis in the other was on projecting what made the United States unique.

The new exceptionalists had antecedents before 9/11. The Committee on the Present Danger began in 1950 to project a more powerful foreign policy and then revived after 1976 to shape evolving conservative (and assertive) policies during the Carter administration. After the Gulf War, which left those on the right feeling that an opportunity for American dominance of the Middle East had been lost, the key figures of those who would shape Bush policies began to emerge. The most radical of all, Dick Cheney, wrote the Defense Planning Guidance draft of 1992, which had to be toned down before it could be published and which served as a preliminary statement of what became the Bush Doctrine after 9/11. Cheney's grandiose ideas imagined a military dominance of the world and called for unilateral action, preemptive strikes, and a strong enough nuclear arsenal to deter nuclear programs elsewhere, including Russia and China. As Hoffmann puts it, "Exceptionalism now meant being, remaining, and acting as the only superpower, and its substance was capabilities, not ideals and missions."

This new exceptionalism privileged the Constitution as the law of the land and eschewed recognition of any higher law, whether divine or global (e.g., United Nations, international treaties, torture conventions). It was a form of benevolent imperialism that some said carried with it the responsibility to keep world order, though the United States had the unilateral right to reject international law if it felt it interfered with its mission. The new exceptionalism created its own sheriffs to patrol the world according to the ethic of *High Noon*. And, finally, those who defined this new exceptionalism argued forcibly for a special relationship with Israel, whose interests and identity merged with those of the United States. It was all, of course, exceedingly grandiose, but as Hoffmann says, the program was also "breathtakingly unrealistic," bound to come up against countervailing public opinion, complex world pressures, and the needs of multilateralism to cope with issues like the environment.

Before 9/11 the new exceptionalism was a "doctrine in search of a cause," the brainchild of a few conservative intellectuals on the outside of power. The election of George W. Bush in 2000 brought many—Dick Cheney, Donald Rumsfeld, Paul Wolfowitz, Douglas Feith, for example—to high positions in the new administration but without the opportunity to implement their schemes. The attacks of 9/11, however, changed that almost overnight, politically dropping like manna from heaven. The climate in the country now affirmed the division of the world into us versus them, into an aggrieved superpower facing global terrorists who needed to be eliminated, into a world of good struggling against evil. The new exceptionalism found welcome soil in which to grow.

THE CULTURE OF FEAR

The most important aftereffects of 9/11 are ones that have become so woven into the social fabric that they lie outside the parameters of this book. We quickly got into the war in Afghanistan before a month was out and then stumbled into Iraq in March of 2003. Both wars continue, though in different ways from what was expected at the outset, and they will probably last to some degree for many years to come. The story of these wars has been well told in some excellent books, with many more sure to appear as the wars themselves change and evolve. I have no intention of summarizing those tales. It would waste the reader's time to summarize them here. I would only assert the obvious point that neither war would have been imaginable without 9/11. The decision to invade Iraq preemptively may seem outside the direct effects of 9/11—until one recalls the aggressive marketing effort by the Bush administration to link the tragedy of the disaster with Saddam Hussein. The false claims for weapons of mass destruction in Iraq only gained traction with the American public because it was a well-established piece of propaganda that Saddam Hussein was a monster who bore direct responsibility for the attacks.

The aftereffects of 9/11 in terms of an enduring culture of fear, along with the fact that we have been a nation at war for most of the last decade, similarly created an environment in which surveillance has increased, personal liberties have been curtailed, and governmental and police agencies have vastly expanded their powers in areas of "coercive interrogation" and practices such as rendition. Again, my task is not to detail these developments, but to note the necessary and sufficient basis for them in the effects of 9/11. The Patriot Act passed Congress overwhelmingly after the attacks and was then signed into law by President Bush on October 26, mainly because the language from a similar effort in 1996 had failed. Its provisions were merely resurrected. Lawyers in the White House added legal cover for vastly extending the powers of the CIA to interrogate harshly and for entities such as the National Security Agency (NSA), whose budget dwarfs that of the CIA, to extend their reach, both abroad *and* domestically. Such developments fed on themselves and a synergy began in which the more fear there was in the land, the more controls were imposed. To justify those controls more fear had to be generated, which easily emerged from a nation at war and countless terrorists vowing to destroy us.

The world we live in, however deep and abiding its antecedents, began with 9/11.

15

ON TRAUMA AND ZONES OF SADNESS

KAI ERIKSON DISTINGUISHES natural disasters of the past from what he calls a "new species of trouble" in the contemporary world. He emphasizes two factors. First, such new trouble is caused by other human beings, which makes it hurt in special ways and generates feelings of "injury and vulnerability from which it is difficult to recover." Hiroshima and the Holocaust, as well as 9/11, are striking examples of such a new species of trouble. Each has effects beyond and very different from the havoc wreaked in earthquakes, floods, and other forms of natural distress, even though often what appears to be "natural" can be devastatingly destructive precisely because of the ways poverty and other decidedly unnatural factors place human beings in unsafe places without adequate safeguards against disaster.

Erikson's second point is even more compelling. The most important aspect of the new disasters, he says, is when they involve some form of toxic contamination. Toxic disasters violate all rules of plot. Some of them have clearly defined beginnings, such as the explosion that signaled the emergency at Chernobyl or the sudden moment of realization that opened the drama of Bhopal. Others begin long years before anyone senses that something is wrong, as was the case at Love Canal. But they never end. Invisible contaminants remain a part of the surroundings, absorbed into the grain of the landscape, the tissues of the body, and, worst of all, the genetic materials of the survivors. An all-clear is never sounded. The book of accounts is never closed.

The 9/11 book of accounts is such a volume. The toxic air from the collapse of those towers continues to compromise the futures of countless thousands in ways that will never be fully known. Such never-ending suffering creates unique forms of mourning. Survivors struggle with physical sensations such as hollowness in the stomach, a lump in the throat, tightness in the chest, and at times other bodily sensations such as aching arms; feelings of sadness, anger, guilt, and self-reproach; thoughts of disbelief, confusion, and preoccupation; often a sense of the presence of the deceased, or paranormal kinds of experiences; behaviors such as sleep or appetite disturbances, absentmindedness, social withdrawal, and loss of interest in life; dreams of the deceased, crying, and social difficulties in interpersonal relationships; and a spiritual searching for a sense or meaning that may involve hostility toward God and a questioning of one's value framework.

Such mourners may live an entire life of grief, letting the sadness of loss become chronic and permanent. But what exactly is being mourned? Robert Jay Lifton answers:

He mourns, first of all, for family members and for others who had been close to him. And he mourns . . . for the anonymous dead. But he mourns also for inanimate objects and loss symbols—for possessions, homes, streets he had known, beliefs that have been shattered, a way of life that has been "killed." In sum, he mourns for the own former self, for what he was prior to the intrusion upon it of death and death conflicts. For what has been taken from him . . . is this innocence of death, and particularly of grotesquely demeaning death.[1]

Lifton is describing here the psychological experience of mourning by survivors of Hiroshima. Their entire world—and their bodies—was shattered in ways that also describe 9/11.

Such collective grief brimming with bereavement overload turns modern disasters into public tragedies. The vast accumulation of private events by their very magnitude overloads all survivors and witnesses. The synergy between private stories transforms an event into a collective experience of historical significance. In that process of turning private into public, the individual participant, whether as a survivor or a witness, blends the personal and collective in unusually complex ways. The experience of the individual inevitably dominates one's own personal sense of tragedy and loss, but that experience is in turn aggravated and intensified by the sense that personal experience blends with the larger collective response. Similarly, the enormous suffering of the public tragedy reverberates in the mind of the individual in a way that intensifies a personal sense of loss.

The twentieth century was a kind of extended public tragedy that provided the background for 9/11. It was a century of violence, one in which two gigantic world wars were fought and the first wholesale modern Holocaust inflicted on European Jews (though there was an important modern antecedent in the mass killing of the Armenians by the Turks in 1915). Since midcentury there have been hundreds of conventional wars, along with several genocides, fought in the shadow of the great new source of anxiety, nuclear and other ultimate weapons. The scale of death in the twentieth century, as well as its form, surpassed anything remotely like it in previous centuries, with the exception of the death of some 40 percent of the population in Europe as a result of the Black Plague between 1348 and 1351, and perhaps some of the radical changes in human and environmental history many thousands of years ago that have left only a cursory and fragmentary archeological record.

We also live in our imagination as survivors of future tragedies. In this sense we are all survivors of future nuclear holocaust. Nor is nuclear destruction the only image that haunts our imagination. Mass deaths resulting from wars and terrorism are constantly evoked in our movies and stories and songs, for example, which also need to be considered in the context of a rapidly expanding human population. Standing at some 2.5 billion in the middle of the twentieth century, the world's population in the early twenty-first century has surpassed 7 billion and could reach 10 billion by around 2050. A large conventional war in Asia could make the dying of World War II seem paltry. A small nuclear bomb set off by terrorists in a major city could kill or maim tens of millions. And biological terrorism, not to mention a pandemic from new diseases in an overcrowded world, could take its victims by the scores or even hundreds of millions. And all that exists in tandem with nuclear holocaust, the gold standard of apocalypse.

Perhaps we need stories to prepare us psychologically for such a future, which gain new meaning in an age of mass communications, especially television but also increasingly with the chat rooms, elaborate Web sites, and streaming video on the Internet. Through such sophisticated means of communication we experience the immediacy of disaster in the minutest of details, along with its violence and human suffering. Abu al-Zarqari crossed a line when, during the Iraq War, he regularly showed beheadings on the Internet as part of his ferocious battle against Americans and their proxies. In the same way, mass communications make the most intimate details of human suffering during disaster available to our consciousness in ways never before experienced. The actual and the imaginative merge in newly significant ways.

ZONES OF SADNESS

The concept of the zones of sadness that is the central organizing principle of this book challenges many assumptions about trauma that prevail in psychology and psychoanalysis. Gaining a proper understanding of trauma has been a hard-fought victory. In its original Greek meaning, "trauma" meant injury to some physical part of the body, a meaning that endures in trauma centers in hospitals or close to battle zones in war. But in the latter part of the nineteenth century, as result of the labors of thinkers such as Jean-Martin Charcot, Sigmund Freud, but especially Pierre Janet, trauma came to mean what William James called a "wound to the spirit" (which in turn adapted a new meaning from Hegel's line in *Phenomenology of Spirit*, "The wounds of the spirit heal, and leave no scars behind"). Trauma became not only something exterior but interior, physical but also psychological. For many reasons, including the triumph of Freud over Janet in the clinical realm for the next five decades, the significance of this new understanding of trauma was all but lost. History, however, forced psychological observers to recover past insights. Survivors of the Holocaust and Hiroshima clearly had wounds to the spirit that could not be explained adequately except in terms of a psychology of trauma. As it turned out, a full appreciation of these collective traumas from World War II was delayed. It took the Vietnam War and people like Lifton working with antiwar vets to bring psychiatry back to the understanding of trauma that had been clear to people like Pierre Janet and William James, and only then in the political context of a women's movement beginning to recover the vast and suppressed world of sexual abuse of girls.[2] In the 1970's the insights about trauma in psychiatry and related fields finally stuck with the formulation of the idea of posttraumatic stress disorder (PTSD), which was first described in the 1980 edition of the *Diagnostic and Statistical Manual of Mental Disorders*.

For astute observers of trauma such as Cathy Caruth, Bessel van der Kolk, Beatrice Beebe, Rachel Yehuda, and others, the new understanding allowed for a much more nuanced appreciation of historical events such as the Holocaust while at the same time changing the clinical approach to those suffering from abuse and other horrors in childhood.[3] Many clinicians, however, continue to struggle with the tension between present and past, because they are so accustomed to think of interior wounds to the spirit in terms that locate them vertically in the self. Adult forms of trauma from this perspective are understood theoretically as psychologically derivative, more retraumatizations than authentic experiences in the moment. Kevin, the psychoanalyst, for example, intentionally insulated himself from experiencing the effects of the disaster. He refused to linger on the street to watch the burning towers and later never watched television. On that Tuesday he went about his business, had lunch with a friend, went to a doctor for a check-up, and later saw his patients. But in time as he listened to his patients talk about it, the disaster intruded on his soul. He opened himself to its symbolic connection with his terrible experience of being burned as a child. Then he suffered in ways that made 9/11 truly transformative for him.

The zones of sadness, in other words, must be understood from one point of view as moral and psychological spaces in the self. Physical proximity to the scenes of death in many cases had nothing to do with the traumatic reactions of New Yorkers to the disaster. Maria, my very vulnerable patient who lived in Queens, might as well have been in Paris or Timbuktu in terms of her experience of 9/11, but when the smell of death wafted in her window on Wednesday, September 12, she fell apart in ways that have taken her years to recover from. Analogously, the responses of many in zone 1 were shaped by earlier traumas. There is no question that Deirdre was especially shaken by her encounter with death on 9/11 because it called up the profound sense of loss she had felt at her early experience of her parents' divorce, not to mention her school-age witnessing of a man being run over by a bus. Felicia, in turn, had not really recovered from the sudden and tragic death of her father when she was sixteen, when suddenly a few years later bodies were falling around her on that Tuesday morning. The relevant early experiences of Miranda are less clear, but in theory no one could have reacted with such terror to a disaster like 9/11 but for early trauma that makes it impossible in the moment to call forth one's range of resources to respond to death in ways that are painful but not debilitating.

There is definitely wisdom to such a perspective. It is now a given—indeed, so obvious as to border on being a cliché—that the past shapes the way we give meaning to the present, and specifically that early trauma can determine how we react to scenes of death, even from a great distance and necessarily symbolized, as on television. As both a historian and a psychoanalyst, I am keenly aware of the relevance of that idea. The hand of the past, whether individual or collective, can be heavy. It would be psychologically superficial not to dwell at length on the concrete ways the responses of survivors to their death encounters connect with earlier, especially traumatic, experiences. Besides, the great variety of human responses to 9/11 shows time and again how such diversity can only be explained in reference to the specificity of the individual's early experience.

But as I have argued, the horizontal or topographic dimension of the human experience of 9/11 (and perhaps of most other disasters and extreme historical events) shaped the broad contours of New Yorkers' experience of the World Trade Center disaster. The trauma of 9/11 was visited upon us as adults and transcended, though it also expressed, early experience.[4] As I have tried to show in great detail in this book, this horizontal dimension of survivors' experiences furthermore radiated out from Ground Zero in ways that can be mapped into discernible spaces, from the scenes of death, to the areas where all but death was witnessed, to the areas with minimal visibility but pervasive fear, and finally, to the universal experience of virtual reality on television. In these spaces New Yorkers had their world collapse in terror in ways that had little to do with earlier trauma but can be best understood within the discernible topographic template of the zones of sadness. Nothing could prepare survivors, witnesses, participants, or onlookers to hold off that dread, nor can their reactions be explained (and minimized) as mere byproducts of earlier experience, more epiphenomenal than actual. The new species of trouble demands our attention for exactly what it is.[5]

Two important qualifications of the strictly spatial, or topographic, nature of the experience of 9/11 in New York need to be kept in mind. First, people were moving all over the place that day, into and out of zones, trying to escape or simply to find loved ones. Felicia ran from the Marriott Hotel to find her boyfriend in Battery Park City. After the second plane hit the south tower she migrated with him south to the tip of Manhattan and around to the FDR Drive, where they walked north past the United Nations and into midtown, thus moving through three zones of sadness. Sanford ran furiously north at first to escape what he feared would be a tower falling over on him, then turned west toward the Brooklyn Bridge and what he felt was the safety of Brooklyn. Eric entered the subway some distance from Ground Zero on his Odyssean journey to find his wife and child on the Upper East Side. Many in midtown were evacuated from office buildings because of bomb threats or simply left in fear of further attacks, fleeing across the East River bridges— Brooklyn, Manhattan, or Queensboro—or trekking north on the avenues to escape the dangers of Manhattan. It was a city on the move, with millions temporarily displaced, crossing zones as they sought safety in distance from the World Trade Center and the possibility of further attacks on Manhattan.

Second, over time the zones of sadness tended to collapse into each other. In New York as the 100 days unfolded, the felt experience of the disaster tended to collapse the often radical initial differences in the experience of those in the zones, even though time never erased the way survivors lived with pain and suffering as opposed to those less exposed to the death. Miranda, Deirdre, and Henry have undoubtedly carried their trauma forward into their lives in ways that have not been matched by Eric or others (including myself). Those working on the pile, furthermore, have carried forward the special burden of *increased* physical suffering from their exposure to the toxic air at Ground Zero the longer they live. Nothing is inevitable, but these workers are vastly more at risk than the general population for developing serious lung disease, cancer, and other ailments.

In Hiroshima as well, the suffering moved outward from Ground Zero but also forward in time and into the lives of subsequent generations. No story better illustrates this dimension of the survivors of the atomic bomb in Hiroshima than that of Sadako Sasaki, a two-year-old girl living a mile from Ground Zero who on August 6, 1945, was filled with radiation from the bomb. Ten years later, dying of leukemia, Sadako began folding small paper cranes in response to a Japanese myth that folding a thousand such cranes grants you a wish. Hers was to live. There are various accounts of how many cranes she actually folded. A popular child's book, *Sadako and the Thousand Paper Cranes*, says that she only folded 644 cranes and that her friends folded the remaining cranes that were put into her coffin when she died. Sadako's brother, however, Masahiro Sasaki, said that she folded more than 1,300 tiny cranes before she died. The actual number hardly matters. Sadako is emblematic of the delayed effects of the bomb, a fact of life in the nuclear age that haunts everyone at some level of consciousness. She is also, however, a symbol of courage in the face of death. Paper cranes have become a powerful and iconic image of hope for the antinuclear movement.

IMPACT ON NEIGHBORHOODS

The most intriguing finding in the first telephone study in Manhattan of the traumatic effects of 9/11, led by Sandro Galeo and conducted between five and nine weeks after the disaster, was the anomaly of heightened levels of PTSD in the Dominican community of Washington Heights.[6] Why should a community so far from Ground Zero have been so powerfully affected by the disaster, especially in contrast with the contiguous African-American neighborhood of Harlem, which did not report high levels of PTSD? That difference in the data suggests some hidden levels of trauma in the Dominican community before 9/11 that have not been explored by any researcher before or since.[7] That unanswered question, however, raises a larger issue of the geography, indeed the ecology, of urban suffering in New York City. It is not a question I can explore in great depth, as that would (and should) be the topic of another book, but to note its significance as a conceptual issue is relevant for my concerns in this study. The zones of sadness are topographical regions extending out from Ground Zero that overlap but are not defined by neighborhoods. The specific vulnerabilities—and strengths—of defined neighborhoods contributed to shaping the experiences of survivors.

It was immediately apparent after 9/11 that a number of neighborhoods in the city were unevenly impacted. Battery Park City was devastated and mostly evacuated; Tribeca was less physically damaged, but many residents were required to leave their homes for prolonged periods; and Chinatown had its tourist and garment economies virtually eliminated, with huge consequences for the lives of scores of thousands of people. At the same time, parts of the Upper East Side continued to function as if nothing had happened in the city, though the lives of many, such as Eric, who worked in the financial district, were turned upside down. Nothing about a given neighborhood determined the psychological experience of survivors who dwelled within it, nor, conversely, did living in far-distant and privileged neighborhoods insulate anyone from suffering, but it mattered where you lived on 9/11, not just where you were as the disaster unfolded.

BATTERY PARK CITY AND TRIBECA

Battery Park City, located immediately to the west of the World Trade Center, was completely evacuated on 9/11.[8] Felicia fled with her boyfriend to Queens. Others left on foot up the West Side Highway, while others, along with tens of thousands of Lower Manhattanites, were ferried to New Jersey. Fires spread from falling debris, and the thick, smoky cloud from the collapse of the two towers completely enveloped the neighborhood. Every window, apartment, block, and street lay covered in ash that would linger for many weeks and months. Most people who lived in Battery Park could not retrieve personal possessions for several weeks and could only return to their homes in late October. Even then many wisely stayed away for many months, and when they did return they faced a large-scale cleanup of their apartments.[9]

The distress and dislocation in Battery Park City also endured for many months and even years after 9/11. In their great fear, most people left the neighborhood with nothing, which significantly aggravated their sense of loss. Their financial, physical, and emotional security collapsed with those towers. Many felt abandoned and ignored—not an uncommon survivor experience—a feeling that lingered for years and contributed to much of the noisy conflict with the city and other officials during the cleanup and recovery process.

Tribeca (*tri*-angle *be*-low *Ca*-nal Street) was the second closest residential community to the World Trade Center site after Battery Park City. It was only slightly less affected. For the most part, debris did not fall that far from the burning and then collapsing towers, but the cloud of toxic ash descended over the apartments and businesses in Tribeca as in Battery Park City (though the further north one was and the closer to Canal Street, the less total was the effect of the ash). More than 1,000 residents in Tribeca were evacuated and an unknown number left voluntarily.[10] A small number of residents of Tribeca refused to evacuate, because the residential community was not as close to Ground Zero and they thought they could manage. Still, the damage was extensive, the toxic ash was everywhere, and the visible scenes at Ground Zero kept the disaster in the forefront of everyone's imagination.

Both communities were therefore severely impacted by the World Trade Center disaster. In both many saw the planes hit, the bodies fall from the sky, and the towers collapse. In both there was mass evacuation and the dust and debris from the collapsed towers settled into the sinews of the neighborhood. Both were cut off from access to the rest of the city, as they lay sequestered in the "frozen zone" below Canal Street. Businesses, which were much more highly developed in Tribeca, were in a state of disrepair and most had to be shut down for weeks afterward because only those involved in the cleanup at the pile or security personnel were allowed in the frozen zone (and the few residents who refused to be evacuated). "Most businesses were shuttered," comments Philip Kasinitz and his fellow researchers, "and both foot and vehicular traffic were severely curtailed. For months after the attack, both areas were blocked, first by debris, then by the demolition and cleanup efforts. Residents had to decide whether to return to homes now caked in what many feared was toxic dust."[11] In these two upscale communities in the heart of New York City, where a third to a half worked in lucrative jobs in the financial district (and many in the World Trade Center itself), most were made homeless by the disaster.

The two neighborhoods, however, recovered at quite different rates and in strikingly different ways that would shape their long-term development. Battery Park City was filled with modern high-rise residences, beautiful communal spaces consisting of parks and playgrounds, and small-scale office buildings (except for the Financial Center). There was no street-level commerce, which meant shopping had to be done in the World Trade Center. But despite its location next to Lower Manhattan, one of the busiest areas in the world, Battery Park City was strangely, even hauntingly, isolated and odd. Despite the fact that it was a planned community on new land created from landfill during the construction of the World Trade Center in the 1970's, there were only three pedestrian bridges into it over the West Side Highway, which was itself a major thoroughfare separating the community from the life of New York. Once inside the neighborhood, it was also difficult to navigate and figure out directions from the maze of fancy apartment buildings that all looked curiously alike. Philip Kasinitz and his colleagues comment, "How public is public space, when it has been embedded in a context that raises such formidable social barriers that the masses of ordinary working people would feel uncomfortable entering?"[12]

The secluded, private nature of Battery Park City both attracted and deterred people from entering. Its stellar location with close proximity to the

World Trade Center and the financial district was its major selling point, but many were also attracted by the very isolation from the chaos of city life that most try to transcend but connect within organic communities. The people who lived in Battery Park City were mostly young, ambitious, successful, and often single. The neighborhood thrived economically but never managed to create much of a sense of community before 9/11. It was insular and had the quality of a suburb within the nation's largest city.

After the 100 days of the disaster, Battery Park City residents very slowly began to move back into their homes, though a significant if undetermined number abandoned them and moved elsewhere. Those who returned, however, found recovery difficult, precisely because the insularity of the neighborhood before 9/11 impeded coherent community efforts at recovery. Because so many people left the neighborhood permanently and because it was so close to Ground Zero, apartment prices dropped precipitously, further undermining community cohesion. In addition, tourists were suddenly everywhere, bombarding the once very proudly private community. Residents wanted a say in everything that was taking place at Ground Zero, which they were seldom granted, and disliked the physical changes surrounding the community. A new social cleavage also opened up between newcomers, who flocked to the neighborhood because of the low rents, and the survivors, who felt these new outsiders were birds of prey feeding on the carrion.

All these difficulties, however, created space for a good deal of positive interactions and a new sense of community. For the first time since it was created, after 9/11 residents of Battery Park City began to place more emphasis on connecting with neighbors and building communal institutions. People began to use the public spaces more and created environments of communication and dialogue with people they had never tried to get to know before. Groups were formed in public spaces everywhere and a tight-knit community began to emerge after the attacks and in the years that followed. "From the time they returned," comments Setha Low, those living in Battery Park City "interacted much more in the plazas, streets and parks of Battery Park City. . . . It is more or less a real community."[13]

Tribeca's very different history before 9/11 shaped its response afterward. The creation of the World Trade Center in the 1970's transformed the organic but somewhat seedy neighborhood just to its north. A host of small businesses left the area, basically driven out by the surge of new economic activity. They left behind spacious, if rundown, warehouses that were then converted into living spaces with tall ceilings and large loft-style rooms. Tribeca quickly attracted young professionals working in the financial district who sought to take advantage of the economic development opportunities. As the neighborhood modernized, more and more buildings were refurbished and the population exploded. Suddenly, Tribeca sported theaters, trendy bars, and five-star restaurants.

The seriousness of the impact of 9/11 on Tribeca should not be underestimated, but once people could clean their apartments and move back in, the neighborhood quickly recovered its previous vitality. As Kasinitz and his colleagues note, "Most business owners of Tribeca applauded efforts to reestablish the neighborhood's place as a trendsetter in the commercial and cultural life of the city. If anything, the economic devastation that followed the attack and the recovery efforts accelerated trends that had been well under way for decades."[14] Tribeca revamped its efforts to build community and changed its focus toward public events—such as Robert De Niro's Tribeca Film Festival, which began in 2006—that were intended to bring outsiders into the community. The area, in other words, never developed the debilitating survivor mentality that hobbled Battery Park City for so many years.

CHINATOWN

Chinatown, though further from Ground Zero than either Battery Park City or Tribeca, suffered massively from the disaster and took longer than either of the other neighborhoods to recover.

Chinatown, a vibrant "ethnic enclave community" located less than ten blocks from the World Trade Center, long consisted of Asian people from different countries, speaking many languages but residing harmoniously together. Business owners and workers did not need to learn more than a basic level of English. They were able to resist assimilation into mainstream society by maintaining their cultural identities and values, while coexisting within the larger social structure. Chinatown had long become a major tourist attraction in the city and its restaurants and trinket shops were known worldwide. But Chinatown also had a robust garment industry that employed large numbers of skilled but uneducated people who lived in cramped quarters with eight or nine people in one apartment, sleeping side by side on the floors. For many generations a pattern had been established. After residents began in Chinatown, gaining some skills and acquiring savings, along with citizenship, they moved up to more middle-class areas in Queens and Brooklyn.

Chinatown before 9/11 was thus a working-class neighborhood that was diverse and highly dynamic, one that gave people who were not trained to do more complex work the opportunity to get ahead in life and create a peaceful and cohesive community.

That all changed on September 11, 2001. For a full eight days, all vehicular and nonresidential pedestrian traffic was prohibited south of Canal Street.[15] Chinatown was essentially sealed off on all sides. Residents were harassed by police for proof of identify and some kind of verification of where they lived. Most could not access such documents, which were either unavailable or did not exist because they were being paid off the books in the restaurants or garment factories. It was a very tumultuous time of upheaval in this community.

The main streets that intersected and surrounded Chinatown—Broadway, the Bowery, Canal, and Lafayette streets—were designated checkpoints by the police because of their proximity to high-security areas such as City Hall, police headquarters, and the courthouses. These areas were virtually impenetrable for anyone other than designated federal or state officials. Not only were the streets closed off but the subway lines that serviced much of Chinatown, especially the N and R lines, were closed down. Margaret Chin reports that, "Certain sections of some streets (Bowery, Henry, and Madison streets) were not open until January 2002."[16] All streets south of 14th Street were initially declared a frozen zone, though on September 14th its northern boundary was moved south to Canal Street, right in the middle of Chinatown.[17]

The garment industry was devastated by the disaster and has barely recovered since. Before 9/11 most garment workers had stable jobs and were unionized; female workers even had flexible hours for tending children. Global developments in the garment industry, however, had already begun to undermine the viability of the model of actually producing clothes in the city. In the latter decades of the twentieth century, leading manufacturers discovered that design could be in New York but production outsourced, sometimes to fifteen or twenty different locations in China, Southeast Asia, India, or other developing nations. The garment industry was thus already declining before 9/11. The World Trade Center disaster dealt it a death blow.

In the first six to nine months after 9/11, government aid to Chinatown was essentially nonexistent, because much of the garment industry lay north of Canal Street.[18] Most shop owners and workers also received no aid, even when the disaster zone label was removed. Most who applied were rejected and never applied again, largely for cultural reasons and because so many of the restaurants operated off the books. Businesses were required to produce "formal paperwork" that they did not possess, and federal regulators, with their complicated rules and procedures, had no sympathy for the special needs of this immigrant and ethnic community.

A decade later, Chinatown is much changed and yet very familiar. The garment industry operates at a reduced level and will probably never recover to its levels before 9/11, though that is as much the result of global trends as of the disaster. Its workers for the most part have therefore migrated out of the community and into other jobs, while others from the neighborhood have returned to their homes, jobs, and community. The restaurant and trinket industry is thriving and tourists once again flock to the winding, crowded streets leading off from Canal. The recovery of Chinatown has also been aided by the economic revitalization of Tribeca and indeed all of Lower Manhattan. It is now a seamless web of city life from Chinatown all the way to Wall Street.

CONCLUSION

The nature of what we mean when we speak of trauma in connection with 9/11 is multifaceted and multilayered. The toxic nature of the debris from the collapse shaped the experience of New Yorkers in terms of what Kai Erikson has called the "new species of trouble," locating it within a context that includes disasters from Hiroshima to Bhopal. On a more immediate level, the experience of New Yorkers was shaped within the zones of sadness on that day; however, during the 100 days things merged into a more universal experience. The data from social scientific studies abundantly document how widespread the suffering was, as well as how it lingered into the future. Finally, yet another sectioning of experience occurred in the varied neighborhoods, especially in those close to Ground Zero. The New York experience of the World Trade Center disaster worked in many different ways and at different levels in the lives of its survivors.

16

HISTORICAL MEMORY OF THE DISASTER

WE CAN DEFINE STAGES in our collective experience of 9/11. On that day it washed over us with the force of a tsunami, and in the months that followed the death settled around and in us. Through it all we lived and relived the event on television, with each re-experience providing different meanings. Gradually, those who died came into some focus with their stories in the *New York Times*'s brilliant "Portraits of Grief," in endless television commentary that seemed mostly offbase, and in time with documentaries, articles, reports, and books that brought some coherence—and explained how 9/11 happened. Movies (mostly bad) were made and novels (a few good) were written, archives were organized, museums of artifacts were founded, and planning proceeded with rebuilding Ground Zero and the memorials in the footprints of the twin towers, surrounded by a memorial park.

Beyond New York the world changed visibly in the wake of 9/11. Wars were undertaken that continue unabated and the culture of fear rearranged crucial American institutions as we learned to live with torture abroad and surveillance at home.

In this tenth anniversary year we must also try to make sense of the meanings of the killing of Osama bin Laden on May 1, 2011 at the hands of Navy SEALs in their raid in Pakistan. The death of Al-Qaeda's leader, without whom there would have been no attacks on 9/11, marks the end of an era, even as it will probably not bring about the closure survivors so desperately need. But the killing of bin Laden ends the life of a masss murderer whose continued taunts at America created enduring pain for all who suffered on 9/11. It is right, and just, that Osama bin Laden is dead.

Historical memory of tragedy and disaster is not an even process, and it is never linear or predictable. The American memory of the Holocaust is instructive in this regard. As discussed brilliantly by Peter Novick in his 1999 book *The Holocaust in American Life*, the story of the Holocaust ebbed and flowed in American memory.[1] In roughly the two decades after the war, the events of the European destruction of the Jews lived almost entirely in the minds of survivors, and even then many sought as part of their survivor experience to suppress public or private discussion. It was not taught in schools and there were few reliable books on the subject. The first blockbuster book about Nazi Germany was William L. Shirer's *The Rise and Fall of the Third Reich*, published in 1960, and it devotes less than 3 percent of the narrative to the story of the Holocaust.

The Holocaust was not even clearly named. The Hebrew word, *shoah*, or calamity, to describe the destruction of the European Jews, was usually translated in the 1950's as "holocaust" by American journalists, Jewish and Gentile alike, and was only generally capitalized after the Eichmann trial in 1962. Some object to the term "Holocaust," which originally described a religious sacrifice in which a victim is consumed by fire, as a Christianization of Jewish suffering. But Novick notes that long before World War II "holocaust" had come to mean widespread destruction. Furthermore, *shoah* in the Hebrew bible is used in several places to describe punishments visited by God on the Jews—"hardly a more palatable connotation," Novick adds.

What is most surprising, however, is the story of how marketing the Holocaust in the United States was linked to strategic efforts by American and Israeli Jews to build support for Israel after the victorious 1967 war that led to a questionable occupation, and especially after the nearly disastrous 1973 Yom Kippur war that revealed Israeli military vulnerability. There was no master plan for the project to link the story of the Holocaust with support for Israel, nor did any single individual or group lead the effort (though Elie Wiesel played a unique role). The story of the Holocaust is, of course, compelling in and of itself. It is part of the story of twentieth-century violence that should be told and retold for countless generations. It is also true that the politics of Israel shaped a concerted effort to institutionalize Holocaust memory. Memorials were constructed; the magnificent Holocaust museum in Washington was built, mostly with federal money; and curriculums were written for schools throughout the land. Laws in many states even mandated that the Holocaust be taught in public schools. The results have been astounding. Compared with the amnesiac 1950's, in 1998 the American Jewish Committee conducted a survey of how Jews think about what it means to be Jewish in terms of various aspects of their identity. Remembrance of the Holocaust won hands down, trumping synagogue attendance, Jewish study, even observance of Jewish holidays. To be a Jew in America now means to know about and honor the memory of the Holocaust, something that reverberates beyond the Jewish community. To be culturally literate in the United States requires knowledge of the Holocaust, regardless of one's religion. Only the most obtuse and anti-Semitic deny the Holocaust. Awareness of other relevant historical experiences, such as the story of slavery and the African diaspora, fade into the shadows of memory by comparison.[2]

The World Trade Center disaster and the events of 9/11 constitute a very different historical event from the Holocaust, but the comparison in terms of memory highlights how unpredictable such things can be. But there are also survivor issues in general that complicate honoring the dead in any process of remembering. We would like to believe that trauma ennobles and that those who survive a terrible disaster become by definition better human beings, more humane and empathic, able to witness for the rest of us. Many 9/11 survivors, of course, were ennobled by their suffering, and our world would be spiritually bereft without them. Others got stuck in their experience of suffering and developed a kind of "exaggerated victim consciousness," an idea developed by Robert Jay Lifton from his work with survivors of Hiroshima. The psychological principle is that survivors tend to revel in their suffering and live off it, feeling that only in the immersion of being a victim can they be fully human. Miranda, for example, whom I interviewed some six months after the disaster, was so stuck in her experience of being a survivor that it had come to define her identity and would probably shape the rest of her life. She was completely self-absorbed in her suffering, unable to work, and had lost touch with friends and community, though she remained devoted to her sister and niece and nephew, who lived down the street from her. For her, and many others, after 9/11 survival required such an exaggeration of her victimization. Otherwise life was without meaning. It is precisely the experience of victimization for the survivors that keeps them from falling apart. It is their glue and salvation.

Understanding the psychology of the survivor helps explain much about the often contradictory aspects of collective memory. Survivors cannot afford ever to forget the details of the event that created their newly fashioned identities, even as those details fade into history and other disasters grab the attention of family, community, and nation. That flow of history, in fact, can be terrifying, as it threatens a basic sense of self. One kind of response among survivors to 9/11 has been to demand that the event be replayed and ritualized, even celebrated, in annual orgies of remembrance, in the sad and mournful televised reading of the names, for example, the telling of the tales in the media, the broadcast of new documentaries, and the publication of new books (such as this one!). Only in such public displays can victims feel fully human, though the irony of such ritualization borders on the tragic. It was the event itself that interrupted the flow of their lives and caused such suffering, but it is the event itself that must be honored for the victim to remain whole.

One important consequence of this traumatic conundrum is the sense that the world is fragile. Its tenuousness in turn confirms analogous fears in the self. One can barely hold on to things. This high degree of vulnerability becomes then part of the individual and social landscape. The evidence of vulnerability is everywhere in the self, but it also raises questions about what happens to the social fabric. Widespread trauma, as after 9/11, weakens social bonds that support the individual in communities that normally provide support, nurturance, and healing. The relationship becomes synergistic, as psychological fears weaken social bonds, which in turn make the world more dangerous in ways that feed individual distress.

These dilemmas confront the survivor with difficult, if not impossible, choices about what is proper and appropriate in the way of collective memory and memorialization. The responses to something as large as the World Trade Center disaster are as varied as all those who were part of it, directly or indirectly, as well as those far removed from it whose lives have been caught up in its wake. One could hardly begin to capture this diversity adequately, but it is of some value to note the plethora of survivor organizations that have arisen since 9/11 and the ways in which Americans, and especially New Yorkers, have chosen to memorialize the disaster. The argument I am making is that memory is both politically and psychologically essential for the survivor, but one cannot remember everything in a meaningful way. Competition results as survivors strive for money, place, and meaning, with the inevitable consequence that some people and ideas are crowded out or relegated to the sidelines of historical memory. It is a process that is both uplifting and dispiriting, in equal parts.

9/11 SURVIVOR AND FAMILY GROUPS

The most striking thing about the 9/11 survivor and family groups over the last decade is their incredible diversity, at times bordering on a fragmentation that has proven distressing to many survivors hoping for a more unified response to the disaster and plans for reconstruction at Ground Zero. In the first year or so after September 11th, the rise of survivor and family groups went viral, with every kind of group, representing every imaginable mission, springing into existence. Within a couple of years, however, many such organizations and the foundations and entities that supported them closed down, disappeared, or changed direction as funding streams for 9/11 programs dried up and donors turned to other causes. In New Jersey alone, a majority of the thirty organizations launched in 2001 ceased operating within two years or disappeared altogether. In some cases, the work stopped when the money was gone. While the major disaster funds ran out of cash, other sources simply turned their attention to other problems and programs.

The intense feelings aroused by the early planning for the rebuilding of the World Trade Center, however, especially between about 2003 and 2006, when most key decisions were made about the rebuilding and the design of the memorial, gave renewed purpose to many groups. The issue that occasioned a major coalition of groups after 2004 was the demand of all survivor and family associations that the footprints of the towers be treated as sacred space and serve as the location of whatever memorial finally emerged at Ground Zero. The initial plans of the developer, Larry Silverstein (who holds the lease to the site), the Port Authority (which owns the land itself), and the Lower Manhattan Development Corporation (which is charged by the state with the rebuilding) called for pushing ahead recklessly in the rebuilding over what is now, at last, widely recognized as a mass grave. After the victory by that informal coalition to force all the official parties involved to commit to a memorial in the footprints of the towers, many groups faded in significance and simply and quietly folded their operations, or, as with a key group of widows of firefighters led by Marian Fontana (9/11 Widows and Victims Association), merged with a larger organization (September 11 Families' Association). Others refocused their concerns and moved into wider areas of education, lobbying, and healing in broadly conceived ways, such as the September 11 Families' Association itself.

The diversity of 9/11 survivor and family groups, however, has remained characteristic over the years. Perhaps there is something American about pursuing such independent pathways. This suggests that the Red Cross as well as governmental groups, such as FEMA, got far too much attention after 9/11 for the vitality of survivor response. In other cultures and after other kinds of disasters, diversity of response is not always the pattern. Survivor groups from Hiroshima and Nagasaki, for example, once they coalesced, basically fell into three main associations. Gensuikyo, which was once assertively communist, and Gensuikin, allied with the socialists, in recent years have abandoned most of their political struggles as their members have aged and the world has changed. Hidankyo, the third major national survivors group, has always been less political. The scores of thousands of survivors of the nuclear attacks by the United States in August of 1945 tended to join one of these three groups in which they found some satisfaction in sharing their common experiences, finding support, and engaging in political work, especially that of seeking to prevent the spread of nuclear weapons in the world.

TWO MAJOR GROUPS

Among the 9/11 groups that have endured for the last decade, two stand out in the scope of their membership and range of their activities. One is the September 11 Families' Association. The mission statement of this group declares its goal as the support of victims of terrorism through communication, representation, and peer support. They seek to unite the September 11th community, present evolving issues, and share resources for long-term recovery. The group originated in the bonds between the very dynamic Marian Fontana, the widow of Dave, her firefighter husband, and Lee Ielpi, a retired fireman himself who lost his fireman son. The members of the September 11 Families' Association came to imagine what they called the Tribute Museum on 120 Liberty, just across from Ground Zero, sometime in 2004. The museum's building was completed in 2006. This well-conceived and well-designed museum, with two floors of informative exhibits, offers a place for tourists to learn about 9/11 until the much larger 9/11 museum next to the memorial and inside the sixteen-acre site of Ground Zero is finished. The staff of the September 11 Families' Association have also enlisted a large number of survivors and family members to give tours of the Ground Zero area throughout the day.

The September 11 Families' Association seeks to steer a nonpolitical course around potentially divisive issues, though not to take a position, for example, on an issue such as the mosque and community center at Park 51, which is itself a political stance. "Balance" can also result in blandness of message and mission, even as it assures funding across the political spectrum and participation in programs by people who would otherwise not agree on much outside of the horror of their 9/11 experience. In their curriculum materials—despite the fact that they proudly display one of Sadako Sasaki's tiny paper cranes in their museum—they surprisingly edit out the word "victim" in their description of survivors of Hiroshima, because some high school teachers find it unacceptable to think of the United States dropping the bomb as anything but a necessary and even desirable action of the military to save the lives of soldiers by quickly ending World War II. The left hand of the museum is not quite sure what its right hand is doing. The presence of the Sadako crane thus proudly displayed in the museum's collection suggests the important historical parallels between the survivor experiences of Hiroshima and those of 9/11, which the museum studiously avoids in its curriculum materials.

The second politically centrist and large survivor group that is focused mostly on a healing mission is Voices of September 11th. Mary Fetchet, who lost her son Brad on 9/11, is the key figure and co-chair of Voices of September 11th, an organization with more than 9,000 members that advocates and provides services for those affected by the events of September 11, 2001. Voices is one of the most active of all the survivor and family groups, and Fetchet advocated strenuously for the creation of the 9/11 Commission, testifying a number of times before Congress. In 2006, Voices launched the 9/11 Living Library Digital archive, to commemorate the lives and stories of September 11, 2001, and the February 26, 1993, World Trade Center bombing. Voices carries out workshops across the country with a specific healing mission; many social workers, Fetchet included, are members. The idea of archiving personal artifacts of a loved one who died is a form of memorializing that they believe can be healing for families.

FOCUSED MISSION

A second kind of 9/11 survivor and/or family group tends to be narrowly focused on a mission in relation to the disaster that represents a small but important piece of memory. There are, for example, groups from the families of those on the four planes, as well as small associations of British victims, or those from California, or from many other places. One such group—the Families of Flight 93—has played an important role in pushing for a meaningful memorial in Shanskville, Pa. In their lobbying, this group has coordinated its efforts over the years, amid some deep divisions, with the National Park Service, which has taken over responsibility for the site and developed a design for a memorial. It plans to open the first phase by the tenth anniversary. The group's informal motto is Todd Beamer's "Let's Roll," as the passengers stormed the cockpit to prevent the plane from hitting a target in Washington.

Another 9/11 group with a focused mission and much influence is the Skyscraper Safety Campaign (SSC), which was created by Sally Regenhard and her family in memory of Christian Michael Otto Regenhard, a twenty-eight-year-old probationary firefighter who died along with his entire fire company. The organization includes families of firefighters, emergency workers, and civilian victims of 9/11. Co-chairperson Monica Gabrielle lost her husband, Richard, who was an employee of Aon Corp., working on the 103rd floor of WTC 2. The SSC seeks to have a comprehensive investigation, with subpoena powers, of why the towers fell, to encourage better compliance with building and fire codes, to educate the public about the significance of following codes, and to ensure that all future construction by the Port Authority in the rebuilt Ground Zero is fully up to code and is as safe for workers inside—and first responders who come to save them in the event of an emergency—as is humanly possible.

The Pentagon families group coordinated its efforts with the highly efficient and hierarchical military to design and build their memorial. The key figure working with families and the military in this effort was Jim Laychak, who lost his brother David in the attack on the Pentagon. Laychak and other family members served on the families advisory group for the design committee that chose the final memorial from among 2,500 registrants. He not only worked to create the memorial, but also proved to be a tireless fundraiser. Given that the military was in charge, that memorial was completely constructed in early 2008 and dedicated on the seventh anniversary of 9/11. Some might consider the memorial clunky, in large part because the process moved so quickly and was not open to suggestions from a wide variety of sources. It is, however, a success story for the families of those who died there on 9/11.

Other organizations should also be noted briefly: September's Mission, a foundation dedicated to building a memorial park; the FealGood Foundation, to lobby for those first responders who have now begun to develop health issues from their 9/11 experiences; the WTC Survivors' Network after 9/11, to join those who felt alone and isolated; United Family Group, Inc., whose mission is to help families but also to develop curriculum materials about 9/11 and terrorism for schools (which led to the name change from United Family Group, Inc., to the September 11th Education Trust); and Families of September 11th, which seeks to aid families of 9/11, especially children, to reach out to victims of terror around the world, and to lobby for national policies that will protect the nation against further terrorist attacks.

POLITICALLY ENGAGED GROUPS

A number of groups, as one might expect, have turned their focus toward politically conservative causes. Many have shown firm support over the years of the George W. Bush presidency for the wars in Afghanistan and Iraq, for the increased powers of surveillance, and even for measures such as the program of torture, rendition, and other abuses of civil rights that became so common in the Bush years. The 9/11 Families for a Safe and Strong America, whose motto is "In the War on Terror, there is no place to run from here," for example, represents the kind of small, politically conservative families' group that in this case appears to be run by some firefighters in Philadelphia who have a tenuous link to 9/11 itself. There have been many such groups in the last decade. Most have lasted only a short while and would not seem to have the vitality or sense of mission to continue very long.

Two of the most interesting organizations, both family groups, have maintained their commitment to nonviolence, tolerance, and peace, despite the conservative drumbeat of most 9/11-related individuals and organizations. Gene Steuerle lost his wife, Norma Steuerle, on American Flight 77 that flew into the Pentagon. Steuerle and his two daughters, Kristin and Lynne, decided to donate the money they received from the federal Victim Compensation Fund to start two charities, one, the Alexandria Community Trust, to increase charitable investment to their local community, and a second to reach out to others who had lost loved ones. The special mission of this latter project has been to connect with those of other faiths and build peaceful alliances. Our Voices Together has joined other local and international organizations on a number of projects to respond to terrorism but also to build peace.

September 11 Families for Peaceful Tomorrows is an advocacy organization formed by family members of September 11 victims. Key figures include Coleen Kelly, Anne Mulderry, and Andrea LeBlanc. Its members include many in the New York City area but also from around the country and even the world. Its mission is "to seek effective, nonviolent responses to terrorism, and to identify a commonality with all people similarly affected by violence throughout the world." Peaceful Tomorrows has established connections with survivors of Hiroshima and Nagasaki, and in the spring of 2010 six of its members traveled to Afghanistan to meet with Afghan civilians who lost family members in the bombing campaign that began on October 7, 2001. Peaceful Tomorrows, on this issue, urges the American government to create a fund that would compensate Afghan people who lost members of their family to the war.

Peaceful Tomorrows defines its purposes in a hierarchy of goals that moves from the global to the local. Most generally, it seeks to promote dialogue on alternatives to war while "educating and raising the consciousness of the public on issues of war, peace, and the underlying causes of terrorism." That goal goes along with one of supporting and offering fellowship to anyone seeking "nonviolent responses to all forms of terrorism, both individual and institutional." Such global objectives are linked to calling attention to threats to civil liberties in the United States, acknowledging the fellowship of all peoples affected by violence and war, and encouraging a "multilateral, collaborative effort to bring those responsible for the September 11, 2001, attacks to justice in accordance with the principles of international law." Finally, Peaceful Tomorrow seeks to promote a foreign policy based on human rights, democracy, and self-rule, and demands "ongoing investigations into the events leading up to the September 11, 2001 attacks that took the lives of our loved ones, including exhaustive examinations of U.S. foreign policies and national security failures."

ARCHIVAL COLLECTIONS

The World Trade Center disaster lives on in the imagination of most Americans through the video narratives we have all seen, as well as in countless digital and film images captured by professional photographers and by ordinary people. The video images are archived by the various networks that own them and on outlets like YouTube.com from nonofficial sources. It is impossible even to estimate the number of personal collections of 9/11 pictures in albums and on private Web sites. Several books of such images have been published, especially in the early years, but the most complete and remarkable is *Here Is New York*, conceived by Alice Rose George, Giles Peress, Michael Shulan, and Charles Traub. This project was a very popular exhibit at 116 Prince Street in the fall of 2001 and into the winter of 2002, then became a website that is still up and running (hereisnewyork.org), and finally was turned into a book with 1,000 of the 5,000 photographs in the overall collection taken by more than 3,000 people.

At what can be called a folk level, memorials to 9/11 have sprung up in literally thousands of sites around the country. Most were temporary and have already faded into the night. Others have endured along busy highways, in backyards, in murals, and in brightly colored tattoos on the backs and arms of citizens. The most systematic effort to capture the folk history of this memory is by Jonathan Hyman, a well-known photographer who has specialized in the way ordinary people memorialized 9/11 in the years after the disaster. In the first five years, that is, between 2001 and 2006, Hyman took more than 15,000 photographs (digital and film), covering territory from Maine to Virginia and across parts of the Midwest. He found the work of graffiti artists, farmhouses painted with gigantic American flags, and firefighters with elaborate memorial tattoos. Most of the images were spontaneous expressions of grief and memory by people in their everyday lives.

His images include those of men and women with tattoos of the burning towers on their backs, trees adorned with American flags, and a small house painted in its entire surround with a flag. Hyman seems to have found every mural in the United States painted after 9/11, often the American flag commonly adorned by images of the burning towers or of a large and fierce-looking bald eagle, as well as pictures of parades and informal memorials. He has had two solo exhibitions of his art. One, at the National Constitution Center in Philadelphia, was titled *9/11: A Nation Remembers*, and ran from September 8, 2006, through January 1, 2007. It featured 100 of Hyman's photographs. A second exhibition, *9/11 and the American Landscape*, was sponsored by the World Trade Center Memorial Foundation and was on view on the forty-fifth floor of the rebuilt World Trade Center 7 in New York City. That second exhibit featured sixty-three photographs by Hyman. A third exhibition featured the work of Jonathan Hyman and Michael Pinciotti; it ran from August 23rd through September 23rd, 2006, at the Liberty Museum and Arts Center in Liberty, New York. This exhibit was titled *Piercing the Skin and Touching the Heart: Tattoos, Murals and Flags of 9/11.*

The vastness of this memorializing folk art has given rise to a number of archival collections, especially in the New York area. Trinity Church, in Lower Manhattan near Ground Zero, maintains a museum filled with artifacts in its St. Paul's chapel to the north of the church on Broadway. St. Paul's served as a resting place for those working on the pile in the months after 9/11. The New York Historical Society maintained an exhibit titled, *Here Is New York*, that contains 1,300 photos documenting the tragedy, video/oral recordings of survivors and rescue workers as well as precious artifacts such as wreckage from the FDNY Rescue Company #2's rig, twisted girders, a melted safety deposit box, a crushed clock with the hands frozen at 9:04, and office fragments from the towers' offices. This exhibition opened September 11th and ran through January 1st, 2008, marking the sixth anniversary of the attacks on the World Trade Center. Another powerful 4-month-long exhibit was put together at the Smithsonian Museum of American History and contained fifty items, including a twisted fire truck door from Fire Company 1 collected from the Trade Center and artifacts collected from the Pentagon and the Pennsylvania crash sites. Alongside the artifacts were photographs, news coverage collages, witness accounts, and frantic email messages by coworkers working for a law firm on the eighty-ninth floor of the WTC.[3] A useful source of data can be found in the 9/11 Digital Archive, as well as the interviews in the Columbia University Oral History archives, both mentioned several times in this book.

The great absence in the world of 9/11 memorials and archival collections is the unbuilt graveyard for the fragments of victims that lie scattered in the garbage at Fresh Kills, the giant landfill on Staten Island. During the cleanup of Ground Zero, the debris from the pile was all carted to Fresh Kills, where it was sifted a second time for any remains that might have been missed. Diane and Kurt Horning, and Barbara and Paul Kirwin, who each lost sons whose bodies were neither found nor ever identified from DNA analysis of remaining fragments in the possession of the Office of Chief Medical Examiner, have led the fight in court over the years to force the city to move the tons of debris from Fresh Kills to a proper burial site. The Hornings and Kirwins assume, not unjustifiably, that fragments of their sons, along with those of many others, lie embedded in all that debris. They argue it is outrageous to leave such human remains lying untended in a garbage dump. Their futile legal struggle (at least so far) has led to widespread appeals not to "trash the dead" and virulent attacks on Mayor Bloomberg as "cold-hearted."

THE MEMORIAL AT GROUND ZERO

At the heart of 9/11 memorializing, however, are the plans for the memorial that will be built at Ground Zero, along with the ongoing (and constantly changing) plans for rebuilding the complex itself. There is, however, a contradiction inherent in the robust enthusiasm for this rebuilding and memorialization. The World Trade Center is much more loved in destruction than it ever was when standing. There was much criticism of the twin towers from the moment of their conception, through the clearing out of the rundown neighborhood to build them, and finally in their gleaming modernist starkness that dominated the New York skyline. Everything about the towers spoke to excess. Documentaries about their construction tick off with relish the outlandish mountains of materials it took to build them, the hundreds of elevators inside, the sheer vastness of the office space inside (that took more than a decade to fill). But it was their physical presence that never ceased to shock anyone who encountered the towers. One tower would have been much more of a quiet presence. Two absolutely identical towers, except for the large antenna on the north tower, commanded attention. Most came to enjoy, or at least tolerate the towers, as emblematic of New York's power and majesty in the world. They overshadowed and dominated, epitomizing the aggressive, competitive nature of capitalism. They were in this sense appropriate for downtown and Wall Street. These giant steel structures glistening in the sun symbolized the lust for money of those who worked in and around them, the greed and excess, which most Americans relish, secretly or not.

More critical voices, however, continually lambasted the cold, harsh appearance of the towers as an example of modernism gone amok. A perfectly good downtown neighborhood, albeit one that was a bit seedy but remained organic and capable of renewal, was wiped out to make room for the towers (and the many other buildings in the World Trade Center complex). The dirt dug up to make these buildings then created the artificial and architecturally tacky Battery Park City across West Street. But most of all it was the towers themselves that critics and many New Yorkers loved to mock. Norman Mailer hated them with a fierceness that only he could muster. He said they had all the beauty of two giant boxes of Kleenex that had been stood up sideways next to each other.

But in their destruction they became instantly beloved. New Yorkers came to mourn not just those who died in the buildings but the towers themselves. Pictures of the towers before 9/11 appeared everywhere, on T-shirts, in books, emblazoned across large panels, pictured in television shows and documentaries, branded into our collective consciousness. We love them now as they were never loved and feel a sadness that reflects the tragedy of 9/11 much more than an authentic memory of the place the twin towers occupied in our imagination before their destruction. The loss is greater than the reality.[4]

It is beyond the scope of this book to describe in detail the plans for the rebuilt site, the history of how the plan for the sixteen-acre site emerged and changed over time, and the complicated politics surrounding every decision every step of the way. It is fitting, however, to note the most dominating building that will rise from the ashes of Ground Zero will be One World Trade Center, first named (and will probably always remain in popular imagination) the Freedom Tower. The name of the building was changed amid much controversy in March of 2009 on the assumption it would be less of a target with a more innocuous description (and also therefore easier to rent office space in it). This tower has the same dimensions at its base as the original twin towers and rises from a location just to the north and somewhat to the west of the old World Trade Center 1, the north tower. The Freedom Tower's original sinewy design by David Childs had to be modified for security reasons, resulting in a somewhat clunky building that will be 1,362 feet high, the exact height of the old WTC 2, and will have an illuminated antenna rising to a symbolic 1,776 feet.

The most important part of Ground Zero, however, will be the memorial, which will attempt the inherently contradictory tasks of bringing closure for survivors while opening up the past in meaningful ways for all others to reflect and study. Named Reflecting Absence and designed by Michael Arad and Peter Walker, the memorial was selected through a competition that drew more than 13,683 registrants with 5,201 submissions from sixty-three nations.

The memorial will be located in the footprints of the two towers, with cascading pools of water falling down the sides. Along the top will be all the names of the 9/11 victims inscribed on one of eighteen bronze parapets on each of the eight sides of the two pools. The groupings of the names—and agreement on these categories came after much acrimony—will list in the memorial in the north tower footprint those who worked in or were visiting WTC 1, the crew and passengers on Flight 11, and those killed in the 1993 bombing of the World Trade Center. The memorial in the south tower footprint will list those working in or visiting WTC 2 or other parts of the complex, including buildings 3, 4, 5, 6, and 7, as well as the concourse, subgrade, plaza, and surrounding areas; the crew and passengers on Flight 175; the victims of the attack on the Pentagon; the crew and passengers on Flight 77; the crew and passengers on Flight 93; and the first responders who died that day, organized in subgroups according to the agencies and units.

The memorial plaza that will surround the memorials will have more than 400 oak trees that are currently growing in a special nursery in New Jersey. The plaza is intended to be an ecologically sustainable park and will include benches for visitors to rest and meditate. The park will probably also become a haven for surrounding office workers.

In the middle of the long process of rebuilding Ground Zero and deciding on a meaningful memorial, it can seem that this or that agency, or this or that individual has needlessly delayed the process. The overlapping jurisdictions of the Port Authority, the governor, the mayor, the owner of the long-term lease, the Lower Manhattan Development Corporation, and the often feuding survivor and family groups have resulted in the stalemate in moving things forward that has persisted throughout the last decade. There is no doubt that rebuilding and memorializing would have been faster and easier to implement had one entity been responsible. If the developer, Larry Silverstein, for example, had actually owned the towers and the land, even as part of a consortium, or if the Port Authority had not leased them out, or if the city had owned and run the complex, a more streamlined process for imagining the rebuilding and the memorial would have been in place. Everything associated with Ground Zero in the last decade has proven to be hugely complicated and filled with fierce political battles. It is amazing things are as far along as they are, though it will be many more years before visitors will wander through the park, visit the museum, walk along Greenwich Street, and pay tribute to the dead in the memorial.

The intensely confused and contradictory process of recovery, however, that we have seen played out over the last decade is part of the disaster. It may well be that the developer, Larry Silverstein, who owned the lease to the twin towers, is mostly interested in making money, but all the other governmental and private entities have pushed passionately for their vision of renewal and memorial precisely as a function of their mourning. Survivors and family groups, from well-organized firemen to more disparate groups, have lacked much of a voice to make themselves heard and influence the decision-making process. The result has been dissent, disagreement, and delays. But how could it have been otherwise? And, honestly, would one want a more efficient process that left many feeling railroaded? It would have been impossible for a master plan for Ground Zero to emerge quickly and efficiently from a process with so many intensely interested parties involved. There is a general feeling, however, that the memorial will be moving and beautiful, that what was once called the Freedom Tower will dominate the sky in good ways, and that the other buildings that are planned to occupy parts of the sixteen-acre site will work well in the general plan. Of course, tough finances may still sink the museum and some of the other office buildings. One cannot tell. The mourning will continue.

The same kind of struggles occurred in Hiroshima. The stark remains of one building—the Genbaku Dome—near Ground Zero that remarkably withstood the blast of the bomb became the immediate symbol of survival for all those in Hiroshima and beyond. It was left standing as a kind of de facto memorial. After the war Hiroshima grew rapidly, with hundreds of thousands of new people moving into the rebuilt city; a tall office building went up right next to the structure. Many felt it was too stark a reminder of death in the center of a bustling city and should be taken down. Many survivors wanted to reinforce the building as a memorial. A compromise was reached at first simply to let the building decay and die, an approach that worked until 1966—twenty-one years after the disaster—when the city reinforced the renamed A-Bomb Dome as a permanent memorial to the bombing of Hiroshima.

There is never an easy path toward mourning, and no memorial can satisfy completely the need to honor the dead. The struggle is not only inevitable but sometimes desirable. Occasionally, as in the "alternative" Vietnam memorial on the Washington mall, what emerges is highly political and distasteful, standing in sharp contrast with the absolute beauty and dignity of the Maya Lin memorial. It is not irrelevant that Lin herself played a role in the selection committee for the 9/11 memorial, but so did thousands of ordinary citizens who weighed in on the decision, viewed and voted on the finalists, and had their voices heard in the selection-making process. It has been seriously delayed. Perhaps it could not and should not have been otherwise.[5]

CONCLUSION

In these public and private ways, in the videos and documentaries, in the photographs, in the murals and tattoos, and in the minds and hearts of New Yorkers and all Americans, the World Trade Center disaster and the other tragedies of 9/11 will not soon disappear. Our memory of it will change, and we will need the pictures, the artifacts, the stories, and especially the memorials to recover it in its authentic meanings. This book, with its stories of those who were caught up in the disaster, is part of that narrative.

A disaster may have something of a life cycle, lending it a living, breathing quality. Destruction and violence in such a metaphor give way to governmental agencies that help communities achieve long-term recovery, which in turn leads to hazard mitigation and more advanced measures of counterterrorism to protect against future disasters.[6] In a sense, such a breakdown of the stages of recovery is obvious, even banal. What is important is the organic metaphor of a life cycle, suggesting a survivor script that must be acted upon, one that makes us players upon a stage where the climax of the plot is predetermined.

In Hiroshima, where well over 100,000 people died in a fraction of a second and at least that many more would suffer from the effects of radiation and die later from cancers and other bomb-related illnesses, a strange thing happened at the end of August 1945. The city turned green. As John Hersey described it:

> Over everything—up through the wreckage of the city, in gutters, along the riverbanks, tangle among tiles and tin roofing, climbing on charred tree trunks—as a blanket of fresh, vivid, lush, optimistic green; the verdancy rose even from the foundations of ruined houses. Weeds already hid the ashes, and wild flowers were in bloom among the city's bones. The bomb had not only left the underground organs of plants intact it had stimulated them. Everywhere were bluets and Spanish bayonets, goosefoot, morning glories and day lilies, the hairy-fruited bean, purslane and clotbur and sesame and panic grass and feverfew. Especially in a circle at the center, sickle senna grew in extraordinary regeneration, not only standing among the charred remnants of the same plant but pushing up in new places, among bricks and through cracks in the asphalt. It actually seemed as if a load of sickle-senna seed had been dropped along with the bomb.

By the first anniversary of the bomb, many of the *Hibakusha* whom Hersey followed closely in his reporting began to feel a "curious kind of elated community spirit," rather like what the survivors of the London blitz felt once the city was rebuilt. We made it, we survived, we will live. The death is over. There is a future.[7]

Authentic hope is always qualified. Otherwise, it is mere optimism, which is false in its very nature because it assumes a rosy future. Rosemary said:

> I mean I don't know. I don't know. For myself, I feel like I've walked into such a new reality. Not that it wasn't there before, but just nothing ever made me look at it and I'm standing here looking at it. And it's really hard to look at. And I don't know what to do about it. And right now I don't feel like I have a whole lot of strength to do anything. But I'm hoping that it doesn't last too long 'cause I really have to do something. I have three grandchildren and a lot of kids that I care about, a lot of kids.

That thought of her grandchildren brought Rosemary to her most important general formulation: "It's suddenly critically important to keep that kernel of humanness. It's not optional anymore. There's something that keeps human beings human and we'd better understand it and share it."

ACKNOWLEDGMENTS

MY GREATEST DEBT is to the survivors and witnesses of 9/11 who shared their experiences with me in the making of this book. I firmly believe that if you want to understand something as large and horrendous as 9/11 you must talk principally with those who suffered from it. I hope the survivors and witnesses who gave me so much will feel that what I make of their stories is respectful and dignified.

As with so many of my books, I remain indebted to Robert Jay Lifton. In this one especially not only did I employ his interview method in the study but he helped me write my protocol, talked with me often as my work proceeded over the years, challenged me four years ago not to abandon my project when he sensed my despair about pulling it together, and read not one but two drafts of the manuscript. One could hardly ask more of a mentor.

For a year or so after 9/11 I convened a study group that met regularly to discuss my interviews. I would distribute the transcript of an interview; then the group would discuss it for an hour and a half. I learned much from those seminars and am very grateful to Michael Flynn, Cindy Ness, Paula Glickman, Katie Gentile, and others who attended more occasionally for their comments. Besides participating in the seminar, Paula Glickman generously shared with me her interviews with therapists and Michael Flynn read a draft of the entire manuscript. Flynn, of course, as I say in the text, also lent me his wonderfully evocative construct of "zones of sadness."

Bill Blakemore put his indelible stamp on the chapter called "Traumasong" and on everything I say about television in another chapter. Many long lunches at Café Fiorello served as the venue for our conversations.

I presented several times on my work at Lifton's annual Wellfleet Psychohistory meetings. The feedback from the members of that amazing group proved invaluable. It would be impossible to thank adequately all those who made helpful comments, but I especially learned from Kai Erikson, Bessel van der Kolk, Peter Balakian, Norman Birnbaum, Judy Hermann, Karl Meyer, Shareen Brysac, Cathy Caruth, and B. J. Lifton.

A number of people read all or large parts of the manuscript at different stages and provided enormously helpful suggestions: Helen McNeil, James W. Jones, Scott Knowles, Katharine Boyd, and my brother, Robert Strozier. Jones even slogged through yet another completely revised second draft, something only a close friend would do.

Tom Ryan, a fireman who suffered terribly on 9/11 and later became my student, friend, and racketball partner, provided invaluable tips on sources over the years. Ryan also read and commented wisely on the final manuscript.

I have been in frequent email contact over the years about this book with Tessa Philips, a close friend and a psychoanalyst in Australia, and in the year or so after 9/11 with her son, Jeremy Philips, who had many keen insights. Tessa especially helped me conceptualize many issues about my topic and kept my spirits up when they flagged.

Andrea Fatica, my assistant at the Center on Terrorism that I founded in late 2001 and continue to direct at John Jay College, graciously helped with any number of tasks over the years in connection with this book and was involved in my interviews with some of the women who got pregnant after 9/11.

Twice I taught a graduate course on 9/11 at John Jay College with Scott Knowles, who gave invaluably of his time and intelligence. I also learned a great deal from the students in those classes and benefited from their research papers and their critiques of my various presentations.

Early on in my work, Rich Elomaa served well as a research assistant. Then in the summer, fall, and early winter of 2010, as I completed the final draft of the book, I benefited from the prodigious amount of work carried out by my research assistant, Payal Desai, who was supported by a generous grant to the college from the Department of Homeland Security. Payal also helped in the frantic last moments of gathering permissions for photographs and other tasks.

Maggie Lyko was unusually helpful in the identification of possible respondents for my study, as she has been in referring me patients from her very wide circle of friends. I consider her the Mother Superior of my practice and my book.

I am grateful to the Columbia University Oral History Office for making their interviews available. I quote from four of their 9/11 interviews.

This book would not have come to fruition but for the tireless work and support of my agent, Richard Morris, of Janklow and Nesbit. He believed in its potential when I was not even sure about it myself and followed through on things during some dark days in publishing. He also came up with the title.

I am most grateful for the professionalism and good will of the staff at Columbia University Press, including Lauren Dockett, Ron Harris, Meredith Howard, Sydnie Keeter, Philip Levanthal, and the wonderful design staff. All worked under a crushing deadline to get the book out in time for the tenth anniversary of 9/11.

And, of course, I could never have written this book without the constant support of my wife, Cathryn Compton. She complained at times of living with a man who talked of death every day, but she brought hope to my life. I have dedicated the book to our lovely daughter, Alison, who carries the torch of peace for the next generation.

APPENDIX

THE LITERATURE ON TRAUMA AND THE MEASUREMENT OF PTSD AFTER 9/11

THE AGGREGATE DATA in various social science studies to date for the traumatic—and continuing—effects of 9/11 on New York City residents capture many of the painful consequences of the World Trade Center disaster. Researchers began a few weeks after the disaster to assess the levels of posttraumatic stress disorder (PTSD) among adults and children, and conducted many and varied follow-up studies. The reason for the emphasis in nearly all these studies on measuring PTSD is that symptoms of emotional distress that fall under this syndrome—flashbacks, recurrent nightmares and other sleeping disorders, startle responses, irritability, hypersensitivity, wariness, social isolation, and difficulty concentrating—can be ascertained readily through telephone interviews by researchers without clinical training. In such research, one generally knows approximately the baseline, or "normal," levels of PTSD among a given population, so that heightened levels of symptomatic behavior after an event like 9/11 can be reasonably assumed to be caused by the disaster itself. The same is true for continuing high levels of PTSD symptoms in subsequent months and years, suggesting but not proving that the effects of the disaster have by no means dissipated.

The relative precision of measuring the traumatic impact of a disaster like 9/11 by assessing PTSD symptoms, however, can be deceptive. In its extreme form, full-blown PTSD can be identified by nearly anyone and hardly requires professional training. The more attenuated forms of the syndrome are the most interesting and problematic for the untrained observer to assess. Miranda presented with a museum of PTSD symptoms, as did Felicia, but for respondents such as Henry or Renee or Arturo the effects of the disaster were more subtle, evoking profound philosophical reflections on death and its symbolic equivalents. A heightened level of existential awareness is not listed as a criterion for measuring PTSD in the psychiatric bible, the *Diagnostic and Statistical Manual of Mental Disorders,* even though a detailed examination of such reflections is much more revealing and interesting than a mere catalogue of symptoms that a respondent might reveal. One can only really grasp such deeper levels of how people suffered from an event like 9/11, and the meanings they gave to their experience, by interviewing them for prolonged periods with sensitivity to their personal backgrounds, their cultural milieu, and their relative position in society. Any other form of measurement is a blunt instrument. Furthermore, with some exceptions, social scientific research on the impact of 9/11 has failed to account for differing emotional responses of people in what I call zones of sadness. We are left with aggregate data that are highly imprecise but seemingly scientific and with an air of mostly undeserved authority.

The pretense of scientific certainty about trauma that lies in measuring PTSD can also have pernicious social effects when analyzing the collective experience of communities of suffering after certain kinds of disasters. Kai Erikson, for example, tells of the court case after the Buffalo Creek Dam broke and released torrents of water on an unsuspecting population. Erikson testified for the members of the devastated community who argued (reasonably) that the mining company knew the earthen dam it built was vulnerable and bound to collapse in the near future but that it never warned the town of the impending disaster or did anything to help the residents relocate in anticipation of the nearly inevitable inundation. In court the psychiatric hired guns for the company argued that their testing showed the absence of heightened levels of PTSD in the community and that therefore there had not been the pervasive suffering and dislocation claimed by the plaintiffs.

Still, one can learn some things about the impact of the World Trade Center disaster by reviewing the social science research. The first to the gate was Sandro Galea, who supervised a telephone interview study in Manhattan from five to nine weeks after the attacks. In the survey Galea and his colleagues found that among a statistically meaningful sample of adults living south of 110th Street in Manhattan, 7.5 percent of the respondents reported symptoms of PTSD and 9.7 percent reported symptoms of depression, which translated into 67,000 people with PTSD and 87,000 with depression immediately after the disaster. The baseline figures for these two disorders in this geographic area were 3.6 percent for PTSD and 4.9 percent for depression. One can reasonably conclude that the immediate impact of the disaster, in other words, was to double the rate of acute suffering in New Yorkers in closest proximity to Ground Zero.[1]

The Galea study also showed some sensitivity to geographic differences in the response of those in New York, depending on proximity to the scenes of death at Ground Zero, by distinguishing between the levels of PTSD among those living below Canal Street—three times the normal rate—as opposed to those between Lower Manhattan and 110th Street. The rates dropped off significantly in those areas above 110th Street, especially in Harlem, but were surprisingly high in the Dominican area of Washington Heights in the far northwest of Manhattan.

The traumatic effects of 9/11 on Dominicans constituted an unexpected finding in the Galea study. Eighty-seven percent of Dominicans stated that they felt acute distress and intense physical reactions when they found out about 9/11; 71 percent said they felt anxiety whenever they read or heard the words "nine eleven" and maintained high levels of sadness throughout. Residents of Washington Heights reported continued loss of appetite, 19 percent said they cried whenever they were reminded of 9/11 and 30 percent reported sleep disturbances due to 9/11.[2] "The rates of PTSD and depression within the Washington Heights area were found to be higher among Hispanics than non-Hispanics five to eight weeks after the 9/11 terrorist attacks. Hispanics expressed nearly twice as many negative emotional and physical symptoms as other groups five to seven months after 9/11."[3] That anomaly, which neither Galea nor anyone else could explain, suggests a predisposition to trauma in the Dominican community, a kind of crisis in waiting among these Hispanic citizens in New York.

Four other interesting studies have provided additional support for the unexpectedly harsh impact of the disaster on the Dominican population of Washington Heights. Irwin Garfinkel and his colleagues at the Columbia University School of Social Work analyzed data from the New York City Social Indicators Survey six months after the disaster and found that among various immigrant groups in New York the Dominican community was impacted the most severely (except for the Chinese community, which will be discussed in detail later). The Dominicans lost jobs, had bad health, and were affected in many other ways as well. Another study conducted by Sandro Galea and his team of researchers showed that the highest prevalence of PTSD occurred in those from the Dominican Republic—14.3 percent, which was the highest rate of all Hispanic groups. A sensitive interview study of older Dominicans using focus groups, conducted in January and February of 2002, by David Strug and his colleagues at Yeshiva University, found acute distress among the participants. Strug and his colleagues found high levels of anxiety, avoidance, and hypervigilance among the participants in the study.[4]

At a more general level, another study of 2,273 people across the United States, conducted in October and November of 2001, found that 11.2 percent of New York City residents had PTSD, whereas the rest of the country was closer to 4 percent, which translates into some 532,240 "excess cases" (or over baseline) of PTSD among adults in the New York City metropolitan area. To be in New York during the disaster, not surprisingly, risked severely undermining one's emotional well-being, but the national figures for increased levels of PTSD, although significantly less than those for New York, are an indirect indication of the impact of television.[5] Another national longitudinal study was conducted by Roxane Cohen Silver and colleagues and consisted of a sample of 3,496 adults through a web-based survey. Data results showed that 17 percent outside of New York City reported symptoms of September 11th–related PTSD two months after the attack, 5.8 percent did so at six months, and a high level was associated with females showing issues such as depression, anxiety, and marital separation.[6]

One all-important category of research was the impact of 9/11 on children. This most vulnerable of groups carries trauma forward into subsequent generations, so it is especially important to have a sense of how the disaster impacted it. For ethical reasons, one cannot directly interview children on such a subject, so researchers usually approach it indirectly, via the parents, especially the mothers and sometimes the teachers in schools. One additional (and unusual) source of qualitative data on the impact of 9/11 on children came from psychiatrists working at the Kids Corner set up at the Family Assistance Center (Pier 94) by Desmond Heath, in collaboration with other members of the Disaster Psychiatry Outreach.

Susan Coates and Daniel Schechter, in an excellent paper published in 2004, report from both qualitative and quantitative work that 96 percent of children from a very early age to five years of age living near Ground Zero suffered at least one PTSD symptom and 35 percent met the DSM criteria for full-blown PTSD.[7] The authors contextualize these figures well, noting that it was only a study by Anna Freud and Dorothy Burlingame in 1943 that first recognized that children respond to wartime trauma principally in terms of whether they are separated from their mothers. In World War II London during the Blitz, for example, it was not the German bombing of London that caused trauma for most children but the evacuation of the city that often led to separation from their mothers. The significance of these findings was not fully appreciated at the time. Later work in the 1960's by writers such as John Bowlby showed how traumatic it was for children to be separated from their mothers when they went into the hospital (research that changed hospital pediatric practices forever). In the 1990's, Coates and Schechter report, this general body of theory was extended to the study of PTSD symptoms in young children in a variety of settings, from abuse to response to external trauma (such as the Oklahoma City bombing in 1995). Before the 1990's, many had doubted that children under five could develop the full range of PTSD symptoms. Systematic investigation of the problem, however, showed children as young as three months could be traumatized according to the formal categories established by psychiatry. The study of the effect of the World Trade Center disaster on preschool children in zone 1 and throughout the world via the impact of television may therefore be the first time fully developed theory about children and trauma met a real disaster.

The authors also report some very interesting longitudinal data about the lingering effects of 9/11 on children. For somewhat obtuse parents who did not know how their children between the ages of six to eleven responded to the disaster, that is, those who failed to talk and interact with their children in meaningful ways, those children were 11.1 times more likely to have behavior problems. The equivalent experience of adolescent children ages twelve to seventeen was four times more likely to result in behavior problems. As Coates and Schechter wisely comment, "This study brought into stark relief the fact that in the wake of a trauma caused by an external catastrophic event, a child's response, especially the young child's response, depends upon the nature of his or her parent's relatedness to him or her after the trauma."[8]

A multitude of studies, such as the Columbia University study titled "Parental Exposure to Mass Violence and Child Mental Health," also relate parental exposure to 9/11 and their children's response to mass violence in relation to their parents' experiences as WTC evacuees and first responders. These studies suggest children's indirect exposure to the events through their parents' experiences are just as important in affecting their mental health as their experiences with direct exposure to the attacks. "In a representative sample of NYC public school children assessed 6 months after the September 11, 2001 attack on the World Trade Center (WTC), seemingly elevated rates of psychopathology were recorded among children of WTC evacuees. Children of NYC First Responders (police officers, EMTs, and fire fighters) displayed a complex pattern of response to the WTC attack. Overall, the findings from this previous study support putative transmission of trauma to children whose parents were exposed to the WTC attack." Many other studies exist showing a direct link relating parent's exposure and children's mental health issues, including long-term issues such as psychopathology. Other studies were conducted by Columbia University in the New York City public school system in collaboration with the NYC Board of Education and are focused on measuring attack-related child PTSD, psychopathology, mental health issues, and life disruptions.[9]

Finally, a host of studies have indicated the continuing impact of the disaster, at least for several years after 9/11. DiGrande and her colleagues found in a New York study that after three years approximately 44 percent of Americans were experiencing at least one PTSD symptom, including avoidance and hyperarousal, whereas 13 percent could be considered as having the full diagnosis. The study conducted by DiGrande and her fellow researchers examined rates of PTSD and risk factors for PTSD among 11,037 lower Manhattan residents two to three years (2003–2004) after 9/11. These New Yorkers were living within one mile of the World Trade Center and south of Canal Street on 9/11. PTSD rates were higher for older residents, female residents, and residents of Hispanic, African-American, and other racial/ethnic backgrounds, than they were for white residents (with the exception of Asian-American residents); for divorced, widowed, or separated residents or those who earned less than $25,000 per year and had less education; for those who reported direct exposure to 9/11 events; and for those forced to evacuate their homes.[10]

Once past about 2004, or some three years after the event, it becomes highly problematic using the research tools of social science to distinguish the continuing impact of 9/11. We were a nation engaged in two wars with their own traumas in the years after 9/11, there was a major natural disaster in 2005 (Katrina), and terrorist events throughout the world and to some degree in the United States itself focused the attention of citizens on the continuing danger of future attacks. The research question, however, for someone reporting elevated fears of terrorist attack in 2008, for example, is to identify the specific role of 9/11 in shaping those fears from the ongoing reports of danger in a 24/7 news environment. Three years after 9/11 Barbara Ganzel and her colleagues used functional MRIs to determine the ongoing trauma among twenty-two healthy adults, half of whom were within 1.5 miles of Ground Zero on 9/11 and the other half some 200 miles away. They showed each subject fearful and calm faces and determined brain activity. The findings showed a marked elevation of bilateral amygdala function among those who had been close to Ground Zero. Other studies tracked the ongoing economic impact of 9/11 on those who were in New York and directly affected by their loss of jobs. As I found often in my interviews, with Deirdre, for example, job loss complicated a person's trauma.[11]

Some polling data, however, suggest different conclusions, and a rapidly diminishing impact of 9/11 as a determiner of trauma and PTSD in the population both within and outside of New York. ABC polling in the year after 9/11, for example, showed a remarkable decline in positive answers to the question, "In the past few days, have you yourself felt depressed because of your concerns about terrorist attacks or the war against terrorists?" Five days after 9/11, 72 percent answered "yes" and 27 percent answered "no." By October 3 those answering "yes" had dropped to 42 percent, by November 7 it was down to 24 percent, and just before the first anniversary, on September 8, 2002, only 12 percent of Americans answered "yes" to the question.[12] Gallup polling in the month following 9/11, another example, showed 85 percent of Americans expected another attack in the United States over the next several weeks but this number again dropped significantly to 38 percent in January 2008. The Gallup polling showed a downward trend in responses when asking the question, "How worried are you that you or someone in your family will become a victim of terrorism?" In January 2002, 41 percent were very/somewhat worried, while 59 percent were not too worried/not at all worried; by 2003, 38 percent were worried and about 60 percent were not worried; and by the end of December 2009, the number of those worried had dropped even further, to 12 percent, with 28 percent not worried. Finally, in January 2010, only 9 percent of Americans expressed concern that they or someone in their family would become a victim of terrorism. These trends in the polling data show significant declines in public fear of terrorist attacks since 9/11 and further support the notion of diminishing impact of 9/11 as a determiner of trauma.[13] Another polling entity, the Pew Research Center, released data showing that in a mere three months, from June 2002 to September 2002, the percentage of Americans worried about another terrorist attack dropped from 76 percent to 62 percent.[14]

Such rapid declines in the self-reports of New Yorkers (and others) about depression and fears relating to 9/11 correlate in a very general way with what one would expect about PTSD in a traumatized community after a disaster. It is not surprising for the first month or so that symptoms of PTSD would be widespread in the community most directly affected. The rates, however, should be cut in half after about six weeks and halved again after six months. Those still suffering symptoms after a year are likely to be troubled for a long time to come and probably were either predisposed to trauma before the disaster or exposed to death during it in radical ways.

NOTES

INTRODUCTION

1. "The World Trade Center catastrophe was a profoundly local event. As the dust settled, rescue efforts turned into cleanup operations, and the debate over reconstruction spilled out, Ground Zero was revealed to be only 16 acres. New Yorkers experienced it as a localized event in real time and space: the planes hitting, the towers aflame, their awesome, inconceivable collapse, acrid poisonous smoke billowing up Broadway, paper floating over to Brooklyn, ash on the pavement. Only later did the constant reruns on television make the catastrophe sensible for us at other geographical scales." See Neil Smith, "Scales of Terror: The Manufacturing of Nationalism and the War for U.S. Globalism," in Michael Sorkin and Sharon Zukin, ed., *After the World Trade Center: Rethinking New York City* (New York: Routledge, 2002), 97.

2. Ronet Bachman and Russell K. Schutt, *The Practice of Research in Criminology and Criminal Justice* (Thousand Oaks, CA: SAGE Publications, 2010), 135

3. "Nothing naked from the world" is from Robert Jay Lifton's memoir *Witness to an Extreme Century* (New York: The Free Press, 2011), which I read in manuscript. I also wrote, with Michael Flynn, "Lifton's Method," *The Psychohistory Review* 20 (1992): 1–16. Lifton's major research studies in which he honed his research method are, in chronological order, *Thought Reform and the Psychology of Totalism: A Study of "Brainwashing" in China* (New York: Norton, 1969); *Death in Life: Survivors of Hiroshima* (Chapel Hill: University of North Carolina Press, 1991 [1968]); *The Nazi Doctors: Medical Killing and the Psychology of Genocide* (New York: Basic Books, 1986); and *Destroying the World to Save It: Aum Shinrikyo, Apocalyptic Violence, and the New Global Terrorism* (New York: Metropolitan Books, 1999).
4. Jim Dwyer and Michelle O'Donnell, "9/11 Firefighters Told of Isolation Amid Disaster," *New York Times*, 2005.
5. *Heinz Kohut: The Making of a Psychoanalyst* (New York: Farrar, Straus & Giroux, 2001).
6. Personal communication, October 26, 2001.

THE EVENT

1. The facts listed here are from the remarkable and underappreciated work of genius by Juan Gonzalez, *Fallout: The Environmental Consequences of the World Trade Center Collapse* (New York: The New Press, 2002), 54–90. Compare the much less detailed discussion in David Rosner and Gerald Markowitz, *Are We Ready?* (Berkeley: University of California Press, 2006), 28, and the CDC study by Robert M. Brackbill et al., "Surveillance for World Trade Center Disaster Health Effects Among Survivors of Collapsed and Damaged Buildings," *MMWR Surveill Summ* 55 (2006): 1–18.

1. SURVIVORS

1. It is impossible for me to know whether any of my respondents later suffered from secondary effects of exposure to the dust and debris on 9/11.
2. Robyn Gershon, the principal investigator of the study "High-Rise Building Evacuation: Lessons Learned from the World Trade Center Disaster" (Maleman School of Public Health, Columbia University, in a presentation at John Jay College, May 3, 2006), summarized her work on those who were evacuated from the towers. Her sample includes 1,767 respondents. From these she has found the following: 58 percent were men who were an average of forty-four years of age, though many were in their twenties and some were as old as eighty. Most had been working in the building for six years. Seventy percent either were married or had a partner, and a little less than half had children. Eighty percent were white, 66 percent had a college education, and 84 percent were employed in a private company. These data correlate well with what we know about the demographics of the victims. Most were

young white men who were very well educated and embarked on good careers in financial companies or other kinds of private companies: Robyn M. Gershon, Kristine A. Qureshi, Marcie S. Rubin, and Victoria H. Raveis, "Factors Associated with High-Rise Evacuation: Qualitative Results from the World Trade Center Evacuation Study," *Journal of Prehospital and Disaster Medicine* 22, no.3 (2007): 165–73. Note also that Edwin Galea and his colleagues also began a study of people who escaped and in an updated paper, "UK WTC 9/11 Evacuation Study," suggested that they were also involved in a major study: Edwin Galea and Sir J. Blake, "Collection and Analysis of Data Relating to the Evacuation of the World Trade Centre Buildings on 11 September 2001," report produced for the UK ODPM, Fire Research Technical Report 6/2005 (London: ODPM Publications, 2004); Edwin Galea, "UK WTC 9/11 Evacuation Study: An Overview of the Methodologies Employed and Some Preliminary Analysis," *Journal of Applied Fire Science* 15 (2010): 335–37.

3. John Hersey, *Hiroshima* (New York: Alfred A. Knopf, 1985 [1946]), 29.

4. Robert Jay Lifton, *Death in Life: Survivors of Hiroshima* (Chapel Hill, NC: The University of North Carolina Press, 1991 [1968]), 500–503.

5. Ibid., 502–503.

6. Bessel A. van der Kolk, "The Body Keeps the Score: Memory and the Evolving Psychobiology of Post-traumatic Stress," *Harvard Review of Psychiatry* 1, no. 5 (1994): 253–65.

7. Lifton, *Death in Life*, 484.

8. Michael Ellison, Ed Vulliamy, and Jane Martinson, "We Got Down to the Outside and It Was Like an Apocalypse: Office Workers Tell How They Scrambled for Their Lives as Colleagues and Friends Perished," *The Guardian*, September 12, 2001.

9. Gershon et al., "Factors Associated with High-Rise Evacuation," 167.

10. There were, of course, also first responders among those moving across the bridge from Brooklyn toward the disaster, just as ferries transported fire officers from Staten Island toward the WTC complex.

11. Mike Magee, *All Available Boats* (New York: Spencer Books, 2002), 43, 48, 85–86.

12. Hersey, *Hiroshima*, 35.

2. WITNESSES

1. The developer Larry Silverstein signed a ninety-nine-year lease for the World Trade Center on July 24, 2001, beating out a competing bid by the Port Authority.

2. The trains in this account are important to understand. The local, or red, line, which then included number 1 and 9 trains, winds its way from the World Trade Center north through several stops (including Franklin Street) in Tribeca. Once at 14th Street the express trains, numbers 2 and 3, can be picked up. The 2 and 3 travel along Seventh Avenue, through Columbus Circle, and along Broadway on the Upper West Side to 96th Street and beyond. Between 14th and 96th streets one can either travel on the local train or take the express on the other side of the track at the express stops.

3. This interview was conducted by my colleague Paula Glickman, who was part of a study group I convened that met regularly after the disaster. She was particularly interested in the impact of the disaster on therapists and conducted a number of valuable interviews. I am grateful to be able to use her interview with Kevin in my own study.

3. PARTICIPANTS

1. Alison Gilbert, Phil Hirschkorn, Melinda Murphy, et al., *Covering Catastrophe* (Chicago: Bonus Books, 2002), 150
2. Ibid., 160, 161
3. Ibid., 161, 173
4. The actual train Eric took was the number 9, which has since been discontinued. The important point for the story, however, is that he caught the local Seventh Avenue (or red) line going north at Franklin Street.
5. Reminiscences of Andi L. Rosenthal (December 7, 2001), on page 17 in Columbia University Oral History Research Office Collection (CUOHROC).
6. Ibid., 17–19.
7. Ibid., 18.
8. Ibid., 19–23.
9. Ibid., 23.
10. Reminiscences of Ivan Almonte (December 10, 2001), on page 8 in the CUOHROC.
11. Ibid., 8–9.

4. ONLOOKERS

1. Sanford, for example, said he heard the squish of falling bodies hit the pavement as he ran toward the Brooklyn Bridge, but when I asked where he was at that point he realized he had not actually heard that sound but inserted it into his memory from later news reports.
2. Conway F. Saylor, Brian L. Cowart, Julie A. Lipovsky, et al., "Media Exposure to September 11: Elementary School Students' Experiences and Posttraumatic Symptoms," *Sage Journals American Behavior Scientist* 46, no. 12 (2003): 1622–42; Jennifer Ahern, Sandro Galea, Heidi Resnick, et al., "Television Images and Psychological Symptoms After the September 11 Terrorist Attacks," *Psychiatry* 65, no. 4 (2002): 289–300.
3. I am grateful to Bill Blakemore for making the arrangements for me to see the ABC tapes and to Joel Kanoff, the archivist of ABC, who set me up to view the tapes. I obtained the CNN archival tape on brief loan from the Vanderbilt University TV News Archive.
4. What follows is my transcription from the tape.

5. Jennings's comment is a completely innocent observation, made out of shock and confusion at what he has just witnessed, though it was to provide a crucial piece of the conspiracy theories that later emerged.

6. After I watched the first tower collapse from where I was standing on 13th Street, several of us immediately feared the collapse of the second tower. I suspect that must have been true for many at the scene.

5. THE DYING

1. Alison Gilbert, Phil Hirschkorn, Melinda Murphy, et al., *Covering Catastrophe* (Chicago: Bonus Books, 2002), 10.

2. Michael Ellison, Ed Vulliamy, and Jane Martinson, "We Got Down to the Outside and It Was Like an Apocalypse: Office Workers Tell How They Scrambled for Their Lives as Colleagues and Friends Perished," *The Guardian*, September 12, 2001.

3. Gilbert, *Covering Catastrophe*, 50.

4. David Friend, *Watching the World Change: The Stories Behind the Images of 9/11* (New York: I. B. Tauris & Co., 2007), 74.

5. Ellison, "We Got Down to the Outside."

6. Gilbert, *Covering Catastrophe*, 53.

7. Reminiscences of Andi L. Rosenthal (December 7, 2001), on p. 18 in CUOHROC.

8. Gilbert, *Covering Catastrophe*, 49, 50, 51.

9. Ibid., 51, 52, 53. Note that these images were not broadcast at the time on television, unless they were on local channels, and then only briefly.

10. Edward T. O'Donnell, *Ships Ablaze: The Tragedy of the Steamboat* General Slocum (New York: Broadway Books, 2003), 4.

11. Michelle M. Houle, *Triangle Shirtwaist Factory Fire: Flames of Labor Reform* (New York: Enslow Publishers, 2002), 30.

12. Jim Dwyer, Kevin Flynn, James Glanz, and Ford Fessenden, "Fighting to Live as the Towers Died," *New York Times*, May 26, 2002; Dennis Cauchon and Martha Moore, "Desperation Forced a Horrific Decision," *USA Today*, 2008.

13. Robert C. Shaler, *Who They Were: Inside the World Trade Center, the DNA Story: The Unprecedented Effort to Identify the Missing* (New York: The Free Press, 2005). Note also Steven Stehr and David Simpson, "Victim Identification and Mismanagement Following the Collapse of the World Trade Center Towers," *Natural Hazards Research and Applications Information Center,* University of Colorado, 482 UCB, 2002, p. 4; personal communication, Larry Kobilinski (Professor of Forensic Science, John Jay College), April 13, 2008.

14. Gail Sheehy, *Middletown, America: One Town's Passage from Trauma to Hope* (New York: Random House, 2003), 412.

15. Mike Magee, ed., *All Available Boats* (New York: Spencer Books, 2002), 49.

16. Thomas Lynch, "Local Heros," in Samuel Heilman, ed., *Death, Bereavement, and Mourning* (New York: Transaction Publishers, 2005), 17–18.

17. Ibid., 18. Note Lynch's two remarkable books, *The Undertaking—Life Studies from the Dismal Trade* (New York: Norton, 1997) and *Bodies in Motion and at Rest* (New York: Norton, 2001).

18. Ibid., 18–19. Note also the forthcoming book by David Sherman, *In a Strange Room: Corpses, Sovereign Power, and the Modernist Imagination,* which he describes on Brandeis University's Web site as "A book-length investigation of modernism at the crossroads of the secularized and medicalized corpse, amplified powers of the wartime and postwar state, and new mourning practices."

19. Uri Heilman, Interview, December 19,2002; and two of his unpublished statements that he shared with me, one from 2001, titled simply "Personal and unpublished statement," and the second from 2002, "Department of Remembrance, Praying for the Dead, Personal and unpublished statement."

20. Francis J. Balducci, personal communication, May 4, 2004.

21. Dorothy Meserve Kunhardt and Philip B. Kunhardt, Jr., *Twenty Days: A Narrative in Text and Pictures of the Assassination of Abraham Lincoln and the Twenty Days and Nights that Followed—The Nation in Mourning and the Long Trip Home to Springfield* (New York: Harper & Row, 1966), 120.

6. APOCALYPTIC INTERLUDE

1. Robert Jay Lifton, *The Broken Connection: On Death and the Continuity of Life* (New York: Basic Books, 1979), 351.

2. Bill Keller, "Nuclear Nightmares," *New York Times,* May 26, 2002.

3. John Farmer, *The Ground Truth: The Untold Story of America Under Attack on 9/11* (New York: Riverhead Books, 2009), 235.

4. John Hersey, *Hiroshima* (New York: Alfred A. Knopf, 1985 [1946]), 35.

5. Ibid., 25, 76, 82, 104–105.

6. This issue of the inefficiency of the radio communication system that day has occasioned much analysis but not much change. Its significance has been lost in what turned out to be the more decisive issue of the failure of the NYPD radio system to communicate with that of the NYFD.

7. Michael Ellison, Ed Vulliamy, and Jane Martinson, "We Got Down to the Outside and It Was Like an Apocalypse: Office Workers Tell How They Scrambled for Their Lives as Colleagues and Friends Perished," *The Guardian,* September 12, 2001.

7. TRAUMASONG

1. I want to thank Bill Blakemore for suggesting the title of this chapter—"Traumasong"—and for vital contributions (including references to Milton and Frost), and to my ideas on language and trauma in discussions over many years. Helen McNeil and Peter Balakian as well had much to contribute to the ideas in this chapter.

2. Rebecca Solnit, *A Paradise Built in Hell* (New York: Penguin Group USA, 2010).

3. Kai Erikson, *A New Species of Trouble: Explorations in Disaster, Trauma, and Community* (New York: Norton, 1994).

4. Robert Jay Lifton, *Death in Life: Survivors of Hiroshima* (Chapel Hill, NC: The University of North Carolina Press, 1991 [1968]), 479–542.

5. Charles B. Strozier, *Heinz Kohut: The Making of a Psychoanalyst* (New York: Farrar, Straus & Giroux, 2001), n. 58, 438–39.

6. Paul Fussell, *Poetic Meter and Poetic Form* (New York: Random House, 1979), 188.

7. Walt Whitman, *Leaves of Grass* (1855), in *Complete Poetry and Collected Prose* (New York: Library of America, 1982), 57.

8. John Felstiner, *Paul Celan: Poet, Survivor, Jew* (New Haven: Yale University Press, 2001), 344.

9. Ibid., 31.

8. TELEVISION

1. Bill Blakemore, personal communication, July 23, 2010.

2. Avishai Margalit, *The Ethics of Memory* (Cambridge: Harvard University Press, 2002), 147. Note also the distinction Shoshana Fellman and Dori Laub make between bearing witness to historical facts and psychological or spiritual truth. See Shoshana Fellman and Dori Laub, *Testimony: Crises of Witnessing in Literature, Psychoanalysis, and History* (New York: Routledge, 1992), 61, 92; note also Kelly Oliver, *Witnessing: Beyond Recognition* (Minneapolis: University of Minnesota Press, 2001).

3. Margalit, *The Ethics of Memory*, 151ff.

4. Ibid., 164, 166–67.

5. Marshall McLuhan, *Understanding Media: The Extensions of Man* (New York: McGraw-Hill, 1964).

6. Norman Mailer, in a presentation at the Wellfleet meetings of Robert Jay Lifton, October 27, 2001.

9. HIDDEN CHILDREN

1. The names I use in this chapter are all pseudonyms.

10. ORGANIC PROCESS

1. Michael Ellison, Ed Vulliamy, and Jane Martinson, "We Got Down to the Outside and It Was Like an Apocalypse: Office Workers Tell How They Scrambled for Their Lives as Colleagues and Friends Perished," *The Guardian*, September 12, 2001.

2. Zac Unger's 9/11 article can be found on *Slate Magazine*'s Web site: http://www .slate.com/id/117085/ along with his first piece about search and rescue. Zac Unger,

"On the Ground at Ground Zero," *Slate Magazine*, 2001, http://www.slate.com/id/117085/, accessed on October 20, 2010.

3. William Langewiesche, *American Ground: Unbuilding the World Trade Center* (New York: Macmillan, 2003), 70.

4. Sermon by the Rev. James Cooper, Trinity Church, May 29, 2010.

5. Langewiesche, *American Ground*, 70.

6. James Glanz and Eric Lipton, *City in the Sky: The Rise and Fall of the World Trade Center* (New York: Times Books, 2003), 291.

7. Ibid.

8. Juan Gonzalez, *Fallout: The Environmental Consequences of the World Trade Center Collapse* (New York: The Free, Press, 2002).

9. David Rosner and Gerald Markowitz, *Are We Ready? Public Health Since 9/11* (Berkeley: University of California Press, 2006), 25.

10. Ibid., 44–49. As of 2010 I continue to treat in psychotherapy two patients whose fees are paid by the September 11 Fund. The long-term health effects of 9/11 are impossible to gauge. Many people and organizations are tracking these effects. The most noteworthy is the World Trade Center Registry, which as of 9/11/08 had 71,437 rescue-and-recovery workers, commuters, area workers, Lower Manhattan residents, and others enrolled. A more specific example is the Beyond Ground Zero Network, which was formed in 2009 to address the severe health and economic effects of 9/11 on poor inhabitants in Chinatown and the Lower East Side.

11. Rosner and Markowitz, *Are We Ready?*, 19–24.

12. This account draws mostly on the detailed (if rather self-centered) history by Robert C. Shaler, *Who They Were: Inside the World Trade Center DNA Story: The Unprecedented Effort to Identify the Missing* (New York: Free Press, 2005).

13. John Hersey, *Hiroshima* (New York: Alfred A. Knopf, 1985 [1946]), 24.

14. Lavonne Mueller, *Voices from September 11* (New York: Hal Leonard Corporation, 2002), 2.

15. P. Lasagor, "9/11 Jersey City Medical Center, Lessons Learned," Department of Surgery–Jersey City Medical Center, Bulletin of the American College of urgeons—National Center for Biotechnology Information 87, no. 7 (2003): 8–12.

16. Bellevue Hospital, New York City, http://www.nyc.gov/html/hhc/html/facilities/bellevue.shtml, accessed on October 20, 2010.

17. Dennis Smith, *Report From Ground Zero* (New York: Penguin Books, 2003), 293

18. New York State Legislature and New York State Legislative Bill Drafting Commission, *Laws of the State of New York Passed at the Sessions of the Legislature* (New York: S.N., 2005), Vol. 2.

19. Dan Barry, "At Morgue, Ceaselessly Sifting 9/11 Traces," *NY Times*, July 14, 2002, 1.

20. Hersey, *Hiroshima*, 73.

21. The information collected about Pier 94 was obtained from a draft written by Mike Hennessey of Gene Codes Forensics, a biological forensics company dealing with DNA analysis in Ann Arbor, MI. His draft is part of a larger paper titled "World Trade Center DNA Identifications: The Administrative Review

Process," which, based on further review, was presented to the International Symposium on Human Identification. This draft can be accessed on several different Web sites, such as http://www.taq.ch/geneticidproc/ussymp13proc/contents/hennesseyrev1.pdf.

22. Ibid.

23. James R. Gill, "9/11 and the New York City Office of Chief Medical Examiner," *Forensic Science, Medicine, and Pathology* 2 (2006), 29, reports that 50,000 people normally worked in the World Trade Center but that because it was early there were only about 17,400 in the buildings when the attacks occurred.

24. Ellison, Vulliamy, and Martinson, "We Got Down to the Outside"; Diane Cardwell, Glenn Collins, Andrew Jacobs, Lynda Richardson, Janny Scott, and Joyce Wadler, "After the Attacks: The Names; Snapshots of Their Lives with Family and at Work," New York Times, September 15, 2001, 1.

25. Eric Lipton, "Numbers of Dead," *New York Times,* September 21, 2001.

26. The Medical Examiner's report (OCME) of January 5, 2010, posted on the Web site of the September 11 Families' Association.

27. John A. Coleman, "Civil Religion," Oxford Journals: Journal of Sociology of Religion 31, no. 2 (1970): 67–88.

28. On Sunday, September 16, I took Robert Jay Lifton on a tour of Lower Manhattan (though we could not go below 14th Street). In the course of our walk around Union Square, he made this remarkable observation about the spontaneous memorials throughout the small park.

12. DEATH AND FUTURE

1. "Faith and Doubt at Ground Zero," Helen Whitney, producer. WGBH documentary, 2002.

2. Susan Neiman, *Evil in Modern Thought: An Alternate History of Philosophy* (Princeton: Princeton University Press, 2004).

3. The feeling Renee had in this regard was that her mother, and others outside of New York, just "didn't get it." Such a view, of course, reflects Renee's perspective and fails adequately to capture the enormous complexity of experience of those throughout the country in their understanding of and attitudes toward the disaster that unfolded in New York City. Such egoism of victimization is also a common dimension of the survivor experience.

4. Reminiscences of Polly Weiss (December 24, 2001), on page 37 in Columbia University Oral History Research Office Collection (CUOHROC).

5. I had a dog experience of my own, though not in the realm of the uncanny. In the immediate wake of the attacks, my old, fat dog was exceedingly nervous, barking at noises, and restless. On the second day after 9/11 she woke up startled and started crying and barking. Since she sleeps in our bedroom, she woke up both my wife and me. The dog had never done anything like that before.

13. PREGNANT WOMEN

Andrea Fatica was very helpful in the research for this chapter. She also was a participant in several of the interviews I conducted.

1. Beatrice Beebe, a well-known researcher at Columbia University specializing in early infant interaction with their mothers, directs a primary prevention program for women who were pregnant on 9/11 and who were widowed by the disaster. Her extensive bibliography of scores of articles from her work is readily available online.
2. At this point Jennifer took some pictures of her healthy and robust two-year-old off a credenza next to the table where I conducting the interview. She beamed with pleasure as I admired her handsome son.
3. All the major hospitals in the city prepared for an expected onslaught of patients in the wake of the disaster. The West Side Highway was lined with ambulances from Mt. Sinai, NYU Downtown Hospital, New York Presbyterian, Bellevue, and many others. St. Vincent's, on 12th Street and Seventh Avenue, had empty gurneys lined up on the street outside the emergency room entrance. See David Rosner and Gerald Markowitz, *Are We Ready? Public Health Since 9/11* (Berkeley: University of California Press, 2006), 10–11.
4. The police at first closed the Brooklyn Bridge to pedestrian traffic in the immediate wake of the collapse of the towers but soon afterward opened it up and the bridge became the main artery out of the disaster area for scores of thousands of people heading toward Brooklyn.

14. THE SURPRISE OF IT ALL

1. Robert J. Shiller, (Princeton: Princeton University Press, 2000).
2. This is John Winthrop's most famous thesis, written on board the *Arbella* in 1630. John Winthrop, "A Model of Christian Charity," Collections of the Massachusetts Historical Society, Vol. VII of the Third Series (Boston: Charles C. Little and James Brown, 1838).
3. Henry Adams, "The First Administration of Thomas Jefferson," *History of the United States of America During the Administrations of Thomas Jefferson,* ed. Earl N. Harbert (New York: Library of America, 1986), 17.
4. Abraham Lincoln, "Address Before the Young Men's Lyceum of Springfield, Illinois," January 27, 1838, in *Collected Works of Abraham Lincoln,* ed. Roy Basler et al. (New Brunswick, NJ: Rutgers University Press, 1953), I:109.
5. Abraham Lincoln, "Address to the New Jersey Senate at Trenton, New Jersey," February 21, 1861, *Collected Works,* IV: 236; Gilbert K. Chesterton, *What I Saw in America,* in *The Collected Works of G. K. Chesterton* (San Francisco: Ignatius, 1990), 21:41–45.
6. This discussion and what follows is from Michael Ignatieff, *American Exceptionalism and Human Rights* (Princeton: Princeton University Press, 2005).

15. ON TRAUMA AND ZONES OF SADNESS

1. Robert Jay Lifton, *Death in Life: Survivors of Hiroshima* (Chapel Hill, NC: The University of North Carolina Press, 1991 [1968]), 483–84.

2. Judy Herman, *Trauma and Recovery: The Aftermath of Violence—From Domestic Abuse to Political Terror* (New York: Basic Books, 1993). This is an excellent discussion of the way these historical themes came together in the 1960's and 1970's and led to a new understanding of trauma.

3. Cathy Caruth, *Unclaimed Experience: Trauma, Narrative, and History* (Baltimore: Johns Hopkins University Press, 1996) and *Trauma: Explorations in Memory* (Baltimore: Johns Hopkins University Press, 1995); Bessel van der Kolk, *Psychological Trauma* (Washington, DC: American Psychiatric Publishers, 1987) and van der Kolk et al., eds., *Traumatic Stress: The Effects of Overwhelming Experience on Mind, Body, and Society* (New York: Guilford Press, 2006); Beatrice Beebe's work previously cited in the chapter "Pregnant Women"; Rachel Yehuda et al., "Impact of Maternal Post-traumatic Stress Disorder and Depression Following Exposure to the September 11 Attacks on Preschool Children's Behavior," *Child Development* 4 (2010): 1129–41. Yehuda and her colleagues have also extended their careful scientific research on PTSD using biological markers to Holocaust survivors. See Yehuda et al. "Parental PTSD as a Vulnerability Factor for Low Cortisol Trait in Offspring of Holocaust Survivors," *Archives of General Psychiatry* 64 (2007): 1040–48.

4. The general issue of "adult onset" of trauma is an important concern of many researchers on trauma. Note, for example, Ghislaine Boulanger, *Wounded by Reality: Understanding and Treating Adult Onset Trauma* (New York: Routledge, 2007).

5. Thomas Laqueur in a recent essay frames my distinction between the vertical and horizontal in terms of the perspective of the observer. Laqueur has nothing but disdain for current obsessions with trauma, victims, and survivors, and all but mocks the small army of some 9,000 mental health workers who flocked to New York after 9/11. Laqueur notes instead that a concern with the problem of incidence leads observers to focus on the vulnerability of victims (the vertical), whereas a focus on what has been witnessed leads to concern with the event itself (the horizontal). Laqueur, however, is most interested in the way the concept of trauma has become, in Foucaultian terms, a "floating signifier." He says, "If the question is posed, as it once was, primarily as a problem of incidence, then investigators will focus on the vulnerability of victims; if it is posed in terms of what has been witnessed, attention turns to the event. No clinical advance can explain the historical shift from one mode of inquiry to the other: the framing of the question about trauma has little if anything to do with substantive knowledge of psychology, psychiatry or neurology. It does have a great deal to do with what Foucault called the production of truth, with the way these disciplines can be mobilised for novel purposes." Thomas Laqueur, "We Are All Victims Now," *London Review of Books* 32 (2010): 1–18; review of Didier Fassin and Richard Rechtman, *The Empire of Trauma: An Inquiry into the Condition of Victimhood*, translated by Rachel Gomme (Princeton: Princeton University Press, 2009), 12.

6. Sandro Galea, Jennifer Ahern, Heidi Resnick, et al., "Psychological Sequelae of the September 11 Terrorist Attacks in New York City," *New England Journal of Medicine* 346, no. 13 (2002): 982–87.

7. I had hoped to study this phenomenon with my talented colleague David Strug, a professor of social work at Yeshiva University School of Social Work, but we were unable to secure funding.

8. There are some anecdotal, and perhaps apocryphal, stories of terrified people huddling in their closets for a week or more.

9. Philip Kasinitz, Gregory Smithsimon, and Binh Pok, "Disaster at the Doorstep: Battery Park City and Tribeca Respond to the Events of 9/11," in Nancy Foner, ed., *Wounded City: The Social Impact of 9/11* (New York: Russell Sage Foundation, 2005), 91.

10. Ibid., 79.

11. Ibid., 80.

12. Ibid., 92.

13. Ibid., 93.

14. Ibid., 80.

15. Margaret M. Chin, "Moving On: Chinatown Garment Workers After 9/11," Nancy Foner, ed., *Wounded City: The Social Impact of 9/11* (New York: Russell Sage Foundation, 2005),184.

16. Ibid., 184–85.

17. Ibid., 185–86.

18. "Chinatown One Year After September 11th," Report of the Asian American Federation of New York (New York: AAFNY, 2002), 1.

16. HISTORICAL MEMORY OF THE DISASTER

1. Peter Novick, *The Holocaust in American Life* (New York: Mariner Books, 2000).

2. "1998 Survey of American Jewish Opinion," American Jewish Committee. Available online at http://www.jewishdatabank.org/study.asp?sid=90116&tp=1.

3. New York Historical Society, "Here Is New York," NYHS http://www.nyhistory. org/web/default.php?section=whats_new&page=detail.html (accessed October 3, 2010); Smithsonian Museum of American History, "World Trade Center" http://www .americanhistory.si.edu/september11/.html (accessed October 3, 2010).

4. The idea of the towers loved only in destruction is from B. J. Lifton, personal communication, March 22, 2010. The Norman Mailer reference is from a presentation at the Wellfleet Psychohistory Meetings, held in the home of Robert Jay Lifton, October 3, 2000.

5. Many of the ideas in the last few paragraphs are a personal communication from Robert Jay Lifton on March 21, 2010. As usual in my conversations with Lifton, there is a nebulous space between us churning with ideas, and it is not entirely clear to me where attribution fairly lies.

6. Linda Baron ["Disaster Basics: The Life Cycle of a Disaster and the Role of

Conflict Resolution Professionals," *Cardozo School of Conflict Resolution* 9, no. 2 (2007): 301–15] first brought to my attention this idea of a life cycle of a disaster, though her analysis is more narrow and concerned with "conflict resolution professionals" at the local level.

7. John Hersey, *Hiroshima* (New York: Alfred A. Knopf, 1985 [1946]), 69, 87.

APPENDIX: THE LITERATURE ON TRAUMA

1. Sandro Galea, Jennifer Ahern, Heidi Resnick, et al., "Psychological Sequelae of the September 11 Terrorist Attacks in New York City," *New England Journal of Medicine* 13, no. 346 (2002): 982–87. Note also Jennifer Ahern, Sandro Galea, Heidi Resnick, et al., "Television Images and Psychological Symptoms After the September 11 Terrorist Attacks," *Psychiatry* 65 (2002): 289–300.

2. David L. Strug, Susan E. Mason, and Frances E. Heller, "An Exploratory Study of the Impact of the Year of 9/11 on Older Hispanic Immigrants in New York City," *Journal of Gerontological Social Work* 42 (2003): 77–100. Note also David L. Strug and Susan E. Mason, "The Impact of 9/11 on Older Chinese Immigrants in New York City," *Journal of Immigrant and Refugee Studies* 5 (2007): 21–44.

3. Galea et al., "Psychological Sequelae," 985.

4. Sandro Galea, David Vlahov, Melissa Tracy, et al., "Hispanic Ethnicity and Post-traumatic Stress Disorder after a Disaster: Evidence from a General Population Survey After September 11, 2001," *Annals of Epidemiology* 14 (2004): 520–31; Irwin Garfinkel, Neeraj Kaushai, Julien Teitler, and Sandra Garcia, "Vulnerability and Resilience: New Yorkers Respond to 9/11," Nancy Foner, ed., *Wounded City: The Social Impact of 9/11* (New York: Russell Sage Foundation, 2005), 29–75; Strug, Mason, and Heller, "An Exploratory Study of the Impact of the Year of 9/11." Note also Strug and Mason, "The Impact of 9/11 on Older Chinese Immigrants in New York City."

5. William Schlenger, Juesta Caddell, Lori Ebert, et al., "Psychological Reactions to Terrorist Attacks: Findings from the National Study of Americans' Reactions to September 11," *Journal of the American Medical Association* 5 (2002): 581–88; George Bonanno, Sandra Galea, Angela Bucciarelli, and David Vlahov, "Psychological Resilience After Disaster: New York City in the Aftermath of the September 11th Terrorist Attack," *Psychological Science* 3 (2006): 181–86; Laura DiGrande, Megan Perrin, Lorna Thorpe, et al., "Posttraumatic Stress Symptoms, PTSD, and Risk Factors Among Lower Manhattan Residents 2–3 Years After the September 11, 2001 Terrorist Attacks," *Journal of Traumatic Stress* 21 (2008): 264–73. Note also Jennifer Ahern, Sandro Galea, Heidi Resnick, and David Vlahov, "Television Images and Probable Post-traumatic Stress Disorder After September 11th: Role of Background Characteristics, Event Exposures and Perievent Panic," *Journal of Nervous and Mental Disease* 192 (2004): 217–26; Mark A. Schuster, Bradley D. Stein, Lisa H. Jaycox, et al., "A National Survey of Stress Reactions After the September 11th Terrorist Attacks," *New England Journal of Medicine* 345 (2001): 1507–12.

6. Roxane Cohen Silver, Alison Holman, Daniel N. McIntosh, et al., "Nationwide Longitudinal Study of Psychological Responses to September 11," *Journal of the American Medical Association (JAMA)* 288, no. 10 (2002): 1235–44.

7. Susan Coates and Daniel Shechter, "Preschoolers' Traumatic Stress Post-9/11: Relational and Developmental Perspectives," *Psychiatric Clinics of North America* 27 (2004): 473–89. Note also Michael W. Otto, Aude Henin, Dina R. Hirshfeld-Becker, et al., "Posttraumatic Stress Disorder Symptoms Following Media Exposure to Tragic Events: Impact of 9/11 on Children at Risk for Anxiety Disorders," *Journal of Anxiety Disorders* 21 (2007): 888–902. Note also Jennifer Stuber, Gerry Fairbrother, Sandro Galea, et al., "Determinants of Counseling for Children in Manhattan After September 11 Attacks," *Psychiatric Services* 53 (2002): 815–22 and Christina W. Hoven, Cristiane S. Duarte, Donald J. Mandell, "Children's Mental Health After Disasters: The Impact of the World Trade Center Attack" *Current Psychiatry* 5 (2003): 101–107.

8. Coates and Schechter, "Preschoolers' Traumatic Stress Post-9/11."

9. Christina W. Hoven, Cristiane S. Duarte, Ping Wu, et al., "Parental Exposure to Mass Violence and Child Mental Health: The First Responder and WTC Evacuee Study," *Clinical Child and Family Psychology Review* 12, no. 2 (2009): 95–112; Note also Jonathan S. Comer, Bin Fan, Cristiane S. Duarte, et al., "Attack-Related Life Disruption and Child Psychopathology in New York City Public Schoolchildren 6 Months Post-9/11," *Journal of Clinical Child & Adolescent Psychology* 39, no. 4 (2010):460–69; Cristiane S. Duarte, Christina W. Hoven, Ping Wu, et al., "Posttraumatic Stress Disorder in Children with First Responders in Their Families," *Journal of Traumatic Stress* 19, no. 2 (2006): 301–306.

10. Laura DiGrande, Megan Perrin, Lorna Thorpe, et al., "Posttraumatic Stress Symptoms, PTSD, and Risk Factors Among Lower Manhattan Residents 2–3 Years after the September 11, 2001 Terrorist Attacks," *Journal of Traumatic Stress* 21 (2008): 264–73.

11. Barbara Ganzel, B. J. Casey, Gary Glover, et al., "The Aftermath of 9/11: Effect of Intensity and Recovery of Trauma on Outcome," *Emotion* 7 (2007): 227–38; Arijit Nandy, Sandro Galea, Melissa Tracy, et al., "Job Loss, Unemployment, Work Stress, Job Satisfaction, and the Persistence of Posttraumatic Stress Disorder One Year After the September 11 Attacks," *Journal of Occupational and Environmental Medicine* 46 (2004): 1057–64; and Jason Bram, James Orr, and Carol Rapoport, "Measuring the Effects of the September 11 Attack on New York City," *Economic Policy Review* (November 2002): 5–20.

12. Personal communication from Gary Langer, the top pollster for ABC News, July 8, 2008.

13. Gallup Poll/USA Today, "Majority of Americans Not Fearful of Terrorist Attack," New York, 2008, retrieved on 14 July 2010, http://www.gallup.com/poll/110203/Majority-Americans-Fearful-Terrorist-Attack.html.

14. Pew Research Center, "One Year Later: New Yorkers More Troubled, Washingtonians More on Edge," New York, 2002 http://people-press.org/report/160.html (accessed on July 14,2010).

INDEX

community, sense of: and Eric, 42, 163; in neighborhoods, 217, 218, 219; of survivors, 162, 163, 184; and trauma, 106–7, 111

Compton, Cathryn, 48–50, 164–65, 180

conspiracy theories, xv, 255n5

Constitution, U.S., 204, 205

construction workers, 141–42. *See also* rescue workers

Cowes, Adam, 103

crowd movement, 40–41, 48

Cuban Missile Crisis (1962), 90, 91, 95, 96

culture: American, 89, 204; of fear, viii, 124, 125, 205–6, 222; and language, 111; and television, 118, 135

Dahler, Don, 56–59

Dave, 19–20, 46–47, 63

David, 130

Davis, Jefferson, 81

De Niro, Robert, 218

death, 13–15, 63–84; causes of, 3, 63–64, 65, 67, 72; and childhood trauma, 212; collective, 88; of first responders, 67, 72, 144, 190; and future, 167–69, 178, 209; hidden children on, 131; images of, 175–79; of Lincoln, 78, 82; and middle knowledge, 71, 86, 157; mystical experience of, 174–75; and numbing, 126; and poetry, 107, 109; and presence of body, 73–84, 155; quantification of, 71–73; and sense of agency, 123; smell of, 85–86, 124, 160, 190, 191, 195, 211; of Strozier's father, 86–87; and survivors, 200, 208; on television, 54–55, 118, 120; and witnesses, 30

death certificates, 152, 154, 155

"Death of Ivan Ilyich" (Tolstoy), 175

"Deathfugue" (Celan), 112

debris: in Brooklyn, 30, 49–50, 251n1; from collapse of towers, 2, 3–4, 23, 24, 25, 99, 118; falling, 1, 10, 11, 13, 14, 19, 21, 24, 63, 98; human remains in, 3, 13, 67, 141, 142, 143, 149, 152, 232; and neigh-

borhoods, 215, 216; smell of, 49–50, 85–86, 124, 160, 190, 191, 195, 211; toxic, 3–4, 71, 140, 220. *See also* Fresh Kills landfill; Ground Zero

Debt of Honor (Clancy), 126

Defense Planning Guidance (Cheney; 1992), 204

Deirdre, 1, 11–12, 26–28, 96, 163, 211, 213, 249; and future, 168–69; language of, 106, 112–13; on outsiders, 125

Deutsche Bank, 65

Die Hard (film), 126

Digrande, Laura, 248

disasters: future, 209–10; *General Slocum* (1904), 69–70; life cycle of, 237–38; natural, 87–89, 96, 207; vs. "new trouble," 207; toxic, 208. *See also* earthquakes; nuclear attack

DNA collection, 148, 150, 151–52

dogs, 173, 259n5

Domingo, Placido, 157

Dominican community, 214, 245–46

Dwyer, Jim, 71

earthquakes, xii, 87, 88, 92, 207; 9/11 compared to, 12, 19, 20

economic effects, 145, 216–20, 249, 258n10

Eddings, Amy, 67

Eleanor, 132

elevators, 1, 14, 16, 17, 18, 72, 140

Eliot, T. S., 53, 109, 128

Ellen, 48, 175–76

Ellis Island, 148

Elsa, 131, 134

empathy, 123, 175, 183, 187; and healing, 107–8; from outsiders, 162–63; and television, 118–19

environmental issues, 89, 178, 205, 208

Environmental Protection Agency (EPA), 145, 146

Eric, 31–33, 161, 163, 213, 214; language of, 105; on subway, 41–43

Erikson, Kai, 88, 106, 207–8, 220, 244

Europe, 202, 209, 247

Freud, Anna, 247
Freud, Sigmund, 108, 210
Frost, Robert, 110
fuel, diesel, 1, 2, 4, 14, 26, 66, 140
funeral ritual. *See* mourning rituals
Fussel, Paul, 109
future: and death, 167–69, 178, 209;
    disasters of, 209–10; hope for, 200; and
    pregnancy, 191, 194–96

Gabrielle, Monica, 228
Gabrielle, Richard, 228
Galeo, Sandro, 214, 245, 246
Ganzel, Barbara, 249
Garfinkel, Irwin, 246
garment industry, 219–20
Gatch, Dr. Charles A., 77
Genbaku Dome (Hiroshima), 236
General Slocum disaster (1904), 69–70
Gensuikin (Hiroshima survivors' organi-
    zation), 226
Gensuikyo (Hiroshima survivors' organi-
    zation), 226
George, Alice Rose, 231
George Washington Bridge, 41
Gershon, Robyn, 18, 252n2
Ginnane, Robert, 68
Giuliani, Rudy, 150, 155, 156–57
Glogg, Carl, 68
Gonzalez, Juan, 145
Grand Central Station, 44
Grant, Ulysses S., 78
Greenwood, Lee, 157
Ground Zero: Bush at, 5, 144; cleanup at,
    xiv, 139–44; disturbed souls at, 174–75;
    end of rescue phase at, 142–43; fires
    at, 5, 140–41; health hazards of, 4,
    144–47; memorial at, xiv, 221, 225, 227,
    228, 233–36; mosque near, 226; rescue
    workers at, 139–44, 213; rivalries at,
    141–42; temporary morgues at, 148–49;
    and zones of sadness, xii, 212
Gulf War, 166, 204

Haiti, earthquake in, 88
Hanjour, Hani, 2
Harris, Patrick, 22, 73
health hazards, 229, 258n10; and Ground
    Zero, 4, 144–47; from toxic debris, 3–4,
    71, 140, 220. *See also* toxins
Heath, Desmond, 152, 247
Hegel, G.W.F., 210
Heilman, Uri, 76
Henry, 11, 13, 19, 24–25, 103, 213, 244; on
    9/11 as movie, 1, 118; fears of, 124, 175;
    on "jumpers," 64–65; language of, 106
Here Is New York (exhibit, website, book),
    231, 232
Hersey, John, 14–15, 24, 91, 148, 149–50, 237
Hidankyo (Hiroshima survivors' organi-
    zation), 226
Hiroshima, 14–15, 21, 49, 207, 210, 220; and
    apocalypse, 128; Asano Park in, 24, 91;
    and children, 95; greening of, 237–38;
    medical infrastructure in, 147–48;
    memorials in, 236; memories of, 93,
    94, 97; parallels with, 24, 91; psychic
    numbing in, 15, 122; remains from,
    149–50; survivors of, 208–9, 213–14,
    223, 230, 238; and survivors' organiza-
    tions, 226, 227; victims of, 94–95
Hirsch, Charles S., 147–50
Hoffmann, Stanley, 204–5
Holocaust, 85–86, 207, 209; and apocalypse,
    129; children hidden during, 127–35;
    and language, 111–12; memory of,
    222–23; and presence of body, 75; and
    psychic numbing, 15, 107; and psychol-
    ogy of trauma, 210, 211; *vs. shoah*, 222
The Holocaust in American Life (Novick),
    222
Holocaust Museum (Washington, D.C.),
    18, 128, 223
Hooker, Joseph, 83
hope, 119, 199–200, 214, 238; and hidden
    children, 135; and pregnancy, 179–80,
    181, 194

54–55; language of, 106; and meaning, 53–54, 58, 118, 128; and memory, 221; multiplier effect of, 121–22; and onlookers, 51; and overstimulation effect, 122; and participants, 39, 47, 48, 49; *vs.* personal experience, 58–59, 118, 122, 251n1; "A Prayer for America" on, 157; and pregnancies, 181, 191, 194; and psychic numbing, 120, 122–23, 135; and PTSD, 246, 247; in real time, 53, 120; *vs.* reality, 52; and witnesses, 118–19, 120

terrorism: and apocalypse, 89; biological, 210; death from, 155; fear of, 206, 249–50; in future, 209–10; hidden children on, 130, 131, 132; in Israel, 76; and new American exceptionalism, 205; and nuclear threats, 91–92, 94; participants on, 45, 49; pre-9/11, 201; and pregnancy, 188; survivors on, 19; and survivors' organizations, 226, 229, 230; witnesses on, 32, 35

Times Square, 34

Tina, 99, 164

Tocqueville, Alexis de, 202

Tolstoy, Leo, 175

Torres, Joe, 68

toxins: in air, 182, 183, 184, 190, 191, 208, 213, 215; in debris, 3–4, 71, 140, 220; at Ground Zero, 145–47; in Pennsylvania, 182–84

Traub, Charles, 231

trauma: adult onset of, 261n4; and agency, 123; childhood, 36–37, 38, 161–62, 211–12; in Dominican community, 214; language of, xii, 105–16; literature on, xiii, 54, 106, 111, 243–50; and "new trouble," 220; of New Yorkers, xiv, 53; psychology of, xiii, 210–11; and sense of community, 106–7, 111, 224; vicarious, 48; and victim consciousness, 223–24. *See also* posttraumatic stress disorder

traumasong, xii, 105–16

Triangle Waist Company fire (1911), 70

Tribeca, 214, 215–16, 217–18

Tribeca Film Festival, 218

Tribute Museum (New York City), 226–27

The Turner Diaries (Pierce), 126

Ungar, Zac, 140

United Family Group, Inc., 229

United Nations (UN), 46, 193, 203, 205

United States (U.S.): and American exceptionalism, 200–205; double standards of, 203–4; history of, 200–203; military response of, 89–90

Upper East Side, 214

U.S. Custom House (WTC 6), 10

Valerie, 30–31

van der Kolk, Bessel, 211

Victim Compensation Fund, 229

victim consciousness, exaggerated, 223–24

victims: of anthrax, 5; demographics of, 252n2; egoism of, 259n3; of fires, 3, 14, 63, 72; foreign, 156; of Hiroshima, 94–95; identification of, 71–72, 143, 149–53; injured, 10, 148, 188, 190; numbers of, 155–56; as sacrifices, 175–76; *vs.* witnesses, 261n5. *See also* death

Vietnam War, 93, 210, 236

Voices of September 11th, 226

volunteers, 139–44, 146

Vonnegut, Kurt, xiv

Wadsworth, Robert, 110

Walker, Peter, 234

wars, post-9/11, xiv, xv, 124, 125, 222, 249; in Afghanistan, 5, 174, 205–6, 229; and civil liberties, 126; in Iraq, 166, 205–6, 210, 229; and Strozier family, 166

Washington, D.C., viii

Washington, George, 202

Washington Heights, 214

weapons of mass destruction, 89, 201, 206; biological, 94, 102, 210. *See also* nuclear attack

Weiss, Polly, 172, 259n4

West Side Highway, 1, 10, 13, 14, 19, 20, 63, 169, 215, 216

West Street, 13, 24

Westin, David, 55

Whitman, Christine, 145

Whitman, Walt, 78, 110

Whitney, Helen, x, 167

Wiesel, Elie, 15, 222

William, 173

Williams syndrome, 175

Winfrey, Oprah, 157

Winstrall, Niko, 68

Winthrop, John, 201

witnesses (zone 2), xiii, 9–10, 29–38, 199, 212, 257n2a; and collective grief, 209; hidden children as, 128; international, 117; moral, 118–19; psychic numbing in, 35–37; and television, 118–19, 120; *vs.* victims, 261n5

Wolfowitz, Paul, 205

women, sexual abuse of, 211. *See also* pregnancies

World Financial Center, 14, 47

World Trade Center (WTC): 1993 bombing of, 11, 12, 17, 31, 43, 91, 100, 163–64, 201, 226; and Battery Park City, 216, 217; fantasies about, 100; popular dislike of, 233–34; and Tribeca, 217; workers in, 30

World Trade Center 1 (north tower): collapse of, 3, 27, 44, 59, 91, 98, 99, 116, 188, 255n6; and Ground Zero memorial, 234–35; hidden children on, 131; hit by first plane (Flight 11), 1, 2, 31, 64, 72, 98,

173, 181; "jumpers" from, 72–73; video of, 10, 67

World Trade Center 2 (south tower): collapse of, 2, 23–25, 34, 44, 52, 56–57, 58, 65, 90, 98, 116, 162, 181, 188, 193, 255n6; and Ground Zero memorial, 235; hit by second plane (Flight 175), 2, 17, 32, 34, 43, 49, 65, 72–73, 112, 131, 181; "jumpers" from, 72–73; order to return to offices in, 16–17, 73; survivors from, 11, 21–22

World Trade Center 6 (U.S. Custom House), 10

World Trade Center 7, 4, 231; survivors from, 11–12, 26–28, 112

World Trade Center Registry, 258n10

World War I, 209

World War II, 100, 209, 210; children hidden during, 127–35; London Blitz in, 247; memories of, 93, 97

WTC Survivors' Network, 229

Yankee Stadium, "A Prayer for America" at, 156–57

Yeats, William Butler, 110

Yehuda, Rachel, 211

al-Zarqari, Abu, 210

Zawahiri, Ayman, 5, 94

zones of sadness, xii–xiii, 9–59, 210–14, 244; contrasts between, 46–47, 212; zone 1 (survivors), 9–28; zone 2 (witnesses), 29–38; zone 3 (participants), 39–50, 113–16, 212; zone 4 (onlookers), xiii, 21, 26, 27, 51–59, 123, 212. *See also* survivors; witnesses

DATE DUE			